Second Edition

Object Relations and Self Psychology
An Introduction

Michael St. Clair
Emmanuel College

Brooks/Cole Publishing Company

I(T)P™ An International Thomson Publishing Company

Pacific Grove • Albany • Bonn • Cincinnati • Detroit • London • Madrid • Melbourne
Mexico City • New York • Paris • San Francisco • Singapore • Tokyo • Toronto • Washington

For Roslin, Forrest, and Travis

 A CLAIREMONT BOOK

Sponsoring Editor: *Claire Verduin*
Marketing Team: *Nancy Kernal, Jean Thompson*
Editorial Associate: *Patsy Vienneau*
Production Editor: *Kirk Bomont*
Manuscript Editor: *Kay Mikel*

Interior and Cover Design: *Kath Minerva*
Art Editor: *Kathy Joneson*
Typesetting: *Bookends Typesetting*
Printing and Binding: *Malloy Lithographing, Inc.*

For more information, contact:

BROOKS/COLE PUBLISHING COMPANY
511 Forest Lodge Road
Pacific Grove, CA 93950
USA

International Thomson Publishing Europe
Berkshire House 168–173
High Holborn
London WC1V 7AA
England

Thomas Nelson Australia
102 Dodds Street
South Melbourne, 3205
Victoria, Australia

Nelson Canada
1120 Birchmount Road
Scarborough, Ontario
Canada M1K 5G4

International Thomson Editores
Campos Eliseos 385, Piso 7
Col. Polanco
11560 México D. F. México

International Thomson Publishing GmbH
Königswinterer Strasse 418
53227 Bonn
Germany

International Thomson Publishing Asia
221 Henderson Road
#05–10 Henderson Building
Singapore 0315

International Thomson Publishing Japan
Hirakawacho Kyowa Building, 3F
2-2-1 Hirakawacho
Chiyoda-ku, Tokyo 102
Japan

Printed in the United States of America

10   9   8   7

Library of Congress Cataloging-in-Publication Data

St. Clair, Michael [date]
  Object relations and self psychology : an introduction / Michael
St. Clair. — 2nd ed.
    p.   cm.
  Includes bibliographical references and index.
  ISBN 0-534-33855-0 (pbk. : alk. paper)
  1. Object relations (Psychoanalysis)   2. Self psychology.
3. Personality disorders.   I. Title.
BF175.5.024S7   1996
155.2—dc20   95-20177
                                                CIP

Contents

Chapter Six

Edith Jacobson:
An Integrated Model   91

Chapter Seven

Margaret S. Mahler:
The Psychological Birth of the Individual   109

Chapter Eight

Otto Kernberg: A Synthesis   131

Chapter Nine

Heinz Kohut: Self Psychology and Narcissism   151

Preface

This book offers an overview and critical assessment of two important streams of psychoanalytic thought: object relations theory and self psychology. The issues, ideas, and controversies of these models of the person are presented as clearly and as readably as possible. This book examines how different theorists vary from one another and from the classical Freudian model.

Presenting these concepts and clinical applications of object relations and self psychology means painting with broad strokes, enabling the reader to see the larger picture without being overwhelmed by technical details. In painting this larger picture, however, I have tried to maintain a balance between technical accuracy and simple clarity. I have tried to shed light on the theoretical models and not cause the reader to encounter the frustration I have often found when reading the technical literature.

The terms "object relations" and "self" have occupied center stage in much psychoanalytic writing during the past few years. *Object relations* usually means personal relations, and *object* is a technical term that means "that with which a subject relates." Discussions of object relations usually center on the early relations of a child and mother and how this early relationship shapes the child's inner world and later adult relationships. *Self*, a beguilingly simple four-letter word, has complex meanings and controversial implications for current psychoanalytic writers. Self can refer to the person I am for myself, or an active entity, or a representation of myself that is present within the ego.

Theories of object relations continue to evolve. I say *theories* because there is no single, generally accepted school or theory of object relations. Many clinicians and theorists have contributed ideas to an evolving body of concepts that deal with object relationships and the implications of object relations. As these theorists stretch and extend the ideas originally suggested by Freud, they create controversy that refines ideas and often threatens traditional meanings without creating a unified theory.

When "self" is used in the phrase "self psychology," it refers to the work of Heinz Kohut. Like many other object relations theorists, Kohut began with traditional psychoanalytic ideas but then fashioned a body of work that strains psychoanalytic orthodoxy to the limits. The fitful and uneven process of testing and refining ideas in heated controversy, however, seems to be the way that psychoanalysis—and other areas of learning—advances. Out of discussion and controversy, an increased understanding can arise of the human person and a person's relationships with others.

Excitement and frustration have compelled me to write this book. Object relations and self psychology offer many stimulating insights into the human personality. The theories presented in this book illuminate areas of early childhood experience, especially relational problems and narcissistic and borderline personality disorders. But I have often become frustrated as I have pushed through much difficult and often confusing material to arrive at these clinical insights. As a teacher, I have been frustrated with the general lack of reading material that would introduce students of psychology and social work to the essentials of object relations and self psychology. A further impetus to write this book has been my wish to provide access to object relations theories and self psychology for a growing number of theologians and other theorists who may not be familiar with recent psychoanalytic literature. A dense thicket of jargon, abstraction, and controversy has kept the insights of object relations and self psychology largely inaccessible to such persons outside these disciplines.

Organization

The first chapter of this book examines some of the terms, concepts, and issues of object relations and self psychology. Chapter 2 provides a summary of some of the Freudian starting points that later theorists have picked up and modified in a variety of ways. The next chapters look at various object relations theorists, including Melanie Klein, W. R. D. Fairbairn, D. W. Winnicott, and Edith Jacobson. Chapter 7 reviews Margaret S. Mahler's developmental model, which has organized many of the insights of the other theorists. Otto Kernberg's synthesis of various theories is presented in Chapter 8, and Chapter 9 looks at Heinz Kohut and his theory of self psychology. Chapter 10 examines the work of

Stephen Mitchell, and Chapter 11 provides a case study and comment. The bibliography at the end of the book provides a guide to the technical literature, and the glossary presents technical terms as simply as possible.

The response to the first edition of this book has been very gratifying. This second edition incorporates changes that have been suggested by colleagues and users of the earlier version. The main changes include the chapter on the cutting-edge work of relational theorist Stephen Mitchell and a full case study that appears as the final chapter. I have chosen not to include any additional historical figures of the object relations tradition (such as Bion and Sullivan), because I believe there is an abundance of more recent work with which students need to become engaged. In the chapter on Margaret Mahler, I have included some of the perspective of Daniel Stern, and I have simplified and updated the bibliography.

Acknowledgments

A number of colleagues and friends read portions of this book while it was in the manuscript stage. Their comments and advice invariably encouraged and helped me, even when I did not always follow their suggestions. I am very grateful for their support, and I would like to mention in particular Martin Wangh, Richard Griffin, Martha Stark, Merle Jordan, Ione Gunnerson, Louis Schippers, John Baker, Judy Teicholz, Carole Bohn, and Lawson Wulsin. Reviewers Lenore S. Blum, Northwestern University; Martha Gizynski, University of Michigan; Ruthellen Josselson, Towson State University; and Beverly Blazey Palmer, California State University at Dominguez Hills were all helpful in their comments. I also want to thank copy editor Kay Mikel and sponsoring editor Claire Verduin of Brooks/Cole Publishing Company.

Michael St. Clair

◎ *Chapter One*

Object Relations Theories and Self Psychology

This first chapter provides a "map" of the journey ahead; it points out the essential features of the landscape and highlights special and noteworthy features that the reader will encounter throughout the book. This chapter introduces the following topics: object relations and the psychology of the self; terms and concepts used in discussing object relations and self psychology; core issues and significant differences in the major theories; and case vignettes illustrating some of these issues.

Object Relations and the Psychology of the Self

Object relations means interpersonal relations. The term *object*, a technical word originally coined by Freud, refers simply to that which will satisfy a need. More broadly, object refers to the significant person or thing that is the object or target of another's feelings or drives. Freud first used object in discussions of instinctual drives and in a context of early mother-child relations. In combination with *relations*, object refers to interpersonal relations and suggests the inner residues of past relationships that shape an individual's current interactions with people.

Psychoanalysis has always investigated the ways an individual's past colors present behavior and relationships. For example, psychoanalysis seeks to investigate the transference that occurs in therapy; that is, how the client transfers aspects of his or her past relationships to the present relationship with a therapist. Psychoanalysis has also traditionally studied relational issues, such as the child's relationships with parents during the oedipal period.

Some scholars within psychoanalytical theory, however, have attended in a special way to relationships and how past relationships structure and shape personalities. These writers approach relationships and the structure and development of the personality in a way that differs from the classic Freudian model of personality. Roughly speaking, those who have departed from the classic Freudian model—I am not speaking here about those who split from Freud while he was still alive, such as Carl Jung, Alfred Adler, Otto Rank, and others—can be classified as object relations theorists and self psychology theorists. Both object relations and self psychology theorists consider themselves within the psychoanalytic mainstream, but they alter that mainstream in significant ways.

Melanie Klein was born in Vienna but moved to London. During the 1930s and 1940s, she and W. R. D. Fairbairn of Edinburgh, Scotland, influenced each other's ideas and published work that began the divergent streams of object relations theories. D. W. Winnicott, a London pediatrician who did psychiatric work with children, produced works that are singular, original, and not well related to other psychoanalytic writing. Margaret Mahler, born in Hungary and trained in Vienna, immigrated to New York City, where her work with children resulted in influential articles and books from the 1950s through the 1970s. Also working and writing in New York City during this period was Edith Jacobson, who came from Germany. Otto Kernberg, another Viennese, took medical and psychiatric training in Chile and continued further psychiatric work at the Menninger Clinic in Kansas. His books and articles, which built on the ideas of those already mentioned, began to appear in the 1970s. Heinz Kohut, born in Vienna and possessing impeccable psychoanalytic credentials, spent most of his professional career in Chicago. At the peak of his career during the 1970s, he published books on the psychology of the self that ruffled the feathers of the psychoanalytic community and altered the flow of psychoanalytic thinking.

Object relations theorists investigate the early formation and differentiation of psychological structures (inner images of the self and the other, or object) and how these inner structures are manifested in interpersonal situations. These theorists focus on the relationships of early life that leave a lasting impression; that is, a residue or remnant within the psyche of the individual. These residues of past relationships, these inner object relations, shape perceptions of individuals and relationships with other individuals. Individuals interact not only with an actual other but also with an internal other, a psychic representation that might be a distorted version of some actual person.

Self psychologists, primarily Heinz Kohut and his followers, approach the self and its structures in a different way than do object relations theorists or those using the traditional Freudian model. Self psychologists explore how early relationships form the self and the structures of the self; they give more emphasis to the self than they give to the ego or self representations or instincts.

A well-known story can serve as a "case study" to illustrate the different approaches each of these three theoretical models might take to the same patient. (In actuality, therapists tend to work in similar ways, while conceptual models have greater differences.) Let us suppose that Cinderella comes to a therapist because she has problems in her marriage to the Prince. A traditional Freudian might investigate Cinderella's repression of her sexual instincts and unresolved oedipal feelings she had for her parents. This therapist or analyst would analyze Cinderella's problems in terms of defenses and conflicts between the structures of the ego and the id.

A therapist working with an object relations perspective would note that Cinderella suffered early psychological deprivation from the loss of her mother. Possibly this loss caused Cinderella to make use of the psychological defense mechanism of splitting, by which she idealized some women (such as her fairy godmother) and saw other women as "all bad" (her stepsisters and stepmother). She idealized the Prince, despite knowing him for only a short time. A marriage based on such distorted inner images of herself and others is bound to run into problems as she sooner or later must deal with the Prince as a real person with human flaws. In object relations theory, the issue would center on the discrepancy between Cinderella's inner world and the persons and situations of the actual world.

A therapist or analyst working within the framework of self psychology would attend to the experience that Cinderella had of herself in therapy as this experience is manifested in the transference to the therapist. Analysis of her transference might reveal an impoverished self that needed a powerful and idealized object. Cinderella's search for such an object reflects her lack of self-esteem and her need to be affirmed by such an idealized object, whether in the form of the fairy godmother, the Prince, or the therapist. She needed to fuse with the idealized Prince out of hope for a feeling of well-being. Out of touch with her own inner emptiness and angry feelings, Cinderella could either idealize her therapist or view the therapist the way she viewed her stepmother.

The three different models approach similar questions from differing perspectives. Freud's model of the personality investigates the structure of the personality, how it is put together. The "parts" or components of the personality—the id, ego, and superego—are conceptualizations that exist only in writings about the personality and are distant from people's experience of themselves. Freud views development in terms of instincts, with the most significant developmental challenge being the oedipal crisis. Disturbance or psychological illness largely lies in conflicts between the different parts or structures of the personality, such as between sexual instincts and the demands of the ego.

Theories of object relations and self psychology, in contrast to Freud, focus on earlier, preoedipal development. These theories see mental illness or pathology generally in terms of developmental arrest rather than structural conflicts. Developmental arrests result in unfinished and unintegrated structures of the personality. In short, there is basic damage to object relationships of the person or to the structures of the self. These changes in perspective produce a different theoretical emphasis and a different use of terms as theory is applied to the understanding and explanation of troubled persons.

All psychoanalytic theories are concerned with explaining how the past influences the present and how the inner world of the patient distorts and influences the external experience. But the different focus and emphasis of various psychoanalytic schools of theory produce different approaches to psychotherapy.

Take, for example, the case of a famous and sophisticated actor who marries and divorces many beautiful women. The classic Freudian model might approach this client in terms of an unresolved oedipal conflict, or a conflict between sexual instincts and the ego and superego.

Object relations theorists might see this actor's inner world filled with distorted, idealized representations of nurturing women, creating a fantasy world that disturbs his relationships with actual women. Having distorted representations of himself and women, he may feel very needy and yearn to be cared for by these temporarily idealized women. He projects his phantasies* that each woman is the one to fulfill his unmet needs, but the painful discrepancy between his inner world and his actual wives results in disappointment, numerous divorces, and new relationships.

Proponents of self psychology might speak of the client's exhibitionism and grandiosity, that he seeks an omnipotent object who, on an unconscious level, will provide him with the self-esteem he lacks. Both the object relations theory and self psychology theory emphasize early relationships with inner objects (or selfobjects†).

All psychoanalytic theorists and therapists are interested in the person's inner world; however, they may explain that inner world differently, emphasizing different aspects because of their theoretical

---

*The spelling of *phantasy* is used throughout this book to refer to mental images that represent instincts and objects. This more technical use differs from whimsical and fanciful *fantasies*.

†Kohut originally used a hyphen in the term *self-object*, but in his later writings (and those of his associates) the nonhyphenated *selfobject* became the conventional usage.

orientation. Let us look at one more illustration of different ways of understanding an individual's inner world. The story of Little Red Riding Hood presents Red Riding Hood's inner experience of her grandmother. While an observer might understand the grandmother's annoyance for some reason, perhaps because the girl came late, Red Riding Hood experiences an unexplainable transformation of the grandmother into a threatening animal, the wolf. In the adult world of reality, such transformations are impossible, but in a child's inner world of experience, such distortions are very likely in the face of strong emotions.

Different psychoanalytic models might try to explain the child's behavior from slightly different perspectives. The classical Freudian model would stress the presence of early, primitive passions. The object relations models might discuss Red Riding Hood's self representation and object representations. Self psychology would approach her in yet a different way, emphasizing the self and possibly narcissistic rage. All these models are called psychoanalytic, but the focus of object relations models and models of the self can vary. In general, these models or theories explore the world of relationships, both past and present, and how the early and past relationships influence present psychic and social functioning. These psychoanalytic theories give clinical insight into how a person's inner world can cause difficulties in living in the actual world of people and relationships.

Terms and Concepts

Theoretical discussions of object relations and self psychology use a specific language, or set of terminologies, that help provide the structure for investigation and application of psychoanalytic theories. The following section discusses and defines some of the key terms.

Object

The *object* in object relations is a technical word in psychoanalytic writing and refers not so much to some inhuman thing but more usually to someone toward whom desire or action is directed. An object is that with which a *subject* relates. Feelings and affects have objects; for example, I love my *children,* I fear *snakes,* I am angry with my *neighbor.*

Human drives have objects. The object of the hunger drive is food, while the object of the sex drive is a sexually attractive person. In a context of instinctual drives, Freud speaks of the infant's objects as being first the breast of the mother, then the mother herself, and finally other persons and things that gratify the infant.

Representation

The term *representation* refers to how the person has or possesses an object; that is, how the person psychically represents an object.

Those who write about object relations generally distinguish between two worlds or frames of reference: the external world of observable objects and an internal psychic world where there are mental representations of objects. The external world refers to the realm of observable objects that exist in a social environment, the world of every day. The internal world refers to the subject's mental images and representations of that external world; that is, how the subject experiences and represents that external world (Boesky, 1983; Sandler & Rosenblatt, 1962).

An observer could describe a mother caring for a child, and the external object in this case refers to the "real" person, the mother. The term *object relatedness* refers to the involvement with this observable person (Meissner, 1980). The *internal object* refers to the child's mental image or representation of the mother. This inner experience and representation is not available to an observer and may not be an accurate reflection of the actual situation, but it does represent the child's (or subject's) experience of relating with the mother and expresses the child's internal psychic world.

When scholars use the term *object,* they need to distinguish carefully whether they are referring to the external person who is observable or the inner object, which is the mental representation of the actual observable person. Of course, they do not always exercise this care, and confusion results when some writers, such as Melanie Klein, use the term *object* without specifying whether it refers to an actual person or an inner representation of a person.

It is the inner world of mental representations that occupies the interest of psychoanalysis, for it is *how* a subject represents and understands the world and his or her relationships that enables a therapist to understand that subject's behavior and motivation. A therapist can only gain information about the internal object relations of a particular individual if that individual can reflect on and talk about his or her feelings and relationships.

Figure 1.1 attempts pictorially to present the inner world of a person, such as the famous and sophisticated actor mentioned previously. The diagram shows the actor, with inner representations of himself and of others—the women in his life and his parents. These

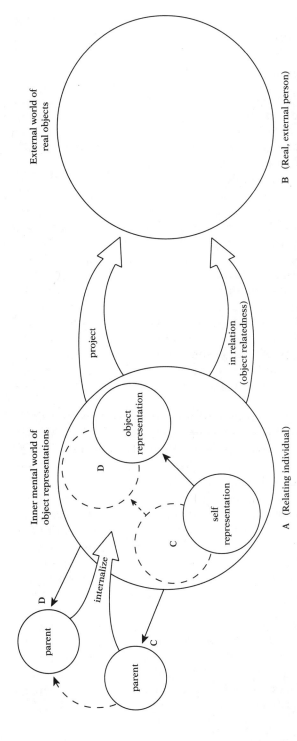

External world of
real objects

B   (Real, external person)

Inner mental world of
object representations

object
representation

D

C

self
representation

A   (Relating individual)

project

in relation
(object relatedness)

D

parent

internalize

C

parent

Figure 1.1 The inner and external worlds of objects. *Object relations* refers to the internal world where there are representations of the self in relation to representations of the object. These inner images may or may not accurately express objects as they actually exist in the "real" world. This illustration shows in a schematized way the inner and outer world of a person in relation to relationship, perhaps the actor mentioned on page 4. Person A, the actor, deals with person B in terms of his inner world, which is shaped and even distorted by his previous dealings with parents C and D. A has not only internalized his parents' interactions, expecting that this will be replicated in his own intimate relationships, but he has also identified with one of his parents and may project an idealized image onto B, thus relating with B in terms of the projected, idealized image.

7

representations from the past serve as emotional filters, coloring and shaping current perceptions and relationships with people.

Self Representation

In addition to the images or representations of objects, another aspect of an infant's inner mental world includes the representations of its own developing self. *Self representation* is the mental expression of the self as it is experienced in relationship with the objects or significant persons in the child's environment.

The infant is initially unable to distinguish objects from the self; objects seem to be parts or aspects of the self. Thus, infants are unable to differentiate their mothers' breasts from their own thumbs, which they accidentally find with their mouths and suck. Gradually, the infant begins to differentiate the object from the self, the nonself from the self, and the object representation from the self representation.

Mental representations of objects and of the self usually have emotional energy attached to them. This emotional energy or affective charge is, in the beginning of the child's development, a sensation of pleasure or unpleasure. What causes unpleasurable feelings in the infant is taken in and internalized as an inner bad object. That is, its mental immaturity only allows the infant to experience the world in subjective terms of "good for me" or "painful for me." The child cannot yet discern that the inner bad object is someone in the external world who frustrates or frightens the child.

If the child feels pleasurable feelings, then the child is "good" because of the gratifying object and because the child's needs are met. If the child has unpleasant feelings (caused by the frustrating or "bad" object), then the child, in his or her self representation, is "bad," and the child's needs are probably unmet.

A self representation shapes how a person relates to others and the world. For example, a man may begin his career in poverty and gain riches, but his self-image may not change, so he may continue to dress shabbily because he still views himself as someone who needs to scrimp and save and not "waste" money on clothes for himself. An objective observer notes that the man has the wealth, but the observer can only guess at the inner images of the self that determine how he spends his money.

Some object relations theorists stress how the self representation is often linked with other mental processes, such as projection and different forms of identification and internalization. This might involve, for example, mentally projecting a person's own feelings onto others and then behaving toward others on the basis of this inner distorted perception. For instance, a mentally disturbed murderer, shooting at the police closing in on him, shouted, "Kill me, kill me, you know I'm guilty!" His own sense of guilt was projected onto the police, and he wanted them to punish him for his crime. A different person might not have externalized his or her own aggressive feelings in such a way and might even have directed aggression against himself by intense guilt or by physical violence against himself in the form of suicide.

Part Objects and Whole Objects

The images and representations of the mental world are not always of whole objects, but there can be representations of part objects; that is, of a part of a person, such as a foot or penis or breast, or even part of the subject's own body as an object, such as a thumb on which the infant is sucking (Arlow, 1980, p. 113).

The term *part object* more usually refers to a representation of an object in terms of whether it is subjectively experienced as good or bad, pleasurable or nonpleasurable for the subject. To experience an object in terms of whether the object gratifies or frustrates is to have only a partial perspective of the object, a perspective that suggests an either/or quality. To view the object in terms of its capacity to both gratify and frustrate is to see the object as a *whole object.*

Generally, the earliest representations of infants are of partial objects. The infant, because of perceptual and emotional immaturity, is capable of only limited perception and can perceive only one characteristic of the real object at a time, such as the satisfaction that the nurturing breast brings or the frustration that the absent breast brings. Satisfying is "good" and frustrating is "bad." The infant at this early stage is unable to hold two ideas or notions simultaneously, such as that its mother is *both* "good" and "bad." Gradually, with growth and development, the infant develops the capacity to see its mother as a whole object that both satisfies and frustrates.

Structures

When a child visibly struggles to get control over intense feelings and puts into words why he or she is crying, an observer sees the work of several psychological functions that are ascribed to the "ego." Usually the concepts of ego, id, and superego, as well as various psychological processes and ways of relating, are considered *structures.* Structures refer to psychological processes and functions that are organized and stable; they are concepts, not things. An observer only knows about possible structures if they are manifested in behavior or in inner experience.

How structures come to be built up within the personality is explained differently by each theorist. Some theorists emphasize the role of repressing instincts and feelings. Other theorists emphasize processes of internalization by which a function that was performed by a parent, for instance, is taken in and established within a child so the child now performs the function for him or herself.

Self

Self occupies a different level of conceptualization than does the term *ego*. An observer cannot see the ego directly, since it is an abstract concept that exists only in psychology books. But ego is conceptualized as an organizer of psychic functions and can be observed in the manifestation of such functions as thinking, judging, integrating, and the like. Self is used in several senses—most broadly, as the whole subject in contrast to the surrounding world of objects. The self is our basic experience of the person that we are. The self can be understood as the broader organization that includes all the psychic agencies, including the ego, in a superordinate integration.

Some ego psychologists would see object relations as one of the critical functions carried on by the superordinate organization of the self, so that object relations belong not to one mental agency (the ego) but rather to all of them together. An object relationship takes place between the self and its objects, rather than between the id and objects or between the ego and objects (Meissner, 1980, p. 241).

We can represent ourself to ourself, even though it is the ego that carries out the internal function of self representation. The self, then, can be the self representation of an individual. This self representation is similar to the object representation and is at a different abstract level from the self as person and locus of experience.

Splitting

Splitting is one of several psychic mechanisms to which both object relations theory and self psychology call attention. This mechanism includes both normal developmental processes and defensive processes. Infants make use of splitting to help order chaotic early life experiences. After the serenity of the womb, the infant experiences life as a buzzing, chaotic discontinuity, and splitting is related to processes that allow the infant to let in as much of the environment as he or she can manage, without the whole undigestible experience. Thus, early splitting refers to the maturational inability to synthesize incompatible experiences into a whole.

For example, the infant has strong contradictory feelings (such as love or hate, pleasure or frustration) but can only keep one of these feelings or thoughts in its immature awareness at a time. The result is a representation of a part object, which is an object with only one particular quality, such as "frustrating"; the seemingly contradictory quality of "pleasure giving" is excluded from the infant's awareness. Only with growing maturity will the infant be able to integrate simultaneously into one stable image the seemingly opposite aspects of the same object or experience, such as the frustrating aspects of the pleasure-giving mother. To maintain this fragile personality structure, the infant uses splitting to keep apart the conflicting feelings that the good and bad aspects of the mother arouse internally within the infant.

Object Relations Theorists

A number of psychoanalytic writers may be loosely grouped together under the title of object relations theorists. They use many of the concepts and terms of the psychoanalytic tradition but give particular emphasis to the study of object relations. As object relations theorists, they may differ among themselves, but all share a common concern about the primacy of relationships over innate instinctual drives. That is, they tend to give a greater weight to the influence of environment in shaping personality than do Freud and the other, more traditional psychoanalytic scholars.

At the center of the object relations theorists' disagreement with Freud is the relative weight given to innate biological factors in shaping the personality as opposed to the influence of relationships. This shift from Freud's early notions of object and the instinctual aspects of early relationships means that object relations theorists focus on preoedipal development as explained in terms of self representation and object representation. Thus, in their study of the development and shaping of personality, the object relations theorists will generally give emphasis to environmental influences rather than innate influences. The less emphasis a theorist ascribes to innate biological factors, the more weight will be given to how an individual develops a self through relationships within a family and how this self in turn relates in a characteristic way toward others. Object relations theorists generally study disorders in relationships and have contributed significant insights to the study of borderline and schizoid personalities.

Object relations theorists such as Melanie Klein, W. R. D. Fairbairn, Edith Jacobson, D. W. Winnicott, Margaret Mahler, and Otto Kernberg will be reviewed in later chapters. These theorists stand out because their original and influential ideas greatly help therapists understand people and relationships.

Self Psychology

The psychology of the self refers to the work of Heinz Kohut and his followers. Kohut brings changes to notions of object relations and the concepts of Freud. Because of his work with narcissistic personality disorders, Kohut gives a different emphasis to certain aspects of object relations that he sees in terms of narcissism. He alters the classical notion of narcissism, which, in Freud's view, is a stage through which the normal person passes, to a concept that narcissism has its own separate development and its own form of pathology requiring special treatment.

A critical issue for self psychology involves the nature and kind of emotional investment in the self. Kohut speaks of narcissistic investment, and Freud of libidinal investment. Freud implied that narcissistic people—people who "loved" themselves in an unhealthy way because of the investment of libido in themselves—could not form relationships with others and hence could not be treated in therapy because they were unable to establish a relationship with a therapist. Kohut understands narcissism differently and believes that narcissistic persons can have relationships or object relations, but they are narcissistic object relations. This means that the person deals with objects as if the object were part of the self or that the object performs a crucial function for the self. This kind of distorted relationship requires a treatment different from that used with neurotics.

"Case" Study

A brief reference to Cinderella again might illuminate some of the concepts of inner representations and structures, and fragmentation and splitting. Cinderella, perhaps, views her stepmother as demanding and unpleasant, a bad woman with whom she feels cautious, sullen, and depressed. On the other hand, she views her fairy godmother as wonderful and all-giving and who makes Cinderella feel exuberant and powerful. With the Prince, Cinderella feels girlish and tender and has a great craving to be with him. With just a bit of imaginative exaggeration, it is possible to notice how Cinderella behaves and feels differently with people as if she had very different subselves within herself competing with each other in an unintegrated way. Those who deal with her may find her emotional shifts bewildering. She also may feel herself to be fragmented and a different person in different circumstances.

Her self representation provides a way of feeling and thinking about herself, partly conscious and partly unconscious. The self representation is closely linked with an object representation, so in the relation with her disliked stepmother Cinderella feels badly about herself. In relation to someone who is a good object, like the fairy godmother,

Cinderella feels good. Cinderella's tendency to experience her self and others in sharp extremes of good and bad is called splitting. Splitting, a childhood defense that can continue into adulthood, suggests a trauma during childhood that could have disorganized inner structures. The traumatic loss of Cinderella's natural mother could indeed have caused enough disorganization and lack of integration within Cinderella so that she does experience rapid mood swings and intense feelings. Her feelings and ways of relating, like different ego states or subselves, would be experienced as unexplained mood shifts and a sense of fragmentation or coming apart. Integration, in contrast, would imply a coherence of the different subselves into a unified personality that responds to different situations with consistency.

The core issues of psychoanalytical theory heighten many of the important similarities and differences of the various conceptual models. Each model would approach a client such as Cinderella—as well as her husband, the Prince—in a different way and with a different focus.

Core Issues

Good theory is consistent, and as one part of a theory is altered, a ripple effect is created throughout the theory. This occurs in psychoanalytic theory as theorists of object relations and the self wrestle with a variety of issues in contrast to the classic Freudian model. As these theorists shift the emphasis from Freud's instinctual drive model to models that give greater emphasis to interpersonal relationships and the self, they address certain issues with a different emphasis. Four of the crucial issues we will examine are: (1) the nature of objects and the shift from Freud's emphasis on instinctual drives, (2) the nature and formation of psychic structure, (3) the developmental stages viewed in terms of relationships with objects, and (4) the different views of conflict and the consequences for therapy.

The Nature of Objects and the Shift from Instincts

An essential cornerstone of Freud's theory of the personality is the concept of instinctual drives as the basic human motivation. The theme of drives—how they are transformed and blocked—permeates Freud's writings. Instincts are innate, and the earliest intrapsychic state of a child is the state of primary narcissism, where the ego is the object of libidinal instinct and there are no external objects in which the child invests psychic energy. Hence, in Freud's theory, there is no preordained tie to people. The drives precede the object and even "create" the object by the experience of satisfaction and frustration, and the drives basically determine the quality of relationships. Freud sees the object as satisfying the impulse. Only later in his writings does Freud wrestle with how to position in his theory an individual's relations with the external world. Essentially, then, in the Freudian drive model, the object is the creation of drives, and object relations are a function of drive (cf. Greenberg & Mitchell, 1983, pp. 42–44).

Object relations theorists talk about objects in a variety of ways, but in general, they deviate from Freud's discussion of object exclusively in terms of instinctual drives. Melanie Klein (1975a, 1975b) is the first to revise Freud's model by giving greater weight to the interpersonal environment as a determining influence on the developing personality. She retains a considerable role for the instinctual drives by viewing transactions between the infant and its objects almost exclusively in terms of drives as transformed by or represented by phantasy (Gedo, 1979, p. 362). Klein's influence prompted Fairbairn (1943/1954) to radically revise the Freudian tradition by staking out a "pure" object relations position. Fairbairn's theory proposes that the main drive that a person has is a drive for a relationship, not the satisfaction of biological instinct. Thus, he views personality and its motivation in terms of interpersonal transactions rather than biological instincts.

The shift in object relations theory from biological drives as motivation to striving for interpersonal relationships has an important consequence. Object relations theorists assign the functions of the id to the ego; that is, they attribute libidinal energy to the ego.

Fairbairn radically departs from Freud's model of libidinal energy by conceptually doing away with the id and developing the concept of a unitary ego with its own energy. Changing the nature of psychic energy leads Fairbairn to significant changes. Thus, he does not distinguish between structure and psychic energy. The ego in his model seeks relations with objects rather than just trying to control an unruly id. According to Fairbairn, if the child's relationship with the parents is good, the child's ego is whole. Conversely, if the relationship is bad, the child's ego establishes compensating internal objects. This basically means structure and energy are located within the ego.

Other object relations theorists, such as Edith Jacobson (1964) and Otto Kernberg (1976), attempt to develop models that integrate object relations without sacrificing instinctual drives in explaining development and motivation. Their integrative attempts usually involve changing the meaning of terms and utilizing such concepts as object representation.

Heinz Kohut (1971, 1977) puts the Freudian investment of objects with libidinal drives to one side. Kohut's focus is not on object relationships between two separate and distinct persons. Kohut develops the concept of narcissistic investment in objects. Narcissistic investment sees objects in terms of their relation to the self; that is, objects experienced as part of the self or performing functions for the self that the self is not yet able to do. In his later writings, Kohut makes instinctual drives secondary and focuses on the self and its very early relations with a selfobject; that is, an object perceived as omnipotent and carrying out crucial self-esteem functions for the self.

The Nature and Formation of Psychic Structure

Structure, a concept used metaphorically and perhaps inexactly, describes the psychological organization and the constituent parts of the person. Freud described these aspects of the personality as the id, the ego, and the superego.

An observer cannot see the inner organization of the personality directly, since it is a hypothetical construct, but a stable patterning and consistency of behavior in the person can be seen. The classic psychoanalytic drive model considers how the repression of drives plays a central role in the emergence of the ego from the id. For Freud, the ego continues to be dependent on the id for energy.

Object relations theorists generally challenge the traditional Freudian understanding of structure. They look to the influence of external objects (the parents and other significant people in the child's world) to build internal psychic organization. The organization and building up of the personality results from *internalization,* a mental process by which an individual transforms regulatory interactions and characteristics of his or her environment into inner regulations and characteristics (Schafer, 1968, p. 9). Object relations theorists give greater emphasis to internalization that deals with relationships than to repression that deals with drives (cf. Klein, 1983; Sternbach, 1983).

Structural formation involves a process by which an aspect of the child's external world has been abandoned as an external object and taken into the ego by a process of identification, thus becoming a part of the child's internal world. This new internal agency carries on the same basic functions that had previously been carried on by the people or abandoned objects in the external world (Ogden, 1983, p. 228). Such an agency in traditional Freudian terms would be the superego, as it judges and threatens the ego like the parents whose place it has taken. Fairbairn, however, makes the same agency part of the ego and labels it the *internal saboteur* or *antilibidinal ego.*

Otto Kernberg, in contrast to Fairbairn, seeks an integration of object relations and the Freudian structural model. His compromise sees *units of object relations* as the essential building blocks of the ego as a psychic structure. These units of object relations, which organize the ego out of chaos, are images of the self in reaction to an object, with each image having a specific feeling tone.

Taking an object into the ego implies establishing an agency within the psyche; that is, an aspect of personality carries on functions internally that were previously performed by external objects. The traditional psychoanalytic model explains the formation of the superego in this way, while object relations theorists use this as a way to explain the formation of the ego. They understand structure formation as a process of internalizing a *relationship with an object*. This, for example, is the basis for Kernberg's concept of units of object relations and for Fairbairn's joining of parts of the ego to objects.

Kohut's structural concerns are for the formation of a cohesive self. This is built up by what he calls *transmuting internalizations*, a process by which the self gradually withdraws narcissistic investment from objects that performed functions for the self and which the self is now able to perform. These psychic functions of the self include reality-testing, regulating self-esteem, and the like—all of which earlier writers had assigned to the ego.

Developmental Stages in Terms of Relationships with Objects

Freud's developmental model centers on the progressive appearance of instinctual energy in bodily zones, such as that which takes place during the oral, anal, and genital stages. For him, the oedipal stage, occurring roughly from the third to the fifth year, is a period of innovation as the child turns from a two-person relationship (mother and child) to a three-person relationship. For Freud, understanding the oedipal crisis is of central importance in understanding object relations (libidinal investment of objects) and neurotic patterns.

Object relations theories are essentially developmental theories that examine developmental processes and relationships prior to the oedipal period. Fairbairn, Mahler, Klein, and Kohut all set developmental crises earlier and in different terms than does Freud. They see the crucial developmental issue as being the child's move from a state of fusion and dependence on the mother to a state of increased independence and increased differentiation (cf. Eagle, 1984, p. 185). The child fills its self-esteem "tank" during this early period of fusion and symbiosis. Disruptions during this period cause the child to feel depleted and empty.

Object relations theory links the emergence of the self with the increasing maturity of relationships with objects. Looking at the relationships and processes of the child with the mother, object relations theories discuss the timing when psychic structures are formed, the ego, in particular, and the quality of the relationships that the psychic structures have with objects.

The self is capable of a different quality of relationship at specific stages of development. This means that the self, originally fused and undifferentiated from the mother object, becomes more independent as it differentiates and experiences itself separate from the mother. Using an empirical model of observation, Mahler (1968) describes the child moving from symbiosis to separation and individuation. In contrast to Mahler, Kohut uses the data of adults in therapy to trace the early reliance of the self on selfobjects. Kohut describes the development of a cohesive self and possible developmental arrests of the self.

Kernberg describes these same differentiating processes by referring to a fusion of self representation with an object representation and the gradual establishment of a clearly differentiated self representation.

During the early preoedipal and oedipal years, a child's object relations do not seem to be between the id and objects or between the ego and objects but rather between the self (or its mental representation) and objects (or their mental representation within the self). Different theorists argue for different explanations—and raise difficult questions. For example, if perceptual functions, even inner perceptions about the self, are ascribed to the ego, how can there be object representations before the emergence of the ego? Is there some primitive ego that always coexists with the id? Does the ego emerge earlier than previously thought, earlier than Freud suggested?

Melanie Klein affirms that the ego is present from birth, and she assigns many organizing processes, even oedipal issues, to the period immediately after birth. Her two developmental "positions" take place during the first year. Fairbairn resolves the question of the development of the ego by looking at the increasing maturity of the ego's relationship to objects.

"Conflict" and Its Consequences for Therapy

Object relations and self psychology theorists view disturbance differently from the classical Freudian model, and with significant consequences for therapy.

The traditional Freudian model understands psychological disturbance as conflict between instinctual demands and the demands of reality, and conflict among the id, the ego, and the superego. The unresolved conflicts of childhood, especially unfinished oedipal conflicts, can continue unconsciously and emerge during adulthood. As the ego defensively responds to threatening thoughts and libidinal feelings, a neurotic compromise is reached that manifests itself in neurotic symptoms.

The Freudian analyst will attempt to uncover the conflicts and seek the unconscious causes of the neurotic symptoms.

In contrast, object relations theorists and self psychologists define conflict and disturbance differently, and they locate pathology differently within the psyche. Psychological disturbance involves damage to the self and the structures of the psyche. Early developmental deficits hinder building a cohesive self and prevent the integration of psychic structures. These preoedipal developmental deficits can result in narcissistic and borderline personalities, which are more serious disturbances than the classical neurosis. For Fairbairn, conflict resides within the ego rather than being between the ego and other psychic structures. Thus, Fairbairn speaks of split-off aspects of the ego (bad objects) at war with other parts of the ego.

Another area of controversy between object relations theorists and Freud concerns the role of aggression. Object relations theorists and self psychologists regard aggression not so much as an instinct but as a response or reaction to a pathological situation. Early developmental deficits and early frustrations in relationships produce aggression. Kohut sees narcissistic rage as a response of the archaic self to not getting what it needs. Kernberg also points to early aggression as a response to relational frustrations, and this reactive aggression prevents the integration of object relations units. He uses a feeding metaphor to describe how a child normally "metabolizes" or psychologically digests and integrates early relational units of feelings and images. Frustration in the mother-child relationship keeps the child from integrating these psychological building blocks, and so these units (of self images and object images) remain "undigested." As undigested aspects of the childish self, they can return as primitive feeling states and unintegrated emotion. The borderline personality has intense childish feeling states that cause an adult to react as an emotional infant.

While Freud focused on repression and the neurotic personality, object relations theorists and self psychologists tend to focus on problems in the structure of personality that manifest themselves in serious difficulties in relationships. Kohut describes narcissistic personality disorders where there are deficits in the structure of the self. The narcissistic personality's disturbed relationships reflect the unfinished, archaic self seeking fulfillment of infantile needs. While the narcissistic personality tends to have a cohesive but archaic self, the borderline personality, as described by Kernberg, is characterized by a fragmented self, where the use of psychological splitting manifests itself in contradictory feeling states. Later chapters further compare and contrast these two disorders, which object relations theory and self psychology have illuminated.

Psychoanalysis has always emphasized the role of relationships in therapy in the form of transferences. Because object relations and self theories emphasize the role of relationships in causing pathology, they emphasize relationships in therapy as part of the diagnostic process and as part of the healing process. As structural deficiencies result from early deficits in the mother-child relationship, so therapeutic restructuring will occur if the therapist (or analyst) can provide the kind of relationship that the patient needs for integrating the different split-off aspects of the personality. The therapist will work on the here-and-now relationship with the patient to make inner changes that heal the then-and-there deficits in the patient's personality.

Therapy, in particular psychoanalytically oriented therapy, provides the opportunity for a patient to confront his or her primitive feelings with a more mature ego, an ego "borrowed" from the therapist. It is as if the unmanageable feelings from childhood can finally be mastered by the patient's adult self. The patient can experience chaotic, split-off aspects of the self and contradictory feelings in the presence of the therapist, who fosters in the patient a sense of being able to manage these feelings in a way not possible when the patient was a child.

Case Illustration

In the following "case study," we can compare and contrast how the three theoretical models—Freudian, object relations, and self psychology—might approach a client.

The client is a pious painter named Christoph, who was troubled with a variety of compulsive and hysterical symptoms. Nine years before the onset of the symptoms, in a state of depression about his life and work, he made a pact with the Devil to surrender himself after nine years, which was now ending. The pact had not demanded wine, women, and song, as might be expected but rather that the Devil serve as a substitute for the painter's dead father. With the period of the pact coming to an end, Christoph prays for a miracle, hoping that God will save him and make the Devil free him from the pact.

Freud (1923/1981) would examine this "case" as a neurosis on which psychoanalysis can shed light. Freud would speculate as to the psychological mechanisms and the instinctual impulses at the base of the disturbance. Freud might believe that Christoph was very depressed at the death of his father and that this depression inhibited his work, stirring up fears and anxiety. The fears and anxiety drove him to make the pact in which he demands that the Devil act as a substitute for the father he had loved. The pact is a neurotic fantasy suggesting the painter's ambivalent feelings toward his father. The painter's longing for his father is in neurotic conflict with unresolved and unacceptable fears as well as defiance of the father. By means of the psychological mechanism of projection, Christoph substitutes God as the longed-for father, and his hostile attitude toward his father comes to expression in the figure of the Devil. The symbol of the Devil troubles Christoph because it represents instinctual feelings that are bad, unacceptable, and repressed. The Devil is so terrifying because the unconscious feelings that are projected into the external world are unacceptable and terrifying. In therapy, Freud would attempt to uncover the unconscious conflict that likely comes from the unfinished issues of the oedipal period of development. By gaining insight into his conflict, Christoph might be freed from his neurotic symptoms.

Fairbairn (1943/1954, pp. 70–74), an object relations theorist, has an alternative way of understanding Christoph. He views the painter not according to Freudian impulses but more explicitly in terms of object relations. The neurotic illness of the painter is viewed as an example of possession by the bad object and the terror of the return of repressed feelings. Christoph does not seek pleasure or the gratification of impulses but rather a father, a good object.

Fairbairn believes that children develop mechanisms to deal with difficulties from frustrations or bad relationships. The child defensively internalizes what is bad or frustrating in his or her environment. A child would rather become bad than have bad objects in the environment, and so the child becomes "bad" by defensively taking on the badness that appears to reside in the objects. The child seeks to make the objects in his or her environment good, purging them of their badness, by taking them on and making them part of his or her own psychological structure. The price of outer security is having troubling bad objects within; in other words, the world is good but now the child is "bad." Once the bad object is within the child, he or she has to further defend against the internalized bad object by repressing any awareness of the object or feelings about it. In religious terms, this might be expressed as, "It is better to be a sinner in a world ruled by God than to live in a world ruled by the Devil" (Fairbairn, 1943/1954, p. 66). The sinner may be bad, but there is security in a world ruled by a good object. In a world ruled by bad objects, there is neither security nor hope (Fairbairn, 1943/1954, p. 67).

This, in Fairbairn's opinion, is Christoph's situation. Even if Christoph's father had been a bad object during the boy's childhood, his bad qualities were balanced by redeeming features that the son was able to perceive and relate to. But when the father died, the bad features returned to awareness (return of the repressed), and the son was at the mercy of this internalized bad object. In other words, Christoph was terribly alone and had to have *someone*, even this bad object, so he would not be objectless and deserted. So he embraces the bad object that simultaneously causes him to feel aggressive toward the father and bad about himself. Guilt over these aggressive feelings probably causes the depression.

Fairbairn, then, sees the pact as a neurotic attempt to hold onto the bad object. The Devil is associated with the deceased father and the bad feelings; the good object and the good feelings are associated with God. Therapy is like a "miraculous cure" in that it releases from the unconscious a bondage to the internalized bad object, which in Christoph's case was both indispensable and intolerable. Fairbairn does not see Christoph in terms of ego and impulse but in terms of his relationships and what those relationships do to his internal world. Dealing with the good object (God) enabled Christoph to regain his good feelings about himself and cast out the bad object.

Kohut would look for the narcissistic elements in this case and would attend to the kind of transference relationship Christoph established with the therapist. The death of the father undid the painter's narcissistic balance, and the pact would be expressive of the grandiosity of the archaic, unmirrored self that seeks to complete what was never finished in childhood. Christoph is desperately seeking an idealized object that will confirm his impoverished self. His attempt to control reality by the magical pact masks his inner emptiness and lack of self-esteem. A powerful, omnipotent object would confirm his very existence and make him feel alive.

Confusion and Controversy

By now the reader may be getting a hint that the study of object relations and the self is not a neat or orderly realm. In fact, the theories and concepts of object relations and the self do not form a unified, discrete, or universally accepted body of truths but are a collection of suppositions and concepts based on clinical experience and observation. Psychoanalytic theory has historically progressed by a lively process of refining and clarifying early fertile concepts and their implications without necessarily abandoning any of them. This is especially true of the psychoanalytic study of object relations and the self. Many theorists and clinicians have contributed to the body of knowledge, and the result is multiple perceptions, overlapping frames of reference, disagreements over terminology, and a lack of orderly schema that all can agree upon. Especially confusing is the use of the same vocabulary by theorists who ascribe very different meanings to the terms because of their differing orientations.

Nevertheless, despite the lack of theoretical consensus, the concepts of object relations theorists and self psychology are valuable. They have added insight into borderline and narcissistic disorders and have aided in the task of diagnosis and formulating therapy strategies. In addition, theorists of object relations and the self have turned attention to early childhood development and the significance of very early interactions.

The following chapters in this book focus on the principal theorists of object relations and the self. The discussion is limited to the key elements of how each theorist uses terms and understands development and psychological disturbance. Each chapter provides a case example of how the particular theorist either did approach or would be likely to approach a client.

References

Arlow, J. (1980). Object concept and choice. *Psychoanalytic Quarterly, 49,* 109ff.

Boesky, D. (1983). Representations in self and object theory. *Psychoanalytic Quarterly, 52,* 564–583.

Eagle, M. N. (1984). *Recent developments in psychoanalysis: A critical evaluation.* New York: McGraw-Hill.

Fairbairn, W. R. D. (1954). The repression and the return of bad objects. In *An object relations theory of personality* (pp. 59–81). New York: Basic Books. (Original work published 1943)

Freud, S. (1981). A neurosis of demonical possession in the seventeenth century. In J. Strachey (Ed. and Trans.), *The standard edition of the complete psychological works of Sigmund Freud* (Vol. 4, pp. 436–472). London: Hogarth Press. (Original work published 1923)

Gedo, J. E. (1979). Theories of object relations: A metapsychological assessment. *Journal of the American Psychoanalytic Association, 27,* 361–373.

Greenberg, J. R., & Mitchell, S. A. (1983). *Object relations in psychoanalytic theory.* Cambridge: Harvard University Press.

Jacobson, E. (1964). *The self and the object world.* New York: International Universities Press.

Kernberg, O. (1976). *Object relations theory and clinical psychoanalysis.* New York: Aronson.

Klein, M. (1975a). *Love, guilt and reparation and other works, 1921–1945.* New York: Delta Books.

Klein, M. (1975b). *Envy and gratitude and other works, 1946–1963.* New York: Delta Books.

Klein, M. I. (1983). Freud's drive theory and ego psychology: A critical evaluation of the Blancks. *Psychoanalytic Revue, 70,* 505–517.

Kohut, H. (1971). *The analysis of the self.* New York: International Universities Press.

Kohut, H. (1977). *The restoration of the self.* New York: International Universities Press.

Mahler, M. (1968). *On human symbiosis and the vicissitudes of individuation.* New York: International Universities Press.

Meissner, W. W. (1980). The problem of internalization and structure formation. *International Journal of Psycho-Analysis, 61,* 237–248.

Ogden, T. H. (1983). The concept of internal object relations. *International Journal of Psycho-Analysis, 64,* 227–248.

Sandler, J., & Rosenblatt, B. (1962). The concept of the representational world. *Psychoanalytic Study of the Child, 17,* 128–145.

Schafer, R. (1968). *Aspects of internalization.* New York: International Universities Press.

Sternbach, O. (1983). Critical comments on object relations theory. *Psychoanalytic Revue, 70,* 403–421.

Chapter Two

The Freudian Starting Point: Concepts Relevant to Object Relations and Self Psychology Theories

Introduction

Sigmund Freud's model of the individual serves as the starting point for many of the theorists who follow him. Freud himself reworked his own ideas, abandoning some and revising others. Insofar as he continued to clarify and alter his concepts, his conceptual model might be considered incomplete. His model includes an understanding of object relations even though he did not work out all the implications of it, nor did he give to object relations the kind of emphasis that later scholars did. He did, however, originate the concepts and the terms that serve as the foundation and starting point for later object relations and self psychology theorists.

Born in 1856, Freud grew up in Vienna and received his medical degree there in 1881. In 1885, he studied in Paris under Jean Charcot, the famous French neurologist. In 1886, Freud returned to Vienna and settled down to private practice. His early patients often suffered from hysteria and neurasthenia. Haltingly at first, Freud gradually moved beyond the neurology and treatment practices of his time to pioneer a psychological method for the understanding and treatment of neuroses. In 1938, the annexation of Austria by the Nazis compelled him to leave Vienna for London, where he died in 1939.

As Freud crafted his theory of the personality, he tried to accomplish various goals. He worked to articulate a theory of motivation that would help explain human behavior and to understand the formative elements that shape personality. In his efforts to explain motivation, he balanced innate biological aspects (the drives) with environmental aspects (the influence of the parents), or in different terms, nature versus nurture. Drives represent the role of biology or nature, and the environmental aspect considers the influence of people or nurturing objects in the environment. Nearly all theorists agree that both nature and nurture shape the human personality, but they disagree as to which is the dominant influence.

Although Freud conceded both nature and nurture as shaping forces on personality (Gedo, 1979), he attached more significance to nature and the instinctual drives. His model is a drive model. He used instinct to explain the relationships and environmental forces that shape an individual's personality. The instincts serve as the framework for his discussions of motivation and object relationships. He assumed that biological or instinctual drives are primary and precede the object. Object relations are a function of instinctual drives.

A "pure" object relations model, in sharp contrast to Freud, focuses exclusively on relationships and environmental influences to explain motivation. Fairbairn, for example, rejects the Freudian emphasis on instinctual drives. This shift in emphasis critically changes Fairbairn's understanding of the structure of the personality and the motivation in relationships. The same is true for Kohut. Shifting from the Freudian emphasis on drives leads Kohut to emphasize the self and its relation to selfobjects rather than the ego in relation to the drives.

In reviewing Freudian theory as a starting point for examining object relations and self psychology theories, I will concentrate on the following: key concepts, formation of psychological structures, stages of development and the choice of objects, pathology, classical therapy or analysis, a case study, and assessment and evaluation of Freud's theory.

Key Concepts

Relationships and Drives

Relationships, or interpersonal transactions in an individual's life, are important for Freud, but they are subordinate to human drives. Freud viewed object relations primarily in terms of instinctual needs and the people who gratify them. There is a conceptual difference between objects and people, and within Freud's drive model there is no theoretical requirement that the object of a drive be a person (Greenberg & Mitchell, 1983, p. 38). The object of a drive could be a piece of clothing or an animal. When Freud looked at an individual's current behavior in terms of a past relationship with a significant person, he saw the relationship's significance in terms of the role that person played in arousing or satisfying the individual's needs rather than who or what that person was. Freud's model of object relations rests totally within an instinctual framework of drives.

The examination of drives is a conceptual method used by Freud to understand and explain *why* people behave the way they do. Freud explained *drives* as the motivation for a behavior through bodily demands that take the form of unconscious wishes and impulses that seek satisfaction. An excitement or urge begins in the body and makes itself felt in the mind as a demand to get something that will satisfy a particular need (Freud, 1905/1957k, 1933/1957f). An observer cannot directly see the drives, but only the *derivatives of drives*, which are the various transformations and substitutions of drives that reach consciousness as ideas, feelings, and *phantasies*. The hunger drive will prompt phantasies of food and eating. The hungrier a person is, the more insistent will be inner mental phantasies and hunger urges. The sexual and aggressive drives operate similarly. The more insistent the sexual drive, the more preoccupying will be the phantasies of seeking activities that will satisfy the need.

Freud distinguished four different components of each drive: aim, source, impetus, and object (1915/1957d, pp. 122–123). The *aim* of an instinct is the satisfaction and discharge of the instinct. The aim of the sexual instinct, for example, is the act toward which the instinct urges, sexual intercourse, which releases sexual tension and causes temporary extinction of the instinct. The aim of the hunger drive is eating, which removes the hunger and restores the feeling of satisfaction.

The *source* of an instinctual drive is the physiological condition or bodily need that results in a stimulus presented in the mind by the instinct. In the example of hunger, this would be the bodily need for nourishment. The *impetus*, or pressure of a drive, is the strength, force, or urgency of the drive, and depends on the intensity of the need.

The *object* of a drive is the thing or condition that will satisfy the drive. It might be likened to a target or goal. Thus, food is the object of the hunger drive, while the sexually attractive person is the object of the sexual drive. From the subject's point of view, objects are sought to fulfill instincts or biological needs. The object can be a person, part of a person (such as a face or breast), or even an inanimate thing. The object representation is how the object is psychologically present in a subject's mind.

When a subject becomes aware of an object that is pleasurable, the subject tries to get and somehow incorporate the object into the subject's ego. People choose and "love" attractive "objects" that promise to give pleasure. On the other hand, when an object causes painful feelings, the subject withdraws from the object and hates it or tries to expel it (Freud, 1915/1957d).

Object Choice

Object choice refers to an object in which a subject invests libidinal or psychic energy. Such an investment is made in the mental representation of the object rather than in the actual, external object. This process is called *cathexis*. To cathect an object is like "falling in love," choosing and investing energy in an object that is another person.

Libido refers to the amount of drive energy, usually sexual energy, and is the force by which the sexual drive finds expression (Freud, 1917/1957e, 1921/1957c). Freud pictured the libidinal energy as radiating out and becoming attached to objects as well as being taken back again into the ego (1914/1957g). When there is an investment of libido in the ego, this is called *narcissism*, a form of object choice with the ego itself as the object. Normally, young children will be very much focused on themselves and their bodies, but gradually with development comes an increased capacity to be attracted to others of the opposite sex, to make object choices of others, and to love someone other than themselves.

Identification and Formation of Psychological Structures

Many object relations theorists downplay the instinctual aspects of object relations and give emphasis to identification, which allows for some environmental influence on the formation of the ego.

Instincts play a steady and central role in Freud's understanding of the formation of the structures of the personality, even though he kept revising and refining his concepts. His early topographical model viewed personality in terms of layers of consciousness, with instincts being unconscious and ego functions conscious. Later, during the 1920s, Freud (1923/1957a) worked out his structural model, which presents the mind or psychic apparatus in terms of function; that is, structures whose functioning is constant. These structures are the id, ego, and superego. The *id*, completely unconscious, gives mental expression to or psychic representations of instinctual drives and serves as the source of psychic energy. Its basic role is to gain satisfaction of instinctual needs.

The *ego* works in contrast to the id and has multiple functions, primarily to mediate between the person's needs and the demands of the environment. The third psychic structure is the *superego*, which represents society within the psyche and passes judgment on the actions of the ego.

These structures emerge at different times. The id is present at birth and operates before the ego differentiates itself from the psychic apparatus. As the ego emerges, it faces the task of controlling or transforming id impulses. The ego makes use of various psychological mechanisms, especially repression, in the process of controlling instincts. The superego forms much later during the oedipal struggle.

Freud discussed various psychological mechanisms that play a role in forming these psychic structures. As the ego emerges, it faces the task of controlling or transforming id impulses. Through *repression*, the ego keeps from consciousness unwanted impulses of the id, and this fosters the ego's growth. The mechanism of identification plays a critical role in the formation of the superego. This mechanism has a different relationship to instincts than does repression and attends to objects in the environment in a way that repression does not.

Because identification attends to objects in the environment and is less involved with instincts, later object relations theorists make use of this mechanism in their explanations of the origin of the ego. *Identification*, broadly speaking, means to become like or to take on characteristics of someone. To clarify the different kinds of identifications, Freud refers to different kinds of relationships that the ego has to objects. For example, identification is the earliest emotional tie to a person or an object. The first way the ego chooses an object and relates to it is by the primal mechanism of *oral incorporation*. This early form of identification is a primitive way of becoming like an object. It is a mental process that is experienced and symbolized as a bodily process of eating or taking inside oneself, such as the infant phantasizing that it is taking the mother inside itself when it sucks in her milk. This implies that one person takes on characteristics of another by taking the other inside, similar to the way some primitive people believe they take on the attitudes of animals that they incorporate or to believers becoming like Christ when they receive Holy Communion (Freud, 1912/1957l, p. 142).

How does identification differ from the investment of psychic energy in an object (object choice or object cathexis)? Freud (1923/1957a) says that they are indistinguishable from each other during the oral phase of development. The later difference between identification and object choice can be compared to a child's identification with his father, in which he wants to *be like* him, and the child's choice of his father as an object, in which he wants to *have* him (Freud, 1921/1957c). The distinction between identification and object choice is one of viewpoint, looking either at the ego changing to be like the loved object or looking at the object that the ego loves or is in relation to.

According to Freud, identification gradually replaces object choice or cathexis. The libidinal energy changes and becomes desexualized, and the object is taken within the ego and invested with this desexualized energy. The ego is now invested with desexualized, narcissistic energy, identifies with the object, and takes on the object's characteristics. For example, a widow who lost a much-loved husband becomes *like* the husband and takes on characteristics that he used to possess. In short, identification replaces object cathexis.

When an identification replaces an object cathexis, the abandoned object cathexis often shapes the identification. For instance, children "love" their parents (as object choices), and by having them as cathected objects, the children become like them (by identification). The term *abandoned* means that the particular way of relating to these objects is replaced by a more mature one, and the earlier mode of relating enters the unconscious. These abandoned cathexes have enduring effects on relationships in adult life and are frequently manifested at some point in transference relationships during therapy.

The substitution of identification for object cathexis, according to Freud, happens frequently and plays an important role in the formation of the ego. The ego can be described as a precipitate of abandoned object choices or abandoned object cathexes. This means that the traces or residues of interpersonal relationships with important people remain and color the individual's identity. Thus, the ego contains within it the history of past object choices or past interpersonal relationships. The traces of past love relationships remain in the child's personality and cause the child to resemble his or her parents.

If the child's ego has too many object identifications and if they become too powerful and incompatible with one another, it can be pathological. An example of such pathology might be the multiple personalities of a Sybil or of a Jekyll and Hyde. In the case of multiple personalities, different identifications of the ego seize consciousness by turns and prevent integration into one personality.

In addition to using identification to explain aspects of ego formation, Freud used identification to explain the formation of the superego. The successful resolution of the oedipal struggle completes the formation of structure. The preoedipal child is in a dyadic relationship with the mother, and the gradual emergence of the triadic relationship with both parents marks the beginning of the oedipal situation. The child resolves the oedipal situation by identifying with the parent of the same sex and by forming a superego. The assimilation of the parents' authority by internalization sets up that authority within the child in the form of the superego.

Children experience intense desires and murderous wishes during the oedipal struggle. Conflict comes from the wish to have one parent in an exclusive, sensual way; the other parent, however, is a seemingly dangerous rival, blocking fulfillment of these sexual wishes and phantasies. Children resolve these conflicts as they gradually identify with their parents and internalize their various prohibitions. For example, a boy gradually transforms his object relationship with his mother from an erotic object choice into an object relationship that is affectionate rather than sexual. A girl similarly resolves the oedipal situation by identifying with her mother and by giving up the effort to satisfy oedipal wishes (LaPlanche & Pontalis, 1973, p. 436). (The reader should note that Freud's discussion, like that of some other writers discussed in this book, is based on stereotypical roles for men and women, such as the mother doing all the child care.)

The superego is the structural consequence of the oedipal complex. At the end stage of the oedipal complex, a portion of the external world has been partially abandoned as an external object, and by identification has been taken into the ego, becoming an integral part of the internal world (Freud, 1938/1957j). This new psychic agency continues to carry on those functions that hitherto the parents (the abandoned objects) performed in the external world. The superego threatens and judges exactly like the parents whose place it has taken. The superego embodies a successful identification with the parents' superego and gives permanent expression to their influence (Freud, 1923/1957a, p. 35).

Stages of Development and the Choice of Objects

Freud (1905/1957k) explained development in instinctual terms. It is the pattern of how the *libido* (the sex drive) becomes manifest in increasingly more organized ways. Development in terms of instinct is a movement from a general pleasure orientation to a specific sexual and genital aim. The movement is from an autoerotic infantile sexuality to a more object-directed relationship, where the focus of sexual feelings is in a sexual person other than oneself. To be more specific, Freud named each developmental phase by the zone in the body where libidinal energy becomes manifest, and so there are the *oral, anal, phallic, latency,* and *genital phases.*

Freud also suggested that the relationship between the ego and its objects changes during development; that is, there is a change in the nature and quality of the ego's choices of objects as the personality grows. This change is from early choices of the self as an object to the later mature choices of others as love objects. For example, a child may suck on her own thumb and in this way makes part of her own body a love object. But when this child becomes an adolescent, she will likely have a boyfriend, a love object separate from herself.

Developmental stages are the ways of indicating the different quality of relationships with objects and the different ways libido manifests itself. Freud suggested how the subject relates to the object in the names he gave to these stages: the oral-cannibalistic, anal-sadistic, phallic-oedipal, latency, and genital stages. As libido detaches from one object and one mode of gratification, there is a cathexis to a new object and a new mode of gratification (Compton, 1983a, p. 389). And so the infant proceeds, according to Freud, through stages, first relating to things it can incorporate through its mouth to a final stage in which it can relate to another person it can love in a mature way. Successful development is the ability to establish relationships with whole objects.

Freud looked at relationships or object choices in terms of how the object gratifies a need or instinct. The following discussion shows the sequence of different object choices that will guarantee the satisfaction of the person's instincts at these different developmental stages.

For the first 18 months of life, libidinal gratification centers on the mouth, lips, and tongue. The libido first attaches to the breast of the mother and to various sucking or intaking activities. The first object of the sexual instinct is the mother's breast or the person who cares for and nourishes the infant (Freud, 1914/1957g, p. 112). Gradually, infants, in their sucking activity, give up the breast and replace it with a part of their own body. The infant begins to suck his or her thumb. In this autoerotic object choice, infants make themselves independent of the consent of the external world for gaining pleasure. As the libido detaches itself from oral and sucking activities, it relates to feces and processes of control. During this anal period, consideration of the external object appears, for the child encounters the external world as an inhibiting power now, hostile to his or her desires. When the child is approximately 3 years old, libido cathects to the genitals, and children may begin to rub their genitals in a masturbatory fashion, with their own bodies as objects. During this phallic period, according to Freud, children become interested in what it is to have or not have a penis. The major sexual issues of the oedipal situation then arise, where the relationship with two parental objects becomes more complex than the simpler and earlier dyadic relationship with the mother alone. After the same-sex object choices of the latency years, the child enters the genital or adolescent period where the choice is heterosexual objects.

Freud's model of development differs from those of later object relations theorists. Freud's model focuses on instincts and sees development as successfully culminating when adults integrate all their early instincts and erogenous zones into their genital sexuality. Early sexual impulses become coordinated as part of an adult sexual experience. Object relations models view development more in perceptual terms. Successful development means achieving whole object relationships. Success in this model means overcoming those forces that lead to splitting early experiences; the mature adult can form unified images that accurately portray the real persons they are in relationship with (Greenberg & Mitchell, 1983, p. 42).

Pathology

Pathology refers to mental problems or emotional disturbance. Freud understood emotional or psychological disturbance as conflicts between the demands of instincts and the internal resistance to them from the ego and superego (1933/1957f). Conflicts take many forms. Building upon material already presented, we can examine three areas of disturbance that Freud explored: (1) neurotic conflict, (2) sexual perversions, and (3) pathological grief.

Neurotic Conflict

The personality has various ways to manage and transform instincts and psychological energy. The ego and superego scrutinize any instinct that arises in the id and proceeds toward consciousness. The ego and superego judge the appropriateness of this instinctual urge and how it seeks expression. Normally, the ego is able to manage forces of the id by healthy defenses. *Neurotic conflict* results when unconscious instinctual energies become unmanageable and defenses are unable to adequately contain these energies. Usually, conflict results in a compromise solution with some expression of the instinct or wish in the form of a symptom. The conflict remains unconscious, but the derivatives of instincts (their transformed manifestations, such as some behaviors or feelings) manifest themselves in the neurotic symptoms. The symptom in psychoanalysis is the symbolic expression of the problem, not the problem itself.

Sexual Perversions

During a child's growth, none of the libidinal attachments to objects is ever permanently left behind. These childish ways of sexually relating to objects and of gaining satisfaction get repressed, but they still remain in the unconscious, potentially available during periods of stress or regression (Freud, 1933/1957f). Adult sexual disturbances are a reemergence of these childish patterns of relating.

Sexual perversions are the manifestations in adults of childish patterns of object choices and immature modes of obtaining gratification. These adult sexual disturbances involve a particular kind of erotic object or a particular immature form of erotic activity. A fetishist is a troubled adult who rejects genital organs as an object of sexual impulse and becomes aroused by some other partial object (a foot, for instance) or some inanimate object (such as a shoe or silk panties). A necrophiliac (Freud, 1917/1957e) chooses dead bodies as erotic objects. A pederast chooses immature children as sexual objects. A voyeur changes the mode of sexual gratification so that looking, which is only preparatory to intercourse, becomes the central sexual activity.

Pathological Grief

Identification contributes to the symptoms of *pathological grief* (Freud, 1923/1957a, p. 28). When someone loses a valued object, a regressive process begins as a way to meet the pain. A grieving person who has lost someone dear often takes on characteristics of the lost person. Identification replaces object choice or object cathexis. For example, a boy who felt unhappy over losing his kitten declared openly that now he was the kitten and accordingly crawled around on his hands and knees (Freud, 1921/1957c, p. 109).

The grieving person tries to withdraw the emotional or libidinal investment from the object. By assuming characteristics of the object, the individual sets the object up within his or her own ego. The ego is then treated as though it were the abandoned or lost object. The individual will inflict himself with reproaches that rightly belong to the object. Identification replaces the object relationship. Now it is no longer a question of "I no longer *have* that dear friend" but rather "I *am* that friend, and I direct toward myself all the disappointment and anger I feel because of the friend's leaving" (Freud, 1921/1957c, p. 106).

Classical Therapy or Analysis

The techniques of psychoanalysis, such as the analysis of dreams and transferences, aim to uncover the unconscious conflict and to trace the conflict back to its origin. The origin of many emotional problems lie in the impulses of early life that were once repressed but that are now returning or threaten to return to consciousness. The individual responds to these threats by means of defenses; the analyst must interpret these defenses and help the client see the feelings behind the defenses.

Case Study

Freud's model of object relationships rests within an instinctual drive framework. He characteristically discussed patients in terms of his drive theory. This case study of Dr. Schreber, taken from Freud's early writings (Freud, 1911/1957h), illustrates how Freud examined drive theory through Dr. Schreber's relationships and conflicts.

Dr. Schreber's *Memoirs of a Neurotic* was published in 1903, and Freud's essay applied the principles of psychoanalysis to this autobiographical material. Dr. Schreber, who was not Freud's patient, was a prominent man who had several serious breakdowns. His symptoms included fears of persecution and death, the belief that his brain was softening, and elaborate delusions.

Two delusions predominated. Schreber believed that God had called him to redeem the world. For the sake of this higher mission, he had to be transformed into a woman, to be emasculated. This idea of emasculation as an injury and persecution was the salient feature of his delusional system. Schreber believed he had suffered injuries for a long time but that his femaleness was more prominent now, that his body had more female nerves, and that God would impregnate him.

Freud sought to make some sense out of Dr. Schreber's strange thoughts by applying psychoanalytic concepts. Freud noted that a person who is hated and feared for being a persecutor was at one time loved and honored. Indeed, Schreber names his physician, Dr. Paul Flechsig, as the instigator of the acts of persecution. Schreber at one time greatly appreciated his doctor. Schreber's relationship with his doctor was a *transference;* that is, "an emotional cathexis [that] became transposed from some person who was important to him on to the doctor who was in reality indifferent to him" (Freud, 1911/1957h, p. 47). Schreber's affectionate dependence on his doctor intensified into erotic desire. One night when he was half asleep, Schreber had a feeling that it must be nice to be a woman submitting to an act of copulation. Freud believed Schreber's mental illness began when he had this wishful phantasy of being female (or passively homosexual). Schreber resisted the phantasy and the outburst of "homosexual libido," whose object was his doctor, Flechsig. Schreber struggled against the sexual impulse, and his defense in this conflict took the shape of delusions of persecution (Freud, 1911/1957h, p. 43).

The delusions developed so that the figure of God replaced the figure of Flechsig. This change in delusion was an attempt at resolving Schreber's sexual conflict. "It was impossible for Schreber to become reconciled to playing the part of a female wanton towards his doctor; but the task of providing God Himself with the voluptuous sensations that he required called up no such resistance on the part of his ego" (Freud, 1911/1957h, p. 48).

Freud reflected how Schreber psychologically split his persecutor into God and Flechsig. If the persecutor Flechsig was originally a person whom Schreber had loved, then God must also have been the reappearance of someone else whom Schreber had loved, and probably someone of greater importance. Freud concluded that the other person was Flechsig's father, and that Flechsig represented Schreber's brother. The warm feelings were experienced through a process of transference to his doctor, Flechsig. In reality, Schreber loved his father very much and grieved over his death.

Freud commented that accurate details of Schreber's early life were lacking, so he could not trace back all the details of the delusions. Freud believed that when a wishful phantasy breaks out, it must be connected with the frustration of some instinct. He saw the essence of Schreber's illness as a homosexual wish that was defended against by the delusions. At root, the illness was a problem with the father. The patient's struggle with Flechsig was rendered as a conflict with God but was really a conflict with the father Schreber had loved and lost.

Freud said that the libido develops through stages, with different object choices at each stage. For example, at one period children take themselves, their own bodies, as the love object, and only subsequently proceed from this to the choice of some person other than themselves as the object. Some people, according to Freud, linger longer at this stage and become fixated so that many features of this stage are carried over into later stages of development (1911/1957h, p. 61). What gets chosen of the self as a love object is the genitals, and development then leads to the choice of an external object with similar genitals, a homosexual object choice. After the stage of heterosexual object choice, homosexual tendencies are not done away with but are merely deflected from their sexual aim and applied to fresh uses. They contribute, Freud believed, to social instincts in that they add an erotic factor to friendship and comradeship. Sublimated erotic instincts foster a love of humankind in general. Freud believed that Schreber, because of frustration, had an intensification of libido and this undid his sublimations and defenses. His libido sought an outlet at the weakest spot in his development. According to Freud, Schreber's illness arose mainly "from a conflict between the ego and the sexual instinct" (1911/1957h, p. 79).

Because Schreber's inner sexual phantasies were threatening, he unconsciously repressed, distorted, and projected them. These former inner perceptions now seemed to him in his paranoid state to be external perceptions. The erotic feelings got transformed into hate, and Schreber thus believed that he was being persecuted by some external agent, whereas he was really being threatened by his own instinctual needs.

Normally, growth into adulthood brings about repression of early forms of relationships with people and immature forms of libidinal investment. For Schreber, circumstances undid the work of repression, and early forms of libidinal choices returned in a troubling and disturbing way. Many of his delusions seemed to be expressions of transformed erotic wishes and early object choices.

This brief presentation of Freud's reflections suggests his instinctual view of object relations and conflicts. Later theorists generally do not link paranoia with homosexual phantasies but instead suggest different and perhaps more sophisticated views on Schreber (Kanzer & Glenn, 1980).

Assessment and Critique of Freud

By inventing the notion of object, by clarifying the different kinds of objects a person chooses during the stages of development, and by emphasizing the relational aspects of the oedipal situation and of structural formation, Freud made significant contributions to a theory of object relations. He invented the terms and defined many of the issues.

Many of the later controversies and evolutions of object relations theory flow from Freud's assumptions and the way he formulated ideas. For example, some theorists criticize his assumptions of the fundamental importance of instinct, claiming that his model understands relationships in a manner too appetitive and sexual, that he did not articulate clearly enough the world of inner objects. Freud's ambiguities, revisions, and refinements of ideas contain the seeds for later controversies and insightful extensions of theory.

An example of Freud's reworking of ideas can be illustrated in his concept of instinctual drives, where two different and conflicting emphases exist (Compton, 1983b, pp. 405–406). Freud (1915/1957d) first emphasized drive as the mental or psychical representation of a bodily stimulus; the second emphasis (1915/1957i, 1915/1957m) was on the drive as the cathexis, which is attached to the representation or idea; that is, the drive as a quota of libido. This is an important difference. With the first emphasis the question arises, how can there be a mental representation without a functioning ego? How is ego-id differentiation to be understood? Is ego functioning required for the deepest layers of id to arise?

In the second emphasis, Freud seemed to imply that the id is purely energy rather than a structure. This suggests that the mind or psyche is the same as the ego. If this indeed were true, then there remains the problem of how there can be any mental functioning prior to ego formation. It would further imply that all conflict is *within* the ego and not between the ego and other systems (that is, the id and superego).

This unresolved issue in Freud's writings set the direction for later object relations theorists and continuing controversies. Fairbairn chooses one side of the conflicting emphasis. He casts out instinctual drives as an essential construct for explaining motivation. He replaces instinctual drives and Freud's biological emphasis by theorizing that there are multiple aspects *in the ego* that are in conflict with each other. This is not inconsistent with an id that is only energy and not structure. Melanie Klein, in another resolution of this ambiguity, claims that the ego is present from birth and that this simultaneous presence of ego and id shapes the mental functioning of the newborn child. The next two chapters will concentrate on these theorists.

Freud used the term *object* in ambiguous ways. He was not always clear as to whether an object is an integral part of a drive, so he repeatedly said both that drives *do* and *do not* have objects in infancy (Compton, 1983b, p. 415). This lack of conceptual clarity as to the precise connection between drives and objects allows later object relations theorists to controversially dismiss drives and focus on objects.

References

Compton, A. (1983a). The current status of the psychoanalytic theory of instinctual drives. I: Drive concepts, classification, and development. *Psychoanalytic Quarterly, 52,* 364–401.

Compton, A. (1983b). The current status of the psychoanalytic theory of instinctual drives. II: The relation of the drive concept to structures, regulation principles, and objects. *Psychoanalytic Quarterly, 52,* 402–425.

Freud, S. (1957a). The ego and the id. In J. Strachey (Ed. and Trans.), *The standard edition of the complete psychological works of Sigmund Freud* (Vol. 19, pp. 1–66). London: Hogarth Press. (Original work published 1923)

Freud, S. (1957b). Formulations on the two principles of mental functioning. In J. Strachey (Ed. and Trans.), *The standard edition of the complete psychological works of Sigmund Freud* (Vol. 12, pp. 218–226). London: Hogarth Press. (Original work published 1911)

Freud, S. (1957c). Group psychology and the analysis of the ego. In J. Strachey (Ed. and Trans.), *The standard edition of the complete psychological works of Sigmund Freud* (Vol. 18, pp. 65–143). London: Hogarth Press. (Original work published 1921)

Freud, S. (1957d). Instincts and their vicissitudes. In J. Strachey (Ed. and Trans.), *The standard edition of the complete psychological works of Sigmund Freud* (Vol. 14, pp. 117–140). London: Hogarth Press. (Original work published 1915)

Freud, S. (1957e). Introductory lectures on psycho-analysis. In J. Strachey (Ed. and Trans.), *The standard edition of the complete psychological works of Sigmund Freud* (Vol. 16, pp. 243–448). London: Hogarth Press. (Original work published 1917)

Freud, S. (1957f). New introductory lectures on psycho-analysis. In J. Strachey (Ed. and Trans.), *The standard edition of the complete psychological works of Sigmund Freud* (Vol. 22, pp. 1–182). London: Hogarth Press. (Original work published 1933)

Freud, S. (1957g). On narcissism. In J. Strachey (Ed. and Trans.), *The standard edition of the complete psychological works of Sigmund Freud* (Vol. 14, pp. 67–102). London: Hogarth Press. (Original work published 1914)

Freud, S. (1957h). Psycho-analytic notes on an autobiographical account of a case of paranoia (dementia praecox). In J. Strachey (Ed. and Trans.), *The standard edition of the complete psychological works of Sigmund Freud* (Vol. 12, pp. 1–82). London: Hogarth Press. (Original work published 1911)

Freud, S. (1957i). Repression. In J. Strachey (Ed. and Trans.), *The standard edition of the complete psychological works of Sigmund Freud* (Vol. 14, pp. 141–158). London: Hogarth Press. (Original work published 1915)

Freud, S. (1957j). Splitting of the ego in the process of defense. In J. Strachey (Ed. and Trans.), *The standard edition of the complete psychological works of Sigmund Freud* (Vol. 23, pp. 275–278). London: Hogarth Press. (Original work published 1938)

Freud, S. (1957k). Three essays on the theory of sexuality. In J. Strachey (Ed. and Trans.), *The standard edition of the complete psychological works of Sigmund Freud* (Vol. 7, pp. 125–245). London: Hogarth Press. (Original work published 1905)

Freud, S. (1957l). Totem and taboo. In J. Strachey (Ed. and Trans.), *The standard edition of the complete psychological works of Sigmund Freud* (Vol. 13, pp. 1–164). London: Hogarth Press. (Original work published 1912)

Freud, S. (1957m). The unconscious. In J. Strachey (Ed. and Trans.), *The standard edition of the complete psychological works of Sigmund Freud* (Vol. 14, pp. 159–215). London: Hogarth Press. (Original work published 1915)

Gedo, J. (1979). Theories of object relations: A metapsychological assessment. *Journal of the American Psychoanalytic Association, 27,* 361–365.

Greenberg, J. R., & Mitchell, S. A. (1983). *Object relations in psychoanalytic theory.* Cambridge: Harvard University Press.

Kanzer, M., & Glenn, J. (Eds.). (1980). *Freud and his patients.* New York: Aronson.

LaPlanche, J., & Pontalis, J. B. (1973). *The language of psychoanalysis.* New York: Norton.

Chapter Three

Melanie Klein: Innovative and Transitional Theorist

Introduction

Melanie Klein was born in Vienna in 1882. Only after her marriage and the birth of her three children did she resume her career and specialize in the psychoanalysis of children. She moved to London in 1926 and continued her innovative work there until her death in 1960. Writing from 1921 to 1960, Klein considerably extended the concepts of object and object relations that Freud initiated. She followed Freud's lead in significant areas, such as the emphasis on instinctual drive in explaining motivation and the formation of personality, but some of her concepts creatively and radically departed from Freud.

Unlike Freud, who based his understanding of childhood primarily on the recollections of his patients (mainly women who were considered neurotic), Klein took the bold step of working directly with troubled children. In the therapeutic world of the time, this was unexplored territory. Her young patients compelled her to develop new techniques and new ways of thinking about the inner world of children. Her observations and creative use of play led Klein to discover that the psychic world of young children, even infants, was filled with primitive and savage conflicts, murderous and cannibalistic tendencies, and excretory and erotic urges (Klein, 1927/1975b, 1959/1975i).

While seeking to chart this new territory, Klein drew upon Freudian theory as a context for her findings and retained the concept of instinctual drives. She discussed her innovative theoretical and clinical work within an instinctual context. She vividly drew attention to the phantasy world of the younger years, and discovered some of the mechanisms infants use to deal with intense anxieties and drives, and archaic urges and fears. She learned that phantasies are a response to intense drives and feelings and dominate the early mental life of infants.

Her innovative work serves an important transitional role, bridging the work of Freud with other analytic thinkers who charted different courses. From her observations of infants and children, she stretched and rearranged Freudian ideas of object and instinct, although not as far as her contemporary, W. R. D. Fairbairn, who fashioned a model of personality based exclusively on objects and object relations.

This chapter reviews some of Klein's key ideas, especially her understanding of object relations and early psychological mechanisms, ideas that later object relations theorists have drawn upon. The topics discussed in this chapter include: key concepts, formation of psychic structures of ego and superego, Klein's two developmental positions, her understanding of pathology and therapy, a case study, and an assessment and critique of Klein's contribution.

Key Concepts

Instincts

Klein's exploration of the infant's psychic world emphasized biological drives and instincts. Drives and impulses dominate this inner world. Interactions between parents and the infant—in fact, all interactions or object relations—are represented as aspects of drives. Klein's emphasis on biological drives in interactions makes her psychology id-centered, a psychology that focuses more on the role of drives as expressed in mental phantasies than on parents' contributions.

A major source of the infant's anxiety arises from the operation of the *death instinct,* a concept Klein shared with Freud, and one that is very controversial and not widely held. The death instinct is supposedly experienced as a fear of death or annihilation. It takes the form of fear of being persecuted or destroyed. The fear of this destructive impulse within the self attaches itself to an object that becomes uncontrollable and overpowering in the phantasies of the helpless infant.

Phantasy

The inner life of the infant involves a world of phantasy, a form of mental activity that is present from birth. In this mental world, phantasies serve as the imaginative representations of bodily instincts and urges as well as the infant's active responses to intense drives and feelings. Thus, the hungry infant can temporarily control its hunger by hallucinating the feel of the breast and the taste of the milk (Klein, 1959/1975i, p. 251).

While these mental processes take place in phantasy and on a psychological level, the infant experiences these phantasies bodily as well as mentally. These phantasies and inner objects seem extremely vivid and real because the infant cannot differentiate at this stage between reality and his or her own phantasy life. Thus, every discomfort and frustration is felt as if it were a personal attack inflicted by a hostile force. The helpless infant experiences these phantasized objects and the feelings as actual happenings; psychological happenings seem to be physical (Segal, 1964, p. 13). For instance, infants making sucking sounds with their mouths and sucking their fingers phantasize that they are actually sucking on the breast or even having the good breast inside themselves. The intense fears and feelings, as well as the mechanisms the infant uses to deal with this intensity, resemble the crazy world of adult psychosis except that Klein clearly said that the young infant is not psychotic and that this chaotic inner world of phantasy is normal for infants (Klein, 1946/1975f).

Object

Klein altered Freud's notion of object (Greenberg & Mitchell, 1983, p. 136). In Freud's drive model, drives are originally objectless because gratification comes first and it does not make much difference what the particular object is. But for Klein, drives are inherently directed toward objects. The infant, for example, seeks milk from the breast, not mere pleasure in the process of eating. Klein criticized Freud's notion of instincts as objectless (Klein, 1952/1975h, p. 53) because, for Klein, every urge and instinct is bound up with an object.

Because the infant's ego and perceptual skills are immature and the infant can attend only to one aspect or part of a person at a time, the infant first relates to part objects. The first part object for the infant is the mother's breast (Klein, 1952/1975e, p. 59). At this early level of development, the infant can only experience gratification or deprivation. The breast gives or denies gratification and becomes, in the mind of the infant, either good or bad. In relationship with the breast, the infant feels gratified or denied, good or bad. Being held and fed gives rise to pleasurable feelings, and these in turn enable the infant to perceive the gratifying object as a good object (Klein, 1936/1975m; 1959/1975i, p. 248).

This tendency to relate to part objects accounts for the phantasy-like and unrealistic nature of the infant's relations to everything—to parts of his or her own body, to people, and to inanimate objects. The object world during the first two or three months of life consists of gratifying and hostile and persecuting parts and portions of the real world.

Klein used the term *inner object* rather than object representation. The suggestion is that object representation is of an object from which separation has been achieved because the child is at a later stage of development. Later theorists, like Kohut, have used the term *selfobject* to refer to a state of fusion between the experience of self and the experience of the needed object (Grotstein, 1982a, p. 495). Klein's inner object corresponds to selfobject.

Psychic Mechanisms

The infant makes use of various psychological mechanisms to control the intense needs, terrors, and feelings of infancy. How the infant relates to the breast demonstrates some of these mechanisms of projection, introjection, splitting, and projective identification.

Projection is a mental or phantasy process by which the infant believes an object has qualities that are, in actuality, the infant's own feelings. Thus, the well-fed infant, filled with pleasure, turns this good feeling back onto the object and believes that the breast is good. The good breast becomes the prototype of what is felt throughout life to be good and beneficent, and the bad breast stands for everything evil and persecuting. When the child turns its frustration and hatred against the depriving bad breast, it attributes to the breast itself all its own active hatred for it.

Introjection, another important and primitive mechanism that is present and available to the very young infant, is the mental phantasy by which the infant takes into him or herself something that the infant perceives in the outside world. Thus, any danger or deprivation from the outside world enters and becomes an inner danger. Frustrating objects and sources of anxiety, even though external to the infant, become internal persecutors of the terrified infant by means of introjection.

The infant uses the mechanism of splitting to protect him or herself. *Splitting* involves separating or keeping apart feelings and aspects of the self. The infant protects itself by splitting its ego and its objects into more manageable aspects; that is, separating these into good and bad facets and keeping them separate (Ogden, 1983, p. 229). The relationship with the mother and her breast is a complex relationship where feelings of love and hate, and frustration and gratification coexist. Splitting simplifies matters by changing the complex relationship with the mother into one that appears to be many simple relationships (the loving object and the gratified self, the hating object and the frustrated self, and so forth). Splitting disperses dangerous feelings by keeping them separate from gratifying feelings.

Another way in which the infant tries to defend itself is by a phantasy process of imposing its own inner world onto the phantasized external world and then reinternalizing this world. The infant is attempting to relieve some of the inner anxiety and inner danger by externalizing them and thereby modifying them in the outer world. This process, called *projective identification*, involves, on a phantasy level, splitting off an unacceptable part of the self and sending this into another object. For example, when an infant experiences hunger pain, it protects itself by splitting off part of its feeling, the pain sensation, and projecting this onto an object, the frustrating breast. But this attribution of the infant's pain to the external object does not help much, and so there is a further process, an introjective return of the amalgam of the split-off part of the self and the object. That is, the hurting, frustrating, and devouring breast is now within the infant. The infant is trying to deal with his or her needs and fears, and it is as if he or she is saying to the breast, "Because I am hurting and need you and you don't feed me, you are bad and are attacking me and devouring me and I feel bad." A similar process also occurs when there is satisfaction. Thus, an infant who is satisfied from having a stomach filled with warm milk might be thinking something like, "You fed me and so are good and make me feel good; therefore, you must be within me now to make me feel this good" (cf. Grotstein, 1981a, 1981b).

These processes are supposed to occur on a phantasy level, but Klein often confused her readers by sometimes describing these representations as if they were actual psychic agencies capable of thinking and feeling. In other words, she sometimes failed to distinguish between objects and the mental representations of these objects, between the contents of phantasies and the actual psychic agencies that do the phantasizing and feeling.

The Inner World of Object Relations

Klein emphasized the infants' active contribution to the formation of themselves and their inner worlds of object relations. Infants face the cycles of gratification and frustration by a constant use of the mechanisms of projection and introjection (Klein, 1948/1975g, p. 31) both to control their inner needs and to establish object relations. That is, infants turn their feelings and energies outward and attribute these qualities to objects, creating their first object relations. The first objects, according to Klein, are the split-off aspects of the self or feelings that are projected onto an external object and then taken back in as internal objects (Grotstein, 1982a, p. 498).

Introjection and projection cause a close bond between internal objects and external objects, and between inner instincts and the environment. Introjection builds up an inner world that partly reflects the external world; projections of inner feelings color infants' perceptions of the external world. In the effort to defend themselves, infants try by phantasy processes to impose their own inner world on the external world and then reinternalize that world. In essence, the infant is creating his or her own world (Klein, 1948/1975g).

Internal objects are an amalgam of the self and external objects. The external object is only of importance in how it modifies the projection rather than as an object in itself. Thus, the shadow of the ego (or the self) falls on the object. The Kleinian inner object reflects more of the id rather than external objects, and the Kleinian inner world stresses the external world's *modification* of the infant's feelings rather than stressing the external world. The traditional psychoanalytic object involves an object representation, where an image of external objects is modified by instincts. This object representation reflects more the external world than the id (Grotstein, 1982a, p. 494).

Klein's psychology thus gives greater importance to nature and instincts than to the modifying role of external objects, such as nurturing parents who temper the instinctual demands of infants. According to traditional psychoanalytic criticisms, Klein did not attend sufficiently to the influence of the parental objects in the environment. She overstressed the importance of the internal world of the infant; that is, what the infant him or herself contributes. Disturbance is from within, from the instincts of the infant, rather than from external influences. Badness and terror originate from within.

Initially, the infant can only relate to part objects; that is, just one aspect of a person. Relating to part objects causes the infant's inner world to be filled during the first two or three months with persecuting and hostile but also gratifying fragments and portions. It is a phantastic and psychotic-like world of danger and anxiety that comes from the infant's own destructiveness and the supposed death instinct. Development, however, enables the infant to gradually relate to whole objects. Healthy development means the infant distorts relationships less by rage, love, and greed. The infant begins to see his or her mother as a whole and loving being, and begins to take pleasure in the whole person, seeing that she has more than just one characteristic. As the infant takes pleasure in this whole person—the mother—the infant's confidence and power to perceive and relate to other whole persons in the external world increases. All other relationships build on this basic object relationship that began with the mother's breast.

These infantile feelings and phantasies leave imprints on the mind that do not fade but are stored and remain active. They exert a continuous influence on the emotional and interactive life of the individual. The alert therapist, for instance, will notice their presence in transference relationships.

Ego and Superego

Building up psychological structures means generating new agencies within the psyche by means of identification and internalization. The new agencies within the personality, the ego and superego, carry on the functions previously performed by external objects, such as the parents (cf. Ogden, 1983, p. 228).

For Klein, object relations exist from birth. The relationship with and the taking in of the first object, the breast, plays an important role in the development of the ego and superego (Klein, 1959/1975i, p. 251).

Klein explained the formation of the ego by means of the introjection of the primal good object, the mother's breast (Klein, 1946/1975f, p. 180). The infant takes in the breast and its milk. The good breast becomes the focal point around which the ego develops. (The ego actually exists at birth.) The good aspects of the mother (her loving, feeding, caring) fill the inner world of the infant and become the characteristics with which the ego identifies. These introjected objects become organizers of further psychic development and are constantly modified by other objects.

More specifically, the infant, as part of its self-protection, deflects the death instinct and the libido or life instinct outward to the external object, the frustrating or gratifying breast. By this protective maneuver, a fluctuation of introjection and projection, the infant creates the amalgam of ego and object that is the core of the developing ego. Just as the infant splits the destructive feelings, retaining one part and projecting the other part outward, so the infant splits the libido, with part of the libido projected outward and the rest retained within. The retained part, the fragment of good feelings, establishes the relationship with the ideal good object, the breast.

In the early stages of ego development, the inner world of the infant is a chaos of images of objects and egos, a world of no cohesion and partial objects. To cope with this world, the infant, within the first year, moves from part objects to whole objects, from fragmented ego to more coherent ego. The infant has a limited capacity in the beginning to differentiate and to perceive reality accurately. As a result, infants supply much to their world from their own fears, neediness, and greed, according to Klein. With an increase of maturity, the disorganized phantasies grow more unified, and the infant overcomes illusions of having omnipotent control over objects; that is, there is a decrease in projective and introjective mechanisms and an increase in more accurate perception.

The superego, like the ego, performs functions that external objects previously performed and is likewise the result of projective and introjective processes. The infant projects his or her own disruptive, demanding traits onto the object, the breast, and reinternalizes the image of the object as an amalgam of him or herself and the object in such a way that the infant's own greed is transformed into an image of a greedy breast, which becomes the demanding superego (Grotstein, 1981b). The superego, then, is the result of infantile greed projected into the demanding, frustrating bad breast, which then becomes the internalized persecuting object. Splitting can separate parts of this internalized amalgam so that the internalized persecutor or conscience appears alien and not part of the self or the "I" (Klein, 1948/1975g).

Children create within themselves unreal and phantastic images of parents who hurt them, who seem to cut, devour, and bite. These dangerous objects become internalized as wild beasts and monsters, and the child dreads being devoured and destroyed. (Maurice Sendak's book *Where the Wild Things Are* comes to mind as an illustration of this.) These internalized beasts and monsters, amalgamated with the greed and fear of the infant, become the superego, the introjected object that bites and devours.

The superego, of course, does not accurately represent the parents as they actually are but is constructed out of the phantasy images of the parents that the infant takes into him or herself, modified and altered by his or her own feelings and phantasies (Klein, 1933/1975c). In fact, it is the child's own feelings and cannibalistic and sadistic impulses that make the early superego so harsh (Klein, 1927/1975b). The child experiences these incorporated objects or parents in a concrete way, as living figures within who hurt and persecute (Klein, 1946/1975f). Of course, if the child experiences an inner world where the people are at peace with each other, there will be greater inner harmony and integration. There will also be less conflict between the ego and superego rather than the terror of a devouring, inner persecutor.

Klein based her view of the harshness of the superego and its very early appearance (a view counter to the prevailing Freudian view) on play therapy with children. Play therapy prompts children to project their inner world of images and introjections onto toys, dolls, and the therapist. Klein encountered a harsh and relentless superego in her work with a young child, Rita, who was 33 months old. The structure of the superego is usually revealed by cruel, negative figures and anxiety-inspiring identifications (Klein, 1929/1975j). In play therapy, Rita played the role of a severe and punishing mother who treated the child, represented by a doll or by Klein, very cruelly. From Rita's ambivalence, her extreme need to be punished, and her feelings of guilt and night terrors, Klein concluded that the superego arises at a much earlier age than Freud had assumed (Klein, 1928/1975d, 1946/1975f).

Klein differed from Freud and Fairbairn in her notions of structure. Freud separated instinctual energy and elements of structure, but Klein suggested that they are inseparable (Grotstein, 1981a, p. 389), and Fairbairn concurs. For Klein, drives are relational; she saw phantasies as representing instincts and the phantasies striving for contact with objects. Personality basically consists of the phantasies of the relationships with these internal objects. The net result is a blurring of the distinction between ego and id and the tendency to see both as an aspect of one psychic agency. Freud clearly distinguished ego from id. For him, psychic conflict came from instincts of the id threatening the ego, and hence conflict could only occur once the id and the ego differentiated. (This would probably be around the second or third year, close to the beginning of the oedipal period.) Since Klein placed less emphasis on id as a structure and more on phantasy that seemed to combine id and ego as aspects of the same psychic agency, this allowed her to conclude that conflicts are possible at the earliest possible developmental stage (Grotstein, 1982a, p. 488). Klein proposed a functioning ego with defenses at the beginning of life, and this implies a much higher degree of psychic organization and structure for the infant than Freud described for that period.

Klein agreed with Fairbairn in that they both blur the distinctions between instinctual energy and structures with the result that personality is viewed as the culmination of the experience and phantasy of internal objects. Klein differed from Fairbairn in that she said both a good and bad breast are introjected; Fairbairn says that there is no need to internalize the good breast, only the bad breast. His reasoning is that the process of introjecting is a defensive one, and only the threatening bad object needs to be defended against, not the good object, which can be allowed to remain in external reality.

But Klein believed that the good internalized breast, as the source of life, is a vital part of the ego. Klein argued that the infant internalizes the good breast as a way of acquiring and keeping within the self the powerful good or ideal object that is protective and life-giving. The inner preservation of this idealized object is necessary and an important protection against the death instinct that is also within the infant. These internal objects forming the superego have a more separate and alien quality within the self-experience than those that form the ego.

Two Developmental Positions

Freud understood development in terms of instinctual energies manifesting themselves in the body, such as during the oral or anal stage. Klein (1946/1975f, 1952/1975h) looked at development in terms of relationships.

Using the term *position*, she described the child's different ways of experiencing and relating to both internalized and external objects. The two positions suggest the occurrence and reoccurrence, during a child's first years, of specific groups of psychological mechanisms, ways of relating to objects, and characteristic anxieties and defenses (Klein, 1932/1975k, p. xiii; 1935/1975a). For example, during the first four or five months, the infant's ego relates primarily to part objects and then increasingly to whole objects. This movement from part object to whole object relationships represents the movement from one position to the next.

The first is the *paranoid-schizoid position*, the name referring to the characteristic mechanisms of this period. During these earliest months of life, from approximately birth to the fourth month, the infant's anxieties are of a paranoid kind about the very preservation of his or her ego. The ego fears that it will be destroyed; destructive impulses and persecutory and sadistic anxieties dominate. Tolerance of frustration is low, and emotional reactions are extremes of good and bad. To preserve the goodness of the needed object, the infant banishes the badness by projecting his or her own hate and terror. Thus, the infant sees the world as having the same destructive and omnipotent qualities as the infant has, somewhat like the world that Kafka described, where vague and powerful enemies "out there" threaten the helpless self (Dicks, 1972, p. 26). Schizoid or splitting defenses are common and are aimed at the annihilation of the persecutors, both inner and outer.

During this position, needs and frustrations are at their crudest level, and the infant has violent phantasies against the object, the mother's breast. The infant can neither distinguish between inner and outer objects nor the source of frustrations. There are oral, urethral, and anal phantasies and desires. In relation to the mother's breast, the infant phantasizes attacks, to suck dry and rob the mother's body of its good contents. There are anal and urethral impulses in the form of phantasies of expelling dangerous substances and harmful excrement.

The second developmental stage is the *depressive position*, named for the predominant feelings experienced during this period. This begins at approximately the fifth month, when the infant has an increased capacity to relate to complete or whole objects. The infant makes progress in integration and a more realistic stance toward the world. The infant increasingly recognizes that the loved object is outside the self. The central task is to establish in the core of the ego a good and secure whole internal object. While the infant feared his or her own destruction during the paranoid-schizoid position, he or she now worries that the good object is endangered.

During the depressive position, the developing ego has more complex, ambivalent feelings and depressed anxiety about the whole object he or she relates to. The infant experiences guilt for previous aggression toward the loved object and now desires to make reparation to the object for previous attacks. The infant desires to care for this loved and needed object. Preservation of the good object is now synonymous with the survival of the infant's own ego. Becoming more identified with the good object, the ego becomes more aware of its own incapacity to protect itself against internalized persecuting objects and feels menaced in its possession of the good internalized object. Anxious lest the good object die or go away, the infant uses manic defenses of denial and omnipotence to defend against guilt, despair, and feelings of annihilation.

Klein connected the Oedipus complex to the depressed position. The feared loss of good objects in the depressed position is the source of the most painful oedipal conflicts. Oedipal desires intertwine with depressed anxieties as the infant struggles to integrate love and hate. Sexual impulses and phantasies emerge to repair the effects of aggression.

These developmental positions are normal, but failure to master and work through these early phases can result in varying degrees of disturbance. British psychologist Henry Dicks (1972), for example, applied these concepts of Klein to convicted Nazi mass murderers. He interviewed men who had been convicted of atrocities in concentration camps and found them to have made only superficial social adaptations while remaining emotionally infantile. Their training and leaders reactivated the latent murderous and sadistic fantasies of these early stages. The social environment and pressures fostered dissolution of inadequate defenses and acting out of crude impulses. These cruel men were playing out primitive object relations, a primitive hate for the supposed or projected "bad objects." One particular prison guard had the feeling of being surrounded by unloving, murderous figures, and his good daddy was not there to help him. As a child he had a need for a parent's love. In his atrocities he acted out, in a displaced and paranoid manner, a repressed murderous hate toward the threatening "bad objects."

Pathology and Therapy

For Klein, psychological danger comes from within. The death instincts cause the child's inner anxieties and persecutory fears (Klein, 1952/1975h, p. 48). The destructive feelings that the child has for different objects stir up fears of retaliation. Inner realities shape the way external realities are perceived by the child so that frustrations and discomforts feel as if they are hostile, attacking forces. These early anxieties influence later object relations. Klein allowed little space for the modifying role of the environment and the good objects of the environment. Most of her emphasis was on instincts in the form of phantasies and inner objects.

The task of therapy is to alleviate some of these anxieties as well as to modify the harshness of the internalized objects and inner persecutors. The process of therapy is to analyze and interpret the transference.

Transference in therapy is a new version of the phantasies, fears, and feelings that were involved in past relational experiences; it is the process of a patient applying to a therapist the feelings and phantasies associated to some past figure or relationship. From the very beginning of life, a child has object relationships, relationships with figures that involve love and hate, anxieties and defenses. Since transference begins in these early experiences of object relations, the analysis of transference will enable the therapist and the patient to explore these early relationships and the feelings attached to them.

As the process of therapy gets to and names the instinctual basis for the phantasies and feelings involved in various relationships, there can be a lessening of depressive anxiety and persecutory guilt. Early and painful patterns and modes of feelings can be diminished. Therapeutic change comes about through analysis of the transference and by connecting current feelings and attitudes with the earliest object relations.

The therapist can represent various different figures from the earliest period of the client's life, whether that figure is the father or mother or some aspect of father or mother or even a part of the individual's superego or id. Although there are relatively few people in the early life of the infant, the infant develops a multitude of different objects since different aspects or roles of the parents are represented in the infant's inner world. It is these inner figures or objects, either whole or in part, that get transferred to the therapist and need to be worked through. In this therapeutic situation, there may be a rapid changing of transferences depending on what is happening in the therapy. The therapist may be perceived in rapid succession as an "enemy" or "helper" or a "bad mother" or a "good mother"; that is, frustrating or satisfying.

Therapy, according to Klein (1929/1975j), especially play therapy, fosters a reexternalization of the figures and objects that were introjected early in the child's life. It can promote externalization of the inner world and inner conflict, a displacement onto the outer world of the child's inner world. For example, Klein presented a case of a 5-year-old boy who pretended he had wild animals—elephants, leopards, wolves—to help against his enemies. In her analysis and therapeutic interpretations, Klein discovered these animals stood for the child's own sadistic impulses: the elephant symbolized his sadistic impulse to trample and stomp, the leopard his desire to tear and bite, and the wolf his destructive excrement and the destroying qualities that came from within him. The boy would become frightened that these temporarily tamed animals would turn against him, that he was threatened by his own destructiveness and internal persecutors (Klein, 1948/1975g). The therapist can play roles such as one of the animals or an animal trainer or a fairy godmother, with each role representing some aspect of either past figures within the child or the child's id or superego.

Case Study

The following case study illustrates Klein's characteristic clinical approach and the manner in which she understood the client's emotional problems in light of her theoretical concepts. Klein believed that a child expresses his or her phantasies and wishes in a symbolic way in play and games. The difference between a child's mind and an adult mind is accessible to play therapy, the essence of which was to interpret the phantasies, feelings, and anxieties expressed by play or blocking the child's ability to play. Interpretation, according to Klein, releases the energy that the child spends on repressing primitive feelings and impulses.

In 1923, Klein worked in play therapy with Rita, who was then 33 months old (1932/1975k, 1955/1975l). During the first year of her life, Rita preferred her mother, and then developed a great fondness for her father and jealousy toward her mother. For example, when she was 15 months old she repeatedly wanted to be in a room alone with her father and to sit on his lap and look at books with him. At 18 months, she changed and again her mother was her favorite. At this time, she began to have night terrors and fears of animals. She became more attached to her mother and developed an intense dislike of her father. When Rita was 2 years old, a brother was born, and she started to manifest obsessive rituals. By the start of her third year, she was very ambivalent and difficult to manage. She was obsessional and moody, alternated between being good and naughty, anxious, and very inhibited in play. At this point, her parents brought her to Klein for therapy.

Klein had 83 sessions with her. In the early sessions, when Rita was left alone with Klein, she was anxious and silent. Klein's practice was to immediately offer an interpretation; that is, to verbalize the significance of the client's actions. Such an immediate interpretation went against the usual psychoanalytic practice of the time. For example, Klein interpreted the "negative transference" as Rita being afraid that Klein might do something to her when she was alone with her in the room. Klein further linked this with Rita's night fears "that a bad woman would attack her when she was by herself in the night" (1955/1975l, p. 124).

Rita was very inhibited in her play, obsessively dressing and undressing her doll. Klein "came to understand the anxieties underlying her obsessions, and interpreted them" (1955/1975l, p. 124). Thus, Rita was involved with elaborate bedtime rituals involving ceremonies of being tightly tucked in, otherwise a mouse would get in through the window and bite her. She would put a toy elephant on her doll's bed to prevent the doll from getting up and going into the parents' room. Klein interpreted the elephant as taking on the role of her "internalized parents whose prohibiting influence she felt ever since ... she had wished to take her mother's place with her father, rob her of the child inside her, and injure and castrate both parents" (1932/1975k, p. 6). The meaning of the ceremony of being tucked into bed was to keep her from getting up and carrying out her aggressive wishes against her parents (1932/1975k, p. 7). Rita expected to be punished for her wishes by an attack on her by her parents (the mouse), who would injure her genitals. In therapy, she played games where she would punish her doll and give way to "rage and fear, thus showing that she was playing both parts herself—that of the powers which inflict punishment and that of the punished child itself" (1932/1975k, p. 7).

Klein reflected that Rita's anxiety referred not only to her real parents but to excessively stern introjected parents, a superego. She commented that the oedipal conflict sets in as early as the "second half of the first year of life and that at the same time the child begins to build up its super-ego" (1932/1975k, p. 7). Rita's inhibition in play came from her sense of guilt, according to Klein. To play with her doll was to deal symbolically with her little brother, whom she had wanted to "steal" from her mother during pregnancy. Prohibitions came not from the real mother but from the introjected mother who treated her with more severity and cruelty than the real one had ever done (1932/1975k, p. 6).

Assessment and Critique of Klein

Klein's work built on and moved beyond Freud. Her work made substantial contributions to the establishment and development of object relations theory. She used Freudian terms and concepts, such as instinct, structure, and object, but extended their meanings in sometimes confusing but still significant ways.

Klein preserved the Freudian emphasis on instinct but understood instinct as intrinsically connected with objects so that drives are relational. From the very beginning of life, impulses occur in an object relations context (Grotstein, 1981a, p. 380) and are object-oriented. The infant is looking for nurture and the breast, not merely for discharge. This emphasis on both instinctual drives and object relations differs significantly from the Freudian position, which views drives as essentially objectless.

Klein did not make the Freudian distinctions between id and ego or between energy and structure. Her use of phantasy as instinct differed from the Freudian notion of phantasy as a transformation of instinct. This blurring of distinctions implies what Fairbairn would later make explicit—namely, that id and ego are different aspects of the same agency rather than separate structures. The id is an infantile aspect of the self striving for nurturing contact with the world (Grotstein, 1981a, p. 388; 1982b). Klein's understanding of early mental life pushed back intrapsychic development to an earlier point than Freud had believed. She assumed the presence of the ego at birth with the very early oedipal conflict resulting in formation of the superego.

Klein had much to teach about the magical and terrifying mental world of children. Her understanding of the inner world of a child's object relations stands as her prime achievement. Her insights into early psychic mechanisms encouraged the expansion of psychoanalytic study from the triadic oedipal relationships to the earlier dyadic mother-child relationships. She adapted psychoanalytic concepts to play therapy, but some of her therapeutic techniques, such as early interpretations, aroused disagreement (Kernberg, 1980, p. 48). Her developmental concepts, despite criticisms (Brody, 1982; Jacobson, 1964, p. 106; Kernberg, 1980), gave insight into serious disturbances and relational conflicts. She developed the terminology of internal objects (part and whole objects) and her work laid the foundation for the British School of Object Relations.

References

Brody, S. (1982). Psychoanalytic theories of infant development. *Psychoanalytic Quarterly, 51,* 526–597.

Dicks, H. V. (1972). *Licensed mass murder: A socio-psychological study of some SS killers.* New York: Basic Books.

Greenberg, J. R., & Mitchell, S. A. (1983). *Object relations in psychoanalytic theory.* Cambridge: Harvard University Press.

Grotstein, J. (1981a). The significance of Kleinian contributions to psychoanalysis. I: Kleinian instinct theory. *International Journal of Psychoanalytic Psychotherapy, 8,* 375–392.

Grotstein, J. (1981b). The significance of Kleinian contributions to psychoanalysis. II: Freudian and Kleinian conceptions of early mental development. *International Journal of Psychoanalytic Psychotherapy, 8,* 375–392.

Grotstein, J. (1982a). The significance of Kleinian contributions to psychoanalysis. III: The Kleinian theory of ego psychology and object relations. *International Journal of Psychoanalytic Psychotherapy, 9,* 487–510.

Grotstein, J. (1982b). The significance of Kleinian contributions to psychoanalysis. IV: Critiques of Klein. *International Journal of Psychoanalytic Psychotherapy, 9,* 511–536.

Jacobson, E. (1964). *The self and the object world.* New York: International Universities Press.

Kernberg, O. (1980). *Internal world and external reality.* New York: Aronson.

Klein, M. (1975a). A contribution to the psychogenesis of manic-depressive states. In *Love, guilt and reparation and other works, 1921–1945* (pp. 262–289). New York: Delta Books. (Original work published 1935)

Klein, M. (1975b). Criminal tendencies in normal children. In *Love, guilt and reparation and other works, 1921–1945* (pp. 170–185). New York: Delta Books. (Original work published 1927)

Klein, M. (1975c). The early development of conscience in the child. In *Love, guilt and reparation and other works, 1921–1945* (pp. 248–257). New York: Delta Books. (Original work published 1933)

Klein, M. (1975d). Early stages of the Oedipus complex. In *Love, guilt and reparation and other works, 1921–1945* (pp. 186–198). New York: Delta Books. (Original work published 1928)

Klein, M. (1975e). The mutual influences in the development of ego and id. In *Envy and gratitude and other works, 1946–1963* (pp. 57–60). New York: Delta Books. (Original work published 1952)

Klein, M. (1975f). Notes on some schizoid mechanisms. In *Envy and gratitude and other works, 1946–1963* (pp. 1–24). New York: Delta Books. (Original work published 1946)

Klein, M. (1975g). On the theory of anxiety and guilt. In *Envy and gratitude and other works, 1946–1963* (pp. 25–42). New York: Delta Books. (Original work published 1948)

Klein, M. (1975h). The origins of transference. In *Envy and gratitude and other works, 1946–1963* (pp. 48–56). New York: Delta Books. (Original work published 1952)

Klein, M. (1975i). Our adult world and its roots in infancy. In *Envy and gratitude and other works, 1946–1963* (pp. 247–263). New York: Delta Books. (Original work published 1959)

Klein, M. (1975j). Personification in the play of children. In *Love, guilt and reparation and other works, 1921–1945* (pp. 199–209). New York: Delta Books. (Original work published 1929)

Klein, M. (1975k). *The psycho-analysis of children.* New York: Delta Books. (Original work published 1932)

Klein, M. (1975l). The psycho-analytic play technique: Its history and significance. In *Envy and gratitude and other works, 1946–1963* (pp. 122–140). New York: Delta Books. (Original work published 1955)

Klein, M. (1975m). Weaning. In *Love, guilt and reparation and other works, 1921–1945* (pp. 290–305). New York: Delta Books. (Original work published 1936)

Ogden, T. H. (1983). The concept of internal object relations. *International Journal of Psycho-Analysis, 64,* 227–241.

Segal, H. (1964). *Introduction to the work of Melanie Klein.* New York: Basic Books.

Chapter Four

W. R. D. Fairbairn: A "Pure" Object Relations Model

Introduction

After service in the Royal Artillery during World War I, W. R. D. Fairbairn completed his medical and psychiatric training in 1926. Most of his professional career was spent in Edinburgh, Scotland, where his relative professional isolation was somewhat balanced by his active involvement with the British Psychoanalytic Society. Melanie Klein's ideas impressed him greatly, even though his own ideas, based on his work with schizoid patients and expressed in his writings from the late 1930s to the early 1950s, were independent and boldly original.

Of all those who have written about object relations, Fairbairn fashioned a model of object relations that is the most "pure"—that is, free of a biological emphasis and purely psychological—a model that is very different from Freud's model of motivation and personality. Melanie Klein, innovative with regard to internal objects, retained the Freudian emphasis on instinctual drives and biology, an emphasis that Fairbairn vigorously rejected. He declared that he was developing a genuine psychological model of the personality and was revising and completing what Freud started (cf. Guntrip, 1971). Later writers retreat from Fairbairn's exclusive object relations model, with writers such as Edith Jacobson and Otto Kernberg attempting to reestablish the link between object relations and the classic instinct model.

This chapter, highlighting how Fairbairn differed from Freud, examines the following: key terms and concepts, personality structure, developmental stages, pathology and internalized objects, Fairbairn's application of analytic therapy, a case study, and an assessment and critique of Fairbairn's contribution.

Key Concepts

Motivation and the Nature of Objects

Fairbairn said that humans have a basic drive toward relating with other people. Libido is object-seeking and highly directional, with the object always being a person. He illustrated this with the protesting cry of a patient who said, "You're always talking about my wanting this and that desire satisfied; but what I really want is a father" (Fairbairn, 1946/1954b, p. 137). Fairbairn thus understood motivation in terms of the ego striving for a relationship with an object, not merely seeking satisfaction. Because drive in classical drive theory seeks to reduce tension, and libido seeks pleasure, the role of the object is just a means toward the end, and anything or any person can be the object of a drive, as long as tension is reduced or gratification is obtained. But Fairbairn rejected the notion that drive has no direction except the direction of satisfaction.

Structure

Fairbairn began his discussion of the ego's inner structures by looking at the experience of a child who must deal with a harsh life situation. Let us say the child has a parent who is frustrating or abusive. The only power a child has to change or improve a terrible problem in that environment is to change him or herself. The child attempts to control the troublesome object in its world by mentally splitting the object into good and bad aspects and then taking in or internalizing the bad aspect. What this accomplishes is to make the environment or object good and the child bad. Beaten, abused children see abusing parents as good and themselves as bad and deserving of beating.

Objects taken within the psyche become dynamic structures. Because the ego is essentially bound up with objects, ego and object are inseparable. To be emotionally important for the ego, an object must have a piece of the ego attached to it. The objects Fairbairn discussed are internal objects. Internal objects are structures, and as structures they are dynamic; that is, capable of acting as independent agencies within the mind (Fairbairn, 1944/1954a, p. 132; Ogden, 1983, pp. 213, 230). Thus, Fairbairn considered objects to be not merely internal figures or mental representations but agencies capable of psychological activity. Abused children may cling to their abusers but hate themselves and later in life may get involved in relationships where they are again victims.

Fairbairn's psychology examined the inner relationships of parts of the ego to various internalized objects and the manner in which these inner relationships actively function and manifest themselves in the relationships of the individual with external objects—that is, people. A simple example of a relationship with an internal object might be a thumbsucker who uses her thumb as a substitute for a missing or unsatisfying object relationship, or a masturbator who, because of an unsatisfying or nonexisting relationship with the outerworld, turns to an internalized or phantasy object.

Fairbairn changed the nature of drive energy and its location from Freud's interpretation. Fairbairn located the libido in the ego, creating an ego that has its own energy rather than deriving energy from a different psychic structure, or the id, as the Freudian model teaches. Locating the libido in the ego and viewing it as a drive toward relationships eliminates the id, modifies the concept of the superego, and, of course, radically changes the ego. The ego becomes a dynamic structure; that is, a psychic structure actively doing something to someone or something.

The "Endopsychic Situation"

Fairbairn looked at the ego's relationships, not the ego's struggle with impulses. The ego seeks relationships with real, external people. If these relationships are satisfactory, the ego remains whole. Unsatisfying relationships, however, cause something important to happen: the setting up within the personality of inner objects that compensate for the bad external objects. Establishment of these inner, active objects causes fragmentation of the ego's unity because different portions of the ego are now in relation to different internal objects. Whenever an object gets split, the ego gets split and relates to the different parts of the object. In short, the ego's frustrating relationships with objects becomes internal, and these inner objects become active structures within the psyche. It is as if there are now a multiplicity of egos at war with one another. The *endopsychic situation* refers to these structures of the ego in relation to internalized objects that have become structures (Fairbairn, 1944/1954a, p. 112).

The result of these inner structures in conflict with one another shows up, for instance, in a troubled marriage. Some of these troublesome inner objects get externalized in the relationship. At an emotional level, a husband may sometimes feel he is not himself but rather some other person or part of a person, usually a past object relations figure. His wife could emotionally represent a parent for him, and in the marriage he might feel like a little boy and not the ordinary adult he is at work or with friends. He may perceive his wife as both a hating and a yearned-for mother. The wife may be very puzzled when she tries to draw near her husband and he pushes her away because he responds only to a partial aspect of her, the hating aspect of which she is unaware (Dicks, 1963).

Differences with Freud

Fairbairn's theories arose from what he saw as the inadequacies of the drive model. His fundamental difference with Freud was over the nature of motivation. For Fairbairn, motivation no longer comes from the ego being in service to the impulses of the body but rather from the ego striving for a relationship with an object. This fundamental difference influenced all else in Fairbairn's psychology—how he looked at drives, the nature of objects, and the nature of conflict.

Fairbairn's psychology flowed from his rejection of Freud's emphasis on drives as the basic human motivation. Fairbairn criticized Freud's assumption, based on the science of Freud's time, that psychic energy is distinct from psychic structure. Hermann von Helmholtz, dominating the science of late Victorian times, claimed that the universe consisted of aggregates of inert, immutable, and indivisible particles to which motion was imparted by fixed quantities of energy separate from these particles. Freud's separation of energy from structure results in a model of hypothetical impulses and instincts that he regarded as things influencing passive structures of the personality. Fairbairn (1946/1954b, p. 150) mocked this notion, saying it is almost as if impulses were a kick in the pants administered out of the blue to a surprised and perhaps pained ego. A consequence of the Freudian separation of energy from structure is that libido is essentially directionless, concerned only with pleasure-seeking and relief from its own tensions.

Pointing to another critical limitation in the Freudian impulse model, Fairbairn (1944/1954a, p. 84) noted that while a therapist might help a patient learn what his or her impulses are, the Freudian model does not suggest what to do with those impulses or how to dispose of them. For example, although a patient may be made aware that impulse tensions are the cause of some unacceptable behavior, it remains unclear what the patient is to do to dispose of those impulses.

In rejecting the Freudian notion of motivation, the biology of drives, Fairbairn developed what he believed to be a truly psychological model that completed what Freud started. His is a psychology of object relations that focuses on objects taken within by means of mental representations and related to by different parts of the ego. He studied these inner relationships of the ego: how they are internalized in relationships, and how they come into conflict with each other.

Freud took his conceptual starting point from a group of patients that differed from Fairbairn's patients. Freud's early therapeutic work with hysterical neurotic patients like Anna O. prompted him to fashion a conceptual model that emphasized the role of impulse and its conflict with the ego. Classical psychoanalysis understands neurosis as a conflict between the structures of id and ego. Freud originally believed that the pursuit of pleasure shaped an individual's actions and behavior. Fairbairn worked with schizoid patients whose problems were developmentally earlier and of a more relational than impulsive nature. By changing the nature of motivation, Fairbairn changed the nature of psychic structures and psychic conflict. The basic structure is an energized, dynamic ego; conflict is not between ego and id impulses but between the different parts of the ego in relation to the ego's inner objects.

Personality Structure

Although Fairbairn wrote as if he were merely modifying Freud's notion of ego, in truth he radically recast the notion of ego. He understood the ego as the primary psychic self, an ego that is unitary and integral, with its own libidinal energy (Greenberg & Mitchell, 1983, p. 163). The ego is split into three separate aspects, and each relates to a different aspect of the object. Fairbairn referred to the dynamic multiple substructures of the ego as the endopsychic situation (1944/1954a, p. 112).

The normal psychological situation of the infant compels the development of inner structures, with frustration playing a basic role in establishment of these inner structures. It is impossible for an infant to continue in the state of perfect, nonfrustrated security. The imperfect conditions of life disturb the libidinal relationships of the infant to its mother and prompt the infant to respond through various defensive mechanisms that contribute to the building up of internal structures. The degree of frustration varies in individual cases, but it is the experience of frustration that calls forth the infant's aggression in regard to its libidinal object, mother and her nurturing breast.

From an emotional point of view, the child experiences frustration as a lack of love or even rejection by the mother. This being so, it becomes dangerous for the child to express hatred for her; this would make her reject the child more. Yet the child also cannot express its need for her, because this would result in the continued humiliation of and depreciation of its love and need for her. The infant responds to frustration with aggression and takes in or internalizes the problematic object. For an objective observer, aggression makes the infant feel ambivalent or split toward the object, while from the subjective viewpoint of the infant, it is the mother who becomes ambivalent; that is, an object that is both good and bad, satisfying and unsatisfying. An immature personality cannot tolerate a good object that is simultaneously bad, so the infant tries to alleviate the unbearable situation in several steps and by doing so forms inner structures.

Normally, a child would reject frustrating, bad objects in the external world if it could. But it is not allowed the opportunity to do so. However much it might like to reject bad objects (such as bad parents who punish or abuse, quarrel, or fight), the child cannot get away from them. It needs the parents and is dependent on them; they have power over the child. Hence, to control the parents, the child must internalize them. This is the only way to get rid of them, by taking them within itself. Once internalized, these objects retain their power over the child's inner world. The child feels possessed by them, as if by evil spirits (Fairbairn, 1943/1954c, p. 67).

The child attempts to defend against or repress these bad feelings, bad experiences, and bad objects (Fairbairn, 1944/1954a, p. 89). The actual repression is not of impulses but of the inner bad objects, which are part objects, and those parts of the ego that are associated with these part objects. These internal bad objects and the parts of the ego associated with them are the endopsychic structure, but not the ego structure that is the central ego. The *central ego* relates to real people in the external world.

The following shows how an infant's endopsychic structures are built:

1. First, the infant splits or mentally separates the mother into two partial objects. Insofar as she satisfies the infant, she is good; insofar as she fails to satisfy the infant, she is a bad object. Because the infant is powerless to alter the situation in outer reality, the infant tries to change things in inner reality, the only realm where the infant has any resources.

2. The infant then tries to transfer the traumatic factor in the situation to his or her own inner reality, where the situation appears to be more under the infant's control. This means that the infant internalizes the mother as a bad object. (Fairbairn insisted that it is only the bad or unsatisfying object that is internalized, since there is no reason to internalize a good object that is available to the infant in outer reality. Melanie Klein, in contrast, spoke of internalization of both good and bad objects.) The problem, however, is not so easily resolved by this process of internalization, for the unsatisfying object continues to be unsatisfying. In other words, nothing is really changed except the location of the problem or the troublesome object.

3. This inner, unsatisfying object has two facets. It frustrates as well as tempts and allures. In fact, its "badness" consists precisely in its combination of allurement and frustration; the infant has not lost

the need for this object. Even after internalization, these dual qualities of allurement and frustration continue. Thus, in the attempt to control this unsatisfying object by introducing it into his or her own mind, the infant has burdened itself with an object that continues to whet the infant's need while frustrating it. The infant's solution to this inner bad object is similar to the solution that was attempted with the original external maternal object that was split into good and bad objects. Now the infant splits the inner bad object into an exciting (or needed) object and a frustrating (or rejecting) object.

4. The infant then represses both of these objects by aggressive repression. Associated with both of these inner objects are the split-off and repressed parts of the ego, namely the libidinal ego and the attacking ego, also called the internal saboteur. The libidinal ego is the needy aspect of the ego that is attracted to the exciting object; the internal saboteur is the part of the ego that identifies with or is in relation to the rejecting object.

The ego structure is split into three separate aspects, each relating to a different aspect of the object. The central ego, or "I," relates to the environment and comprises conscious and unconscious elements. The central ego aggressively severs subsidiary egos from itself and, for defensive reasons, represses them. The two subsidiary egos are the libidinal ego and the internal saboteur. The libidinal ego is the part of the self that feels needy as well as attacked or persecuted. The internal saboteur (antilibidinal or attacking ego) functions in a way similar to the superego and is aggressive and attacking, especially toward the needy part of the self (the libidinal ego). Each aspect of these subsidiary egos is in relation to an internalized aspect of the object. So the internal, exciting object stirs up the neediness that is the libidinal ego; and the rejecting object is in relation to the internal saboteur, which identifies and combines with the rejecting object and attacks the libidinal ego in a punishing way.

Fairbairn sought to explain motivation and behavior by means of these active inner objects. A delinquent and misbehaving child probably has had "bad" parents, but such a child will not say his or her parents are bad. Fairbairn said that in such cases, the child's bad objects have been internalized and repressed. The child would rather be bad him or herself than have bad objects or be in a bad situation. The likely motive for a child becoming bad or delinquent is to make his or her objects "good." In becoming bad, the child is really taking upon him or herself the burden of badness that appears to reside in the child's objects. By this means, the child seeks to purge them of their badness (Fairbairn, 1943/1954c, p. 65). The outer security of an environment of good objects is purchased at the price of inner security when bad objects are internalized. Hence, the ego is at the mercy of an internal persecutor against which defenses must be erected. The ego defensively and repressively banishes the internal bad object to the unconscious. But the inner, repressed bad object acts dynamically and causes bad behavior or bad feelings about the self.

A more extreme example of this process can be illustrated in the case of a victim of physical or sexual abuse. After the physical or sexual misuse, the child will often feel badly about herself but still retain an idealized sense of the parent who abused her. She is the bad person; the abuser is the good parent who could do no evil. In her own mind, she must have deserved or caused the abuse. Insofar as the child identifies with the internalized bad objects, she feels herself to be bad—even to the consternation of those who try to help or convince her of her innocence. In other relationships, the child may project part of the bad object onto a person and relate to the person as a victim; that is, her internal saboteur castigates and attacks her libidinal self for needing someone to love her.

If the ego protects itself by repressing these objects and the parts of the ego that are associated or in relationship with them, is the ego repressing itself? Fairbairn responded that it is inconceivable that the ego as a whole represses itself; but one dynamically charged part of the ego can repress another dynamically charged part (Fairbairn, 1944/1954a, p. 90). This means the internal saboteur represses the libidinal ego, and the central ego represses both the aggressive internal saboteur and the libidinal ego. Indeed, Freud had postulated the existence of a structure (the superego) to account for the repression of impulse, but here Fairbairn was looking at repressed structures, not impulses.

Developmental Stages and Object Relations

In considering development, Fairbairn (1941/1954d, p. 46*ff.*; 1946/1954b, p. 144*ff.*) examined the development of object relations; that is, the changing quality of the object that the individual seeks at various levels of development.

Relationships with a person (object) involve dependency of some sort, and Fairbairn's developmental model considers the quality of an individual's dependency upon his or her inner objects. Development, then, proceeds from an infantile dependence on a part object (the mother's breast) to a mature dependence on a whole object (a whole person with sexual features). Growth moves from an infantile attitude of taking to a more mature attitude of mutual giving and receiving between two differentiated individuals.

The classical Freudian developmental model is built on the nature of the *libidinal aim*; that is, how a person gets satisfaction and how libido is manifested in an erogenous zone of the body. Fairbairn emphasized the nature of the object and the quality of the relationship to it rather than the zone in the body wherein impulse is manifested. The classical psychoanalytic model bases the phases of development on the technique the individual uses rather than on the particular object the relationship involves. Thus, Freud spoke of the oral phase rather than a breast phase, an anal rather than a feces phase. Fairbairn seemed to imply that Freud emphasized sucking as a manifestation of libido rather than as an indication of the quality of the relationship experienced by this oral incorporation. So, Freud emphasized the manifestation of libido in a particular erogenous zone while Fairbairn stressed the quality of the relationship and only secondarily how it is libidinally manifested.

Fairbairn proposed three stages in the development of object relations. Stage 1 is the stage of infantile dependence, which means primarily an identification with the object. Stage 2 is an intermediate or transitional stage. Stage 3 is the stage of mature dependence; this stage implies a relationship between two independent persons who are completely differentiated from each other.

The first stage, the *infantile dependence stage,* is characterized by identification with the object and by the oral attitude of incorporation or taking. Incorporation is the earliest way of assimilating objects, and the object with which the individual is identified becomes equivalent to an incorporated object. Incorporated objects are contrasted with observable objects, such as the breast and the mother. Incorporated objects can be substitutes for observable objects because of frustration, absence, and so forth. Thus, thumbsucking replaces the absent comfort of the breast. Because this model considers development in terms of object seeking, it is incidental that the infant uses his or her mouth for breast seeking; the issue is to find an object that can be taken in, incorporated.

Still covered by Fairbairn's Stage 1 is the anal stage, wherein the task of differentiating the object tends to resolve itself into a problem of expelling contents; this is an anal technique. A person is anal when there is the preoccupation with the disposal of contents. In this stage, the psychological internalization and incorporation of objects into the psychic structure also occurs. Such a process of internalization marks the basic endopsychic situation (Fairbairn, 1946/1954b, p. 147).

During Stage 2, a *transitional stage,* a child's relationships with objects expand. The child, however, experiences conflict between the progressive urge to give up the infantile attitude of identification with the object and the regressive urge to hold onto that attitude. The conflict sometimes gets expressed in the urge to expel and the urge to retain contents (an obsessive-compulsive stance). As long as this conflict is unresolved, the child develops defensive techniques to deal with the conflict. Fairbairn notes that his schizoid patients struggled with this unresolved conflict in their relationships; they felt infantile dependency and yet longed to renounce such dependent feelings.

In Stage 3, the *mature relational stage,* the capacity to give predominates. According to Fairbairn, a mature relationship involves mutual giving and receiving between two differentiated persons who may express their relationship sexually. The quality of the relationship is primary; how the relationship is expressed sexually or libidinally is of only secondary importance.

To summarize, Fairbairn's developmental model shows the movement from an infantile object relationship based on identification (being like the object without being differentiated from it) to a mature object relationship with a whole and differentiated object. The process of development implies an increased differentiation from the object by the individual. As differentiation increases, there is a progressive decrease in identification with the object by the individual. There is also a change in the libidinal aim or way of getting satisfaction, going from a taking stance to one characterized by giving.

Fairbairn's developmental emphasis on relationship differed from the Freudian emphasis on instinctual drives. The classical Freudian developmental model was built upon the nature of the libidinal aim; that is, how a person gets satisfaction and how libido is manifested in an erogenous zone of the body. Freud emphasized the manifestation of libido in a particular erogenous zone, while Fairbairn stressed the quality of the relationship and only secondarily how it is libidinally manifested. Fairbairn emphasized the nature of the object and the quality of the relationship to it rather than the zone in the body wherein impulse is manifested.

The classical psychoanalytic model, from Fairbairn's point of view, overemphasized the place of the technique for satisfying drives rather than the quality of the object. The classical model, for instance, explains thumbsucking on the basis of the child's mouth as an erotogenic zone with libidinal pleasure resulting from sucking. But why the thumb? Why is this object used to obtain satisfaction? Fairbairn might have responded that the baby must have a libidinal object, and the thumb serves as a substitute for the breast. His emphasis was less on the mouth and the technique of sucking than on the need to be in relation to an object that can be incorporated.

Just because a physical capacity for a genital level of expression (intercourse) is reached, it does not necessarily follow that the object relationship is satisfying or mature. An infatuated teenage romance might illustrate this. Two young teenagers, with many needs, might seek each other because they are alike in their intense reactions to their families and share similar needs for support. They may do a lot of taking from each other and express their neediness through a sexual relationship. But such a relationship does not have the same qualities of giving and maturity that two more developed adults may share after working out issues of identity and separateness from their families.

Pathology and Internalized Objects

Freud understood psychological pathology in terms of the ego being in conflict with impulses that get repressed. Fairbairn understood pathology in relational terms; that is, in terms of the bad internal objects that are disruptive within the ego. These bad internal objects, which are in relation to different portions of the ego, are repressed and are the "badness" inside the person.

As stated earlier, self-protection is an essential element in Fairbairn's understanding of psychopathology. Those processes by which a child takes on the badness that appears to be in the hurtful objects of his or her environment are compensatory. Rather than having bad objects in his or her environment, the child controls the badness by becoming bad him or herself through internalization of these bad objects. This process of splitting and internalizing tends to make the environment good, but now the child has the internalized bad objects within him or herself. The child further defends against these inner bad objects or persecutors by repression, which banishes the bad objects to the unconscious. If these internalized bad objects are sufficiently charged, and if repression fails, they may cause psychological problems in various ways. The intensity of the badness of these objects, the intensity of the energy charge, and the extent to which the ego identifies with them are all aspects of these bad internalized objects producing neurotic and psychopathological symptoms. Symptoms and reactions are further shaped by the particular developmental stage of the conflict as well as by the kinds of defenses erected by the ego to protect itself from these bad objects.

The child's greatest need is to obtain assurance that the parents love the child as a person and that the parents genuinely accept the child's love. This assurance determines the success or failure of the conflict of dependent relationships with objects. On one side of the conflict is the regressive urge to be united with and identify with the object. On the other side is the progressive urge to separate and move to safe relationships with more differentiated, real objects. Fairbairn (1941/1954d, p. 39) described schizoid patients behaving like timid mice, creeping out of their holes to peep at the world of outer objects and then beating safe retreats. This represents their attempt to emerge from the state of infantile dependence and deal with separation anxiety.

Substitute satisfactions compensate for failure of emotional relationships with outer objects. These substitute satisfactions represent relationships with internalized objects; the individual turns to them instead of to safe and satisfactory relationships with objects in the outer world. Masturbation, sadism, masochism, and so on are some of these substitute satisfactions.

The ego has ambivalent feelings of accepting and rejecting internalized objects. The child develops different methods or techniques for dealing with or regulating relations with the internalized objects during the period of transition from infantile dependency to mature dependency. For example, the *phobic technique* involves externalizing the rejected object and avoiding it. The *paranoid technique* involves externalizing the rejected internal object and treating it as actively bad. The *hysteric neurotic technique* entails rejecting the incorporated object without externalizing it, but it also overvalues the accepted object that has been externalized. Hysterics manifest this pattern in intense love relationships: they do not like themselves because of overidentification with the internalized object but pursue the overvalued externalized object.

Analytic Therapy

As pathology involves disturbances in relationships with others, so therapy involves restoring the capacity to make direct and full contact with others, according to Fairbairn (Greenberg & Mitchell, 1983, p. 156). The goal of therapy (Fairbairn, 1943/1954c, p. 69*ff.*) is the release of bad objects from the unconscious. Only when these internalized bad objects are released from the unconscious can their cathexis or emotional power be dissolved. These objects were internalized because they once seemed indispensable, and they were repressed because they were intolerable (Fairbairn, 1943/1954c, p. 74). To aid in the release of bad objects, the therapist must become a sufficiently good object for the patient by providing a secure environment.

The therapist must be careful and avoid strengthening guilt in the patient or seeming to side with the patient's superego (antilibidinal ego or internal saboteur), for guilt strengthens resistance and keeps the bad object repressed (guilt is a defense and can aid resistance). What feels resistant is the fear of releasing the bad objects from the unconscious. Such a release would make the world of the patient a bad world or environment "peopled with devils which are too terrifying for him to face" (Fairbairn, 1943/1954c, p. 69). At one time, the individual needed these bad objects (to have them within so as to make his or her world better), and this need continues in some manner. It is this need for them that gives the continued presence and repression of these objects their power. Some patients would lose their identities if they surrendered their bad objects because they have become so familiar with and reliant upon their neurotic patterns of interacting and feeling.

It is the failure of the defenses of repression and guilt that allow the troublesome *partial* return of these bad objects. This return of the repressed is usually behind many symptoms. When these bad objects partly escape the bonds of repression in the unconscious, they make certain situations terrifying. One example would be transference situations where the patient is once again in relation to the bad object he or she once needed to deal with by means of internalization and repression. Certain traumatic situations also can provoke the release of these bad objects; for example, experiences of abandonment, dreams of being attacked by monsters, and so on. An understanding of the reemergence of terrifying bad objects gives some insight into the phenomenon of a troubled person killing another because he or she saw the victim as a terrifying threat.

Case Study
Fairbairn (1944/1954a, pp. 95–105) gave an account of a client's dream that concretely illustrated his understanding of the inner multiple egos and how those egos relate with inner objects.

The client was a married woman who sought therapy because of frigidity. She dreamed she saw an actress attacking her. Her husband looked on but was helpless and did not protect her. After the attack, the actress turned away and resumed her role in a play. The dreamer saw herself bleeding on the floor, but this bleeding figure turned into a man, then turned back into her, and then back into the man again. The dream ended with the woman awakening with anxiety.

Working traditionally through association, Fairbairn arrived at a nontraditional understanding of the dream. The man in the dream was wearing a suit like the dreamer's husband. The client-dreamer had many qualities of the actress in her own personality, playing the roles of good wife and mother. The patient also associated her mother with the actress. Fairbairn found six figures in the dream: (1) the dreamer being attacked, (2) the man into whom the bleeding figure turned, (3) the attacking actress, (4) the dreamer's helpless husband, (5) the dreamer as an observer, and (6) the actress as the dreamer's mother.

Fairbairn (1944/1954a, p. 100) looked at these figures as ego structures and object structures. Thus, the ego structures are (1) the observing ego or the "I," (2) the attacked ego, and (3) the attacking ego. The object structures are (1) the husband as an observing object, (2) the attacked object, and (3) the attacking object. Fairbairn concluded that the three ego structures in the dreamer's mind represented separate ego states or structures. There is the central ego with two subsidiary egos, which he called the libidinal ego (associated with the husband), the attacked ego, and the internal persecutor or saboteur (associated with the mother as an attacking and repressive figure). So, instead of Freud's psychic structures of id, ego, and superego, Fairbairn viewed an ego split into three separate egos.

Fairbairn also considered that these ego structures existed in relationships with internal objects. The dreamer's husband was an important object for her in outer reality, so he not only was an internalized object but also corresponded closely to the external object. But she was ambivalent to him, and these attitudes were expressed in her need for and aggression toward him. In the dream, aggression was directed not only against the libidinal ego but also against a libidinal object that, by association, was both the husband and the father as well as herself. This libidinal object excited. The dream figures representing her mother (a rejecting figure) and herself were the objects that rejected. The dream thus dramatically explains the dreamer's anxiety by showing how she attacked herself and a figure dear to her, her husband.

Henry Dicks (1963) carries this analysis of Fairbairn further by applying it to marital relationships. He believes that these inner relationships are externalized in some marital relationships. Marriage often fosters the attribution or projection onto the spouse in such a way that, for instance, the wife might experience her husband as a persecuting father as well as a punishing superego. She experiences ambivalence in that her husband might also represent for her the needed object for whom there is much affection; thus, in her inner experience, her ego is split into a libidinal ego and an internal saboteur in relation to the libidinal object and the rejecting object, while the central ego carries on the relationship with the actual wife.

Assessment and Critique of Fairbairn

Fairbairn made explicit many of the concepts that Klein implied. While Klein tried to maintain conceptual contact with Freud, she was the first to conceptualize the child's internal object world as organized around internal object relationships. Fairbairn explicitly rejected the Freudian notions of instinct and drive motivation, and instead developed very different concepts of object, structure, and development.

In objecting to the mechanical and impersonal qualities in the instinct model, Fairbairn rejected (perhaps too strongly) Freud's pleasure principle and notions of instinctual energy. He replaced these with dynamic object-seeking structures—that is, persons (cf. Robbins, 1980, p. 482). Fairbairn saw the Freudian id as energy without structure and the Freudian ego as structure without energy (cf. Ogden, 1983, p. 230). This traditional ego has function but not its own energy or motivation. The notion of dynamic structures combines the elements of id and ego into one structure, a primary self. This self seeks objects and not mere gratification, and Fairbairn's model explains the development of this primary self or ego.

This primary ego is intact at birth, and Fairbairn sees structuralization as proceeding from experiences with bad objects and the processes of splitting. That is, difficulties with parents cause psychological problems as well as contribute to the normal process of structuralization. Unsatisfactory relationships cause the differentiation of this primary ego into three dynamic structures (Robbins, 1980, p. 483).

Fairbairn understood the child as internalizing bad objects in the course of development and structuralization. It is not merely objects that the child internalizes but object relationships. An aspect of the ego is split off and becomes identified with an object representation, and this changes how the person thinks about and experiences him or herself (Ogden, 1983, p. 234). Fairbairn thus saw self and object components in the internal relationship as active agencies, dynamic structures.

Fairbairn, like Klein, telescoped all development into a very early and brief period (Kernberg, 1980, p. 82). Fairbairn, again like Klein, ignored the differentiation between self and object representations of this early period (Kernberg, 1980, p. 82). Fairbairn saw this early ego as intact but also undifferentiated. Edith Jacobson later grappled with this issue and arrived at a solution that better reflects early structural development and differentiation as well as preserving the tripartite model (see Chapter 6).

Fairbairn accomplished several things. He was able to describe subjective awareness of early conflicts. He advanced Klein's innovative efforts by reaffirming the real relationship with the mother and by providing more of a structural framework for Klein's free-floating, multiple inner egos and objects (Kernberg, 1980, p. 83). His overall contribution lies in his efforts to formulate the early age at which internalized object relations foster an emerging self that does not stem from impersonal instincts. Fairbairn's work, however, still falls short of an integrated model that both describes experience and gives a coherent conceptual explanation of early experiences.

References

Dicks, H. V. (1963). Object relations theory and marital studies. *British Journal of Medical Psychology, 36,* 125–129.

Fairbairn, W. R. D. (1954a). Endopsychic structure considered in terms of object relationships. In *An object-relations theory of the personality* (pp. 82–136). New York: Basic Books. (Original work published 1944)

Fairbairn, W. R. D. (1954b). Object-relationships and dynamic structure. In *An object-relations theory of the personality* (pp. 137–161). New York: Basic Books. (Original work published 1946)

Fairbairn, W. R. D. (1954c). The repression and the return of bad objects (with special reference to the "war neuroses." In *An object-relations theory of the personality* (pp. 59–81). New York: Basic Books. (Original work published 1943)

Fairbairn, W. R. D. (1954d). A revised psychopathology of the psychoses and psychoneuroses. In *An object-relations theory of the personality* (pp. 28–58). New York: Basic Books. (Original work published 1941)

Greenberg, J. R., & Mitchell, S. A. (1983). *Object relations in psychoanalytic theory.* Cambridge: Harvard University Press.

Guntrip, H. (1971). *Psychoanalytic theory, therapy and the self.* New York: Basic Books.

Kernberg, O. (1980). *Internal world and external reality* (pp. 57–84). New York: Aronson.

Ogden, T. H. (1983). The concept of internal object relations. *International Journal of Psycho-Analysis, 64,* 227–241.

Robbins, M. (1980). Current controversy in object-relations theory as outgrowth of a schism between Klein and Fairbairn. *International Journal of Psycho-Analysis, 61,* 477–491.

Chapter Five

D. W. Winnicott:
Pediatrician with a
Unique Perspective

Introduction

Donald W. Winnicott, an English pediatrician who wrote from the 1930s to 1971, least fits into a convenient category of object-relations theorists. Much of his writing and theories began as radio talks or professional lectures, and thus has a chatty and informal tone. Although largely free of jargon, his style can be imprecise and confusing at times. He sometimes borrowed terms from Melanie Klein but also coined words and used them with his own meaning, such as good-enough mothering, holding environment, and the squiggle. Winnicott emerges through his writings and clinical anecdotes as a genial, warmly attentive, even playful man to whom people responded well.

Winnicott died in 1971 at the age of 74. He was both a pediatrician and psychoanalyst, spending forty years at Paddington Green Children's Hospital in London. He underwent analysis during the 1930s and came under the influence of Melanie Klein, who served as a consultant (Khan, 1971). During his busy career as a pediatrician and analyst, Winnicott cared for thousands of mothers and their children, and he says of himself that during World War II he "hardly noticed the blitz, being all the time engaged in the analysis of psychotic patients" (1945/1958g, p. 145).

Winnicott did not build a formal system but primarily devoted his attention to certain areas of child development. One of Winnicott's innovations was to stress the delicate balance between the environment and the evolving self. His innovative views on the development of the self were the conceptual forerunners of some of Heinz Kohut's ideas. This chapter will examine Winnicott's terms and concepts and his theories on parental care and developmental processes, mental illness, and therapy. A case study and a critique of Winnicott's work then follow.

Key Concepts

Environment and Instinct

Winnicott emphasized the environment in the formation of self, saying that the environment, when it is good enough, facilitates the maturational processes of the infant. The infant depends on the provisions of the environment, and the environment (in the person of the mother) adapts itself to the changing needs of the infant. With growth, the infant gradually depends less on the environment or mother.

While not rejecting Freud's notions of instincts and the inner dynamics of the individual, Winnicott shifted perspectives and focused on the interaction of the child with the environment. This perspective puts instinctual development into a social and interactive context with the result that he understood the emotional development of the young child almost exclusively in terms of the child's relationship with the mother rather than in terms of instinct. This concentration on interrelationship and the importance of environment was a sharp departure from Freud's emphasis on instinctual development. Growth moves toward a maturity that is social (defined in terms of relationships) and not merely instinctual.

Facilitating Environment

The conditions of the environment, whether favorable or unfavorable, shape the development of the infant. The crucial factor in the environment is maternal care. "At first it is the mother herself who is the facilitating environment," Winnicott said (1963/1965g, p. 85). The infant will grow and succeed in the maturational process if there is a facilitating environment (Winnicott, 1963/1965i, p. 239). Characteristic of the facilitating environment is *adaptation*. Winnicott used the term to describe the *environment's* adaptation to the infant's needs. The infant's needs and maturational processes are central, and it is the parents' responsibility to adapt to them. That is, the mother at first is totally given over to infant care and then gradually she tends toward de-adaptation, a reassertion of her own independence.

In different words, the facilitating environment gives the infant an experience of omnipotence. The infant begins by relating to subjective objects; that is, phantasy or mental objects. Then the infant makes a difficult transition and begins to relate to "objects objectively perceived" by a process of mentally creating and recreating the object. A good object has to be created by the infant out of need. As the object changes over from being subjective to being objectively perceived, the child gradually leaves the stage of omnipotence (Winnicott, 1963/1965d, pp. 180–182).

Hallucination of Omnipotence

In the earliest stages of growth, the infant has no relation to reality and must create the world, as it were, with very few resources. The one resource available to the infant is phantasy or hallucination. Because of such instinctual tension as hunger, the infant is ready to believe something could exist, and so the infant can hallucinate an object and have a magical expectancy for some kind of object. The good mother will come along with her breast so that the infant can find it.

In this crucial period of the infant's first and primary relationship to external reality, it is as if two lines (needs of the infant and the provision of the environment) proceed from opposite directions and come near each other. If there is some overlapping or meeting of these lines, the infant has a moment of illusion, an experience that the infant can take as either an illusion or a thing belonging to external reality. The mother allows the infant to dominate and the infant's subjective object will superimpose on the objectively perceived breast if all goes well. To go well and healthily means that the mother fits in with the infant's impulse and allows the baby the illusion that what is there (the breast, for example, or a comforting hand) is the thing created by the baby.

Good-Enough Mother

Winnicott coined the striking term *good-enough mother* (1962/1965f, p. 57) to describe the parental function of providing sufficiently for the child to get a good start in life. In a way that Freud did not quite do, Winnicott emphasized the need for the *environment and the parents* to adapt to the infant and the infant's needs. Freud, without ignoring the parents, tended to emphasize the inner world and instinctual needs of the infant.

The good-enough mother sufficiently provides for what the child needs at a particular developmental period in the relationship with the mother. The mother adapts and changes according to the changing needs of her child, and gradually there is a decrease in the growing child's dependence. To emphasize the changes demanded of the mother, Winnicott gave the term *primary maternal preoccupation* (1963/1965g, p. 85) to the mother's preoccupation with the needs of her baby, which at first seems like a part of herself. The child's growth will often correspond to the mother's resumption of her own independence (1963/1965g, p. 87). Gradually, as the infant grows and develops, there are interpersonal changes, with the demands on the mother being less as her baby grows more independent.

In successful adaptation to her infant, the good-enough mother meets and fosters the omnipotence of the infant. The mother successfully and repeatedly meets the infant's spontaneous gestures or makes real the infant's sensory hallucination (1960/1965e, p. 145). This fosters the infant's omnipotence, and the infant begins to believe in an external reality that appears as if by magic and behaves as if under his or her control (because of the mother's successful adaptation to the infant's gestures and needs).

The infant gradually develops the capacity to conjure up what is actually available, and the good-enough mother has to keep providing this kind of experience, which feeds the infant's sense of narcissistic omnipotence. The infant then can serenely enjoy the illusion of omnipotent creativity and control. Not only is there the physical experience of instinctual satisfaction but also an emotional union and the beginning of a belief in reality as something about which one can have illusions. The final steps can now be taken, the gradual letting go of omnipotence and the gradual disillusioning of the infant when it comes to recognize the illusory element and establishes contact with reality (Winnicott, 1948/1958f, p. 163).

True Self and False Self

In discussing the importance of the environment's adaptation to the infant, Winnicott discussed the notions of the *true self* and *false self*, both developing from the child's interaction with the environment. What are the consequences for the infant's self in the process of letting go of omnipotence and illusion? Through the infant's impulses (met and confirmed by the mother) the infant discovers the environment and the *not-me* world and the establishment of the *me* (Winnicott, 1950/1958a, p. 216). Object relating comes about when the mother lets the baby find and come to terms with the object (breast, bottle, and so on). The true self has a me and a not-me clearly established.

The caring mother must also protect the infant from complications and impingements from the world that the infant cannot understand. If the environment is not safe, the infant may respond with compliance. This compliance could lead to the isolation of the infant from its own spontaneous and life-giving core (Winnicott, 1948/1958f, p. 171). The false self develops at the earliest stage of object relations when there is not good-enough mothering, when the mother does not meet and implement the omnipotence of the infant. Should the infant's gesture be repeatedly missed, the mother substitutes her own gesture, which is met by the infant's compliance (Winnicott, 1960/1965e, p. 145).

When the mother's adaptation is not good enough, the cathexis of the external object is not initiated, and the infant remains isolated and lives falsely. A false self reacts compliantly to environmental demands and builds up a false set of relationships. The false self hides the true self and cannot act spontaneously. Only the true self can be spontaneous and feel real or genuine. The presence of a false self results in the person feeling unreal and futile and unable to be genuine in relationships.

Object

Although Winnicott borrowed terms and concepts such as *object* from Melanie Klein, he tended to give them his own interpretation and meaning. Thus, he used the term *subjectively conceived object* (1960/1965j, p. 45), which is similar to Klein's concept of internal object (Winnicott, 1951/1958i, p. 237). This is in contrast to an *object objectively perceived* (Winnicott, 1960/1965j, p. 45), which is an external object or actual person.

Winnicott believed that the infant develops from a relationship with a subjective object to gradually establish the capacity to relate to an object that is objectively perceived (1963/1965h, p. 224). Good-enough mothering, especially holding, allows the infant to move from fusion and merger with the mother to a state of being separate from her and capable of object relationships (Winnicott, 1960/1965j, p. 45). By *object relationships*, Winnicott meant relating with external objects that have a separate existence, an existence outside the omnipotent control of the individual that is subjective and phantasy (Winnicott, 1963/1965h, p. 224). With maturation, the individual is gradually able to relate genuinely to objects, have vital contact with reality, feel real and alive, feel real in the world, and feel that the world is real and actual.

At the very early stage of development, a two-body relationship exists, while at a later stage, during the oedipal period, a three-body relationship predominates (Winnicott, 1958/1965b, p. 29). The original two-body relationship is made up of the infant and the mother (or mother substitute). Winnicott believed there cannot be a one-body relationship at the very earliest stages, as the capacity to be alone is a very sophisticated phenomenon and comes only after establishment of a three-body relationship. To be alone depends on the existence of a good object in the psychic reality of the individual (Winnicott, 1958/1965b, p. 32).

In describing this good internal object, Winnicott used the language of Melanie Klein. The good internal object can refer to the good internal breast or the good internal relationship. Having good internal objects and confidence in internal relationships allows the individual to rest contented even in the absence of external objects and stimuli. "Maturity and the capacity to be alone implies that the individual has had the chance through good-enough mothering to build up a belief in a benign environment" (Winnicott, 1958/1965b, p. 32).

Omnipotent control of reality implies phantasies about reality, a way of trying to deal with inner reality or fleeing from inner reality to external reality. In fact, the individual gets to external reality through the omnipotent phantasies that are elaborated to get away from inner reality (Winnicott, 1935/1958c, p. 130). Winnicott gave several examples. A child can have unconscious sadistic phantasies against the internal parents while dealing with the external parents in a protective way. An extroverted adventurer may be a shallow personality fleeing from inner depression. A king may get much external respect because in many people's inner reality the internalized father is being killed and cut up, and this internalized man becomes personified as a real man whom . people can respect and serve (Winnicott, 1935/1958c, p. 131).

Transitional Object

One of Winnicott's most notable contributions to object relations theory addressed the notion of the *transitional object,* an intermediate area of experience between subjective objects and true object relationships. The transitional object is not an internal or subjective object, and it is not merely an external object; it is the first not-me possession. A common transitional object is a soft blanket—one readily recalls the security blanket of Peanuts' cartoon character Linus—or a diaper or an old piece of cloth. Included among transitional phenomena are an infant's babbling, a mannerism, or some part of the child's own body that is not yet recognized as belonging to external reality. What is important for the infant is that the thing or sound becomes vitally important as a comfort at the time of going to sleep or as a protection against anxiety or loneliness.

Transitional objects and *transitional phenomena* (a broader, more inclusive term than transitional object) belong to that intermediate area of experience to which inner reality and external life both contribute. The infant is passing from omnipotent control (phantasy) to control by physical manipulation (reality-testing), in which the child needs the illusion to create an intermediate situation that is partly subjective and partly reality-oriented. Thus, the blanket is a real, objectively perceived thing but serves like the comforting breast that is under the control of the infant. The transitional object is neither under the infant's magical, omnipotent control like the internal, subjective object (such as the illusion of the breast as part of the infant), nor under outside control the way the real, external mother is (Winnicott, 1951/1958i, p. 237).

Developmental Processes and Parental Care

Winnicott wrote extensively about the parent-child interaction and had significant insights to share about the child's developmental processes. As Winnicott focused his discussion on mother and child, he moved around and examined the picture from different angles or perspectives. His writings, however, did not integrate these different perspectives into one carefully worked-out, coherent system. He did, however, look at a number of interrelated processes, emphasizing that child development is intertwined with the relationship with the mother. His overriding theme was the contribution of the environment to child development, and he defined development in terms of the child's relationship with the environment—that is, the parent, who, for Winnicott, was invariably the mother.

When Winnicott dramatically said "there is no such thing as a baby" (1952/1958b, p. 99), he meant that whenever you find an infant you find a mother who cares. Without the maternal care, there is no infant (Winnicott, 1960/1965j, p. 39). A baby is not an isolated individual but an essential part of a nursing couple. Development of the young child is inextricably linked to maternal care: "the infant and the maternal care together form a unit" (1960/1965j, pp. 39, 43). Thus, Winnicott emphasized emotional growth not so much as a progression of the individual's instinctual life but as an interpersonal growth from dependency to independence. "There is no value whatever in describing babies in the earliest stages except in relation to the mother's functioning," he wrote (1962/1965f, p. 57). Winnicott, in fact, was somewhat casual about various stages of development and considered that "a division of one phase from another is artificial, and merely a matter of convenience" (1960/1965j, p. 44).

The child develops within the environment of good-enough mothering, progressing from an original unintegrated state to a structured integration, with the capacity for object relationships and "living with"; that is, relationships with whole, external objects (Winnicott, 1960/1965j, p. 44). The infant journeys from *absolute dependence*, through *relative dependence*, to *independence*, and these three kinds of dependence correlate roughly with the three overlapping stages of parental care: "holding," "mother and infant living together," and finally "mother, infant, and father living together" (Winnicott, 1960/1965j, p. 43).

Included in Winnicott's discussion of the development process are: maturational processes, kinds of parental care, the links between maturational processes and parental care, kinds of dependence, and development of the ego.

Maturational Processes

Maturational processes, or developmental stages, are inter-twined with parental care and are inherited tendencies in the child for forward development. These processes include integration, personification, and object relating (Winnicott, 1945/1958g, p. 145; 1952/1958b, p. 226; 1962/1965f, p. 60).

Integration suggests the increased organization of the individual into a unit, since the personality does not begin as a completed whole. *Personification* refers to the way in which the individual's psyche becomes localized in the body. *Object relating,* for Winnicott, has to do with feeling real and relating to real people and actual objects in the environment; this differs, of course, from the usual meaning of object relations as an inner process.

Kinds of Parental Care

The maturational processes of the child are fostered by parental caring. The environment, in the form of parental care, supplies holding, handling, and object presenting (Winnicott, 1962/1965f, p. 60).

Holding is both an environmental provision as well as a period or stage in parental care. Thus, holding denotes not only the physical holding of the infant but also the whole environment, which facilitates growth prior to the concept (and stage) of "living with."

During the holding period, the infant is merged with the mother and is not yet capable of perceiving objects as external to the self (Winnicott, 1960/1965j, p. 44). Gradually, the infant changes from an unintegrated state to a structured integration. The infant becomes a unit, a person, an individual in his or her own right, has an inside and an outside, a me and a not-me (1960/1965j, pp. 43, 45). The infant further develops the capacity for object relationships, changing from a relationship with a subjectively conceived object to one with an object objectively perceived. This development is closely bound up with the infant's change from being merged with the mother to being separate from her, or relating to her as separate and not-me. The successful accomplishment of this moves the infant from the holding phase to the phase of living with (Winnicott, 1960/1965j, p. 45). *Living with* is the phase of development when the child as an individual relates with the mother as a real object external and separate from the child's self.

Links between Maturational Processes and Parental Care

The maturation processes of the infant are closely related to the kind and quality of parental provision. Thus, integration is closely linked to holding, personalization is linked to handling, and object relating is linked to object presenting.

Integration and holding

Integration is closely linked with the environmental function of holding (Winnicott, 1962/1965f, p. 61). Holding includes the whole routine of care throughout the day, especially physical holding of the infant, a form of loving. Some adults do not know how to hold an infant, and the infant feels insecure and often cries (Winnicott, 1960/1965j, p. 49). Holding fosters integration, which makes the infant a unit or unit self, a whole person living in the body. Integration, bringing together the psychological pieces of the infant, is the opposite of psychological fragmentation and disintegration.

The holding environment's main function is to reduce to a minimum impingements that the infant cannot manage or which cause the child to shut down or feel annihilated. A successful holding environment builds up positive feelings of being actual and in existence in the infant. In short, good maternal care brings the infant into existence as a person (Winnicott, 1960/1965j, pp. 47, 49).

Winnicott saw the mother as evoking the baby's existence partly by mirroring the baby. (This notion calls to mind Kohut's mirroring environment; perhaps he drew upon Winnicott's idea.) What the baby sees when he or she looks at the mother's face is him or herself. For when the mother looks at her baby, her appearance is related to what she sees in the baby (for example, her pleasure in her child is reflected in her face, and the infant sees that joy and feels like he or she is joyful and good). The mother gives back to the baby the baby's own self. It is as if the baby, in looking at the mother's face, looks in a mirror and sees itself. "When I look I am seen and so I exist" (Winnicott, 1971a, p. 114). Thus, in the early stages of emotional development, a vital part is played by the environment that, in fact, is not yet distinguished from the infant by the infant.

Personalization and handling

This environmental provision is a form of parental care that fosters a firm union of the baby's ego and body. When a parent touches and gently handles the baby's body, the baby's person is grounded in its own body, nurturing a body ego that serves as a base for the baby's ego. Physical handling links the ego and the person of the baby to the body, body functions, and sensations in a way that is comfortable and familiar. Winnicott used the term *personalization* to describe this process of linking the ego to the body with its various id drives and satisfactions. If the firm link between the ego and the body should be lost, strange feelings of unreality can result as well as feelings of being out of touch with the self and distant from one's own body. Winnicott used the term *depersonalization* to refer to the loss of this union of ego and body, although there is a slightly different and more sophisticated meaning of this term in psychiatry (1962/1965f, p. 59).

Object relating and object presenting

This form of parental care involves the mother presenting objects (breast, bottle, and so forth) in a way that shapes how the baby will relate to external reality and external objects (Winnicott, 1945/1958g, p. 152). The baby develops a vague expectation that originates in some need. The good-enough mother presents an object that meets the baby's need, and so the baby begins to need precisely what she can provide. For example, the mother has a breast with milk, and she would like her hungry baby to nurse at her breast. The mother needs to shape how the infant deals with this external object. There needs to be the illusion that the infant can either experience the breast as its own hallucination or a thing belonging to external reality. The infant needs to come to the breast when excited and ready so that when the actual nipple appears it is the nipple that the baby has hallucinated. In this way, the infant starts to build a capacity to conjure up what is actually available. The mother needs to continue providing the infant with this type of experience, with the baby seeming to create the object and actively participating in its own instinctual satisfactions rather than having them imposed upon it (Winnicott, 1945/1958g, p. 153; 1962/1965f, p. 60).

Some dissatisfaction is helpful here for the baby's emotional growth. When the child is still in a fusion with the mother, gratification of instincts does little with regard to locating or positioning the object, whereas dissatisfaction places the object, as it were, in the way. That is, frustration evokes aggression, which helps place the object separate from the self. Frustration helps educate the child in respect to the existence of a not-me world. For example, a gratifying feeding seems to make the object go away without an object cathexis, for although instinctual gratification and satisfaction are good, they do nothing with regard to the position of the object, and so the infant continues on in a fusion state (Winnicott, 1963/1965d, p. 181).

Winnicott gave the term *ego-relatedness* to the relationship of the infant with the mother (Winnicott, 1958/1965b, p. 33). This, Winnicott believed, is the material out of which friendship is made and also the matrix of transference. The ego immaturity of the infant is balanced by the ego support of the mother (Winnicott, 1958/1965b, p. 32). It is only when someone is available and present to the infant, without making demands, that the infant can discover its personal life (rather than a false self), can feel real, and can develop the capacity to be alone. As the experience of good objects in the inner psychic reality is increasingly established, the infant has the capacity to be alone, content in the absence of the external object.

Dependence

Another manner in which Winnicott explained development is in terms of the quality of dependence of the child on the mother. Development stages of the young child are inextricably intertwined with the kind and quality of maternal care. The three categories of dependence are absolute dependence, relative dependence, and toward independence.

Absolute dependence

During this earliest phase of the infant's emotional development, the mother is the facilitating environment, and she is in the state of "primary maternal preoccupation" (Winnicott, 1963/1965g, p. 85). During the first few weeks of the infant's life, the mother is preoccupied with her baby, which seems like a part of herself. The baby is absolutely dependent on the mother to the point of not even being aware of the mother's care, and in many ways the mother is in a dependent state because of her close links with her child. She provides food, tests the temperature of the bathwater, and provides the infant with the environment it needs. She keeps reality from impinging on the infant.

During this period of absolute dependence, the mother (or mother substitute) needs to be devoted to the care of the infant. As she adapts to her infant's growth, the mother will gradually resume her own life and independence as her child grows toward increased independence.

Relative dependence

In a state of relative dependence, the child begins to be aware of its dependence on the mother and anxiety results from this awareness. This is a stage of lessening adaptation on the mother's part as she gradually returns to "being herself" or as she was before the birth of her infant (Winnicott, 1963/1965g, p. 88). Early intellectual understanding enables the hungry infant to delay and to know that kitchen noises indicate that food is coming soon. The child also knows now that mother is necessary; the child now has a conscious need for her. This phase lasts roughly from the sixth month to the second year.

The infant gradually achieves integration, which makes the infant a unit or unit self, a whole person, with an inside and an outside, a person living in the body. Personal psychic reality is located inside; and outside means not-me (Winnicott, 1963/1965g, p. 91). The establishment of "I" includes "everything else is not me" (Winnicott, 1962/1965f, p. 61). The environmental function of holding fosters integration, and there is a sense of "I am seen or understood to exist by someone," and "I get back (as a face seen in a mirror) the evidence I need that I have been recognized as a being" (Winnicott, 1962/1965f, p. 61). This is a startling forerunner of Kohut's concept of "mirroring." The normal infant, for long stretches of time, does not mind if it is many bits or a whole being, or whether it lives in its mother's face or in its own body. Gradually, the infant normally has one person to gather its pieces psychologically together in self-integration (Winnicott, 1945/1958g, p. 150). Winnicott spoke of an adult client who in an unintegrated way gives every detail of his daily life during the week and feels content if everything has been said, while the analyst feels no therapeutic work has been done except that the patient needs to be known in all his bits and pieces by one person, the analyst.

Integration, of course, is opposed to fragmentation and disintegration. The defense of disintegration is an active production of chaos in the absence of maternal ego support against unthinkable anxiety that results from failure of holding in the stage of absolute dependence (Winnicott, 1962/1965f, p. 61).

Toward independence

The infant develops means for doing without actual care. The child develops mental mechanisms and intellectual understanding and is more involved in society. The child develops a true independence with a personal existence in ever-widening circles of social life. This phase describes the strivings of the toddler and continues through puberty and adolescence (Winnicott, 1963/1965g, p. 91).

Development of the Ego

Another way Winnicott examined development is by considering the ego's development, which he saw as influenced by the environment. He sometimes referred to the development of the baby, sometimes to the development of the ego. As used by Winnicott, the term *ego* describes "that part of the growing human personality that tends, under suitable conditions, to become integrated into a unit" (1962/1965f, p. 56).

Unlike Freud, who envisioned the ego emerging from the id, Winnicott said that there is no id before ego. The ego offers itself for study long before the word "self" has relevance, and self arrives after the ego. In response to the question of whether the ego is present from the start, Winnicott said the start is when the ego starts (1962/1965f, p. 56).

Mental Illness

Winnicott approached mental illness from a variety of perspectives over a period of time, and he emphasized the difficulties of reducing a complex subject to simple terms. In his earlier writings, Winnicott was close to Freud and Klein in his analysis, but he gradually developed his own approach in which he stressed deficiencies in the child's environment. Because of failures in child care, the self of the child may not be true, spontaneous, or integrated, and the child will be filled with various kinds of anxieties.

In general, Winnicott stressed that any classification should be based on the degree and quality of environmental distortion and deficiency. He saw mental illness in terms of the processes of early infant maturation but in reverse (1963/1965i, p. 241); that is, there are environmental hindrances to the proper growth of the infant. In his later writings, he divided mental illness into three categories: psycho-neurosis, intermediate (antisocial or delinquent) illness, and psychosis.

Psycho-Neurosis

Psycho-neurosis is a term used to describe the illness of persons who have reached the stage of the Oedipus complex. At this level of emotional development and strength, individuals have an intact personality and the capacity to experience relationships among three whole people rather than have merely two-body relationships. Winnicott assumed that such individuals are relatively normal, that environmental provision has been good enough so that their personalities are sufficiently organized as to be capable of defending against anxiety and conflict. Winnicott looked upon this area of disturbance as the province of orthodox Freudian analysis while his own special area of expertise lay in the area of psychosis (1960/1965j, p. 218).

Intermediate Illness

Intermediate illness or mental disturbance results from an environmental provision that is at first good and then fails. It succeeds in that it allows the child to develop an ego organization, but growth stops before the individual is able to establish an internal environment, that is, become independent. This kind of deprivation produces individuals who are sociopathic, delinquent, or antisocial. Such individuals have the attitude that society (the environment) owes them something.

Psychosis

Winnicott claimed that *psychosis* results from an early privation or failure of the environment. This failure of environmental provision disturbs maturational processes to such a degree that the child is unable to achieve the crucial maturational processes of integration, personification, and object relating.

The environment might fail in its function of fostering maturational processes. In the earliest stages of life, the basis for an individual's mental health is laid down. The environment does not make the individual grow, but if good enough, it facilitates the maturational processes of the individual. To facilitate these growth processes, the environment must, in good-enough fashion, adapt to the changing needs of the growing child (Winnicott, 1963/1965h, p. 223) and facilitate certain maturational processes. Failure of the environment to adapt to the needs of the child can lead to interference with the normal growth processes that lead to the establishment of a self that goes on being (integration), achieves a comfortable harmony with the body (personalization), and develops a capacity for relating to objects (object relating) (Winnicott, 1963/1965h, p. 227).

Disintegration is the reverse of integration, with a lesser degree of disintegration being splitting. Breaking the link between the body and the psyche is depersonalization or some psychosomatic disorder. Successful object relating means joining up the idea of the object with a perception of the whole person of the mother. Success means feeling real, feeling real in the world, and feeling the world is real. The reverse of successful object relating is *de-realization*, or feelings of unreality and loss of contact with social reality.

Therapy

If mental illness is related to early environmental failures that result in a sense of futility and the development of the false self, then therapy is to be a reverse of this. Therapy reproduces early mothering processes to produce a genuine, healthy true self. Winnicott's notions of therapy closely followed his understanding of the essentials that the environment must provide for the maturing child.

The therapist should get to know what it feels like to be the client. The therapist accepts being a subjective object in the client's life, which might involve being the client's love object without acting out or being the client's hate object without taking revenge. The therapist must tolerate the client's illogicality, muddle, and meanness for the sake of assisting a regression (Winnicott, 1963/1965h, p. 229).

Therapy is a process of controlled regression. That is, the conditions of therapy, the professional setting, and the therapist's patience and reliability foster a regression in the patient. *Regression* is an organized return to early dependence and the stage of the environmental failure. It is not a return to some earlier point of instinctual life but rather a tendency toward a reestablishment of dependency (Winnicott, 1959/1965c, p. 127).

Healing in therapy is not something the therapist does but something that the client, in the dependent relationship, brings about through a self-cure. The goal of therapy is to unfreeze the early emotional failure by providing a successful experience of early narcissism or omnipotence. In therapy, change comes when the traumatic early factors enter the therapeutic material in the client's own way, within the individual's omnipotence. Certain aspects of the environment that failed originally are relived, with the environment this time succeeding instead of failing to facilitate inherited tendencies for growth and maturity (1959/1965c, p. 128).

The therapist fosters the client's regression so that the individual can relive earlier infantile experiences and correct those developmental deficits. The individual feels confidence in the therapist because the therapist provides the right environment and the necessary environmental provisions in a reliable and patient way (Winnicott, 1960/1965j, pp. 37–38).

Progress is experienced as independence is increased, and the therapist helps the individual's true self meet limited environmental failures without organizing the defenses that involve a false self protecting the true self (Winnicott, 1954/1958d, pp. 286–287). All of this must be repeated again and again, just as the good-enough mother must repeat good experiences for her infant.

Winnicott furnished an example of how he tried to respond to an adolescent client's infantile needs. The reluctant client telephoned and asked if Winnicott could see him on the next day, a Saturday. This represented a somewhat magical and unrealistic demand on the famous and busy pediatrician. Winnicott, however, knew he must try to meet this demand since the gesture came from the boy and Winnicott wanted to fit in with him, just as the successful parent fits in with the infant's needs (1948/1958f, p. 168). Winnicott tried to foster a therapeutic climate where the client would create the kind of therapist he needed and the therapist would try to foster a regression by fitting into that role, at least in the early stages of therapy.

The Squiggle Game

Winnicott invented a drawing technique that he used in his diagnostic and therapeutic work with children; he called it the *squiggle game* (1971b). This game was used by Winnicott as a playful way of establishing contact and communicating with a child.

The game, based on Winnicott's understanding of development and the role of the environment, involved Winnicott and a child sitting down with paper and pencils. Winnicott would shut his eyes and make a few lines or squiggles on paper, and the child had to turn these lines into something—a rabbit, a house, anything. Then the child made a squiggle, and Winnicott made these lines into something. Gradually, Winnicott showed, the child will represent his or her personality and concerns through the drawings.

Winnicott noticed that children often dreamed about him the night before coming to his office for a first consultation. He understood this imaginative dream as representing their attitude toward him. He fit into the role of being the subjective object; that is, he became what they needed him to be for the first two or three therapeutic sessions as a way of getting in touch with their inner world, in a way very similar to a mother's matching of an infant's spontaneous gesture. The child believed he or she could be understood and helped, and Winnicott's entering into the child's world strengthened that belief. Feeling understood could allow the child to make great progress in loosening a tight knot of emotional development.

In describing various case studies in which he used this technique, Winnicott conveyed the fun and playful quality of his work with children. Based on his long efforts in child therapy, Winnicott used a lovely image to describe his seemingly effortless and intuitive therapeutic skill with children: that, in therapy, he was playing music rather than slogging away at technique.

Case Study
The following case study illustrates Winnicott's therapeutic approach with an adult rather than a child (1954/1958d, pp. 255–261). The essential approach, however, is similar in that it is based on Winnicott's understanding of the environment's role in the development of the person. Winnicott provided a holding environment that allowed for a regression to a developmental dependency, a point of development that the client needed to relive more favorably. When this particular client withdrew or was emotionally not present, Winnicott was able to convert the withdrawal to a therapeutic regression that could be worked through. Movement is from a false self to a true self.

The client was a male doctor, a schizoid-depressive who was married and had a family. This client had a breakdown in which he felt unreal and had lost the ability to be spontaneous. He was unable to work for several months. Although able to join in conversations initiated by others, the client was all but friendless since he was so boring and unable to be impulsively spontaneous.

During one session in which the client was stretched out on his back on a couch, he had the phantasy of being curled up and rolling over the back of the couch. Winnicott suggested that he felt like fleeing from the painful situation. The client also made circular motions with his hands to show his curled-up position. Winnicott interpreted his motions as implying something the client was unaware of, that there was some sort of medium. The client responded that it was like the oil in which wheels move (1954/1958d, p. 256). Winnicott developed the idea that a medium holds the client, that the therapeutic environment has the capacity to adapt to the client's needs even though the client is only dimly aware of them.

This client had a dream about discarding a shield he no longer needed. This seemed to reflect Winnicott's ability to provide a suitable medium at the moment of withdrawal. By putting this medium around the withdrawn self, Winnicott converted the withdrawal into a positive therapeutic regression. The client felt safe in having the feelings from which he had been fleeing.

Winnicott began to see how this client needed him to be. The client was very dependent, which was painful. As the client got in touch with his dependence on his mother, he was able to be angry at Winnicott, who took on the role of the good-enough parent responding to a child's gestures.

On another occasion, when Winnicott was talking, this client reported that his thoughts wandered and he felt far away, working at a factory. Winnicott made the interpretation that he had gone away from Winnicott's lap. This aptly expressed the level of emotional development of the client, that in the withdrawn state he was emotionally an infant and the couch had been the therapist's lap. The therapist supplied the lap for him to come back to and the medium in which he could move around.

On another occasion, the client reported that he continued to have problems in being spontaneous in conversation at home and with friends. He could only join in when two others were taking the responsibility for carrying the conversation. If he made a remark, he felt he was usurping the function of one of the parents, but what he really needed was to be recognized by the parents as an infant.

The client feared that he might find he had suddenly kissed a person—it would perhaps be someone who chanced to be next to him, possibly even a man. He now began to sink into the therapeutic situation, feeling like a child at home, and if he spoke he would be wrong because he would be in the parent's role. He felt hopeless about having a spontaneous gesture met. There were further associations of people going in and out of doors. Winnicott suggested that this was associated with breathing. Ideas are like breath and like children. If a therapist does nothing to them, the client feels like the ideas are abandoned. This client's fear was that of an abandoned child, of the abandoned remark, or the wasted gesture of a child that is not picked up and responded to by an adult.

On another occasion, when the client talked about never having accepted his father's death, he reported a headache. Winnicott interpreted this as the client's need to have his head held as he would naturally have it held if he were a child in distress. The client gradually realized that his father had indeed held him and comforted him, and now there was no one to hold his head and comfort him in his grief. The essential point is not that Winnicott would actually hold the client's head but that Winnicott understood immediately what he needed.

In withdrawal states, the client is holding the self, and the therapist needs to convert the withdrawn state to a regression where the therapist can hold the client. A regression is the opportunity to correct a past inadequate response to an individual's need. A therapist needs to understand the client in a deep way and convey that to the individual through the interpretive remark. The correct interpretive remark provides a holding of the client, which allows the client to regress and be dependent on the therapist (1954/1958d, p. 261). Therapy's validation of the client's childlike need contributes to and consolidates the existence of the true, spontaneous self. The therapist, responding to the client's wishes as needs, is like a mother responding to the gesture of her child.

A client needs the therapist to be omnipotent, to know and tell him what he needs and fears. The client often knows these feelings, but the crucial issue is that the therapist needs to know and say them. The client's false self and defenses may distract the therapist, but the therapist must be wary of this and see the central issues without being told (Winnicott, 1963/1965i, p. 237).

Assessment and Critique of Winnicott

Freud's and Klein's theories significantly enriched Winnicott early in his career, but in his later writings, he spoke with his own voice and made an original and significant contribution to the study of the person. Although his ideas do not constitute a system, they provide original insights into the development of children. Winnicott provided a unique perspective on how the interplay between mother and child fosters or hinders the child's development.

It is not always easy to relate Winnicott's ideas to the concepts of others because he grew and changed, and also because he sometimes displayed a casualness toward theory that can startle—or refresh—the reader, such as dismissing a point essential to Klein by saying "But what does it matter?" (Winnicott, 1962/1965a, p. 176). Harry Guntrip claims Winnicott used Freudian terms that "he no longer really believed in, especially 'id' which was meaningless in his outlook . . . it was mere habit" (Guntrip, 1976, p. 361). Winnicott also distorted classical Freudian concepts to suit his own classification of mental illness, such as when he said the classic Freudian concept of neurosis is not necessarily an illness (Winnicott, 1956/1958e, p. 319).

Roughly contemporary with Winnicott was W. R. D. Fairbairn, another significant member of the British School of Object Relations. Although he shared many of Fairbairn's dissatisfactions with Freud, Winnicott strongly criticized Fairbairn for trying to supplant Freud's theory (Winnicott & Khan, 1953). Winnicott further found fault with Fairbairn for not integrating his ideas into the developing body of psychoanalytic theory. This is curious, for Winnicott was not an orthodox Freudian by any norm, but his relation with the psychoanalytic stream was indeed important to him.

Winnicott enriched that mainstream in a variety of ways—with his creative therapeutic work with children and with his original ideas on development, which moved beyond the instinctual emphasis of Freud and anticipated Kohut's notions of healthy narcissism and the importance of the self.

References

Guntrip, H. (1976). In A. M. Mendez & H. J. Fine, A short history of the British school of object relations and ego psychology, *Bulletin of the Menninger Clinic, 40,* 357–382.

Khan, M. M. R. (1971). Obituary: Donald W. Winnicott. *International Journal of Psycho-Analysis, 52,* 225–226.

Winnicott, D. W. (1958a). Aggression in relation to emotional development. In *Collected papers: Through pediatrics to psycho-analysis* (pp. 204–218). London: Tavistock. (Original work published 1950)

Winnicott, D. W. (1958b). Anxiety associated with insecurity. In *Collected papers: Through pediatrics to psycho-analysis* (pp. 97–100). London: Tavistock. (Original work published 1952)

Winnicott, D. W. (1958c). The manic defense. In *Collected papers: Through pediatrics to psycho-analysis* (pp. 129–144). London: Tavistock. (Original work published 1935)

Winnicott, D. W. (1958d). Metapsychological and clinical aspects of regression within the psychoanalytical set-up. In *Collected papers: Through pediatrics to psycho-analysis* (pp. 278–294). London: Tavistock. (Original work published 1954)

Winnicott, D. W. (1958e). Pediatrics and childhood neurosis. In *Collected papers: Through pediatrics to psycho-analysis* (pp. 316–321). London: Tavistock. (Original work published 1956)

Winnicott, D. W. (1958f). Pediatrics and psychiatry. In *Collected papers: Through pediatrics to psycho-analysis* (pp. 157–173). London: Tavistock. (Original work published 1948)

Winnicott, D. W. (1958g). Primitive emotional development. In *Collected papers: Through pediatrics to psycho-analysis* (pp. 145–156). London: Tavistock. (Original work published 1945)

Winnicott, D. W. (1958h). Psychoses and child care. In *Collected papers: Through pediatrics to psycho-analysis* (pp. 219–228). London: Tavistock. (Original work published 1952)

Winnicott, D. W. (1958i). Transitional objects and transitional phenomena. In *Collected papers: Through pediatrics to psycho-analysis* (pp. 229–242). London: Tavistock. (Original work published 1951)

Winnicott, D. W. (1965a). A personal view of the Kleinian contribution. In *The maturational processes and the facilitating environment* (pp. 171–178). New York: International Universities Press. (Original work published 1962)

Winnicott, D. W. (1965b). The capacity to be alone. In *The maturational processes and the facilitating environment* (pp. 29–36). New York: International Universities Press. (Original work published 1958)

Winnicott, D. W. (1965c). Classification: Is there a psycho-analytic contribution to psychiatric classification? In *The maturational processes and the facilitating environment* (pp. 124–139). New York: International Universities Press. (Original work published 1959)

Winnicott, D. W. (1965d). Communicating and not communicating leading to a study of certain opposites. In *The maturational processes and the facilitating environment* (pp. 179–192). New York: International Universities Press. (Original work published 1963)

Winnicott, D. W. (1965e). Ego distortion in terms of true and false self. In *The maturational processes and the facilitating environment* (pp. 140–152). New York: International Universities Press. (Original work published 1960)

Winnicott, D. W. (1965f). Ego integration in child development. In *The maturational processes and the facilitating environment* (pp. 56–63). New York: International Universities Press. (Original work published 1962)

Winnicott, D. W. (1965g). From dependence to independence in the development of the individual. In *The maturational processes and the facilitating environment* (pp. 83–99). New York: International Universities Press. (Original work published 1963)

Winnicott, D. W. (1965h). The mentally ill in your caseload. In *The maturational processes and the facilitating environment* (pp. 217–229). New York: International Universities Press. (Original work published 1963)

Winnicott, D. W. (1965i). Psychiatric disorders in terms of infantile maturational processes. In *The maturational processes and the facilitating environment* (pp. 230–241). New York: International Universities Press. (Original work published 1963)

Winnicott, D. W. (1965j). The theory of the parent-infant relationship. In *The maturational processes and the facilitating environment* (pp. 37–55). New York: International Universities Press. (Original work published 1960)

Winnicott, D. W. (1971a). Mirror-role of mother and family in child development. In *Playing and reality* (pp. 111–118). New York: Basic Books.

Winnicott, D. W. (1971b). *Therapeutic consultations in child psychiatry.* New York: Basic Books.

Winnicott, D. W., & Khan, M. M. R. (1953). Book review of Fairbairn's *Psychoanalytic studies of the personality. International Journal of Psycho-Analysis, 34,* 329–332.

Chapter Six

Edith Jacobson:
An Integrated Model

Introduction

Edith Jacobson received her training in medicine and psychoanalysis in Germany in the 1930s. She came to America before World War II and began private practice in New York City. She wrote most of her important work from the 1940s through the 1960s.

Jacobson enriched psychoanalysis and the theory of object relations by fashioning an integrated model of object relations. She interwove strands from the Freudian tradition with those of new ideas. The result is a seamless, coherent model that accounts for the traditional elements of id, ego, superego, and instincts, as well as object relations. Her theories, abstract and complex, demand much of the reader. This is one reason Jacobson is not as popularly known as other writers. However, her revisions of the traditional model have significantly influenced many contemporary theorists, Otto Kernberg in particular (1980, p. 103). She and Kernberg have pushed the drive model as far as it will go to accommodate relational concepts in the form of object relations (cf. Greenberg & Mitchell, 1983, p. 351).

Without abandoning the drive model, Jacobson stressed the importance of relationships. She tied the drive model to an object relations model through the infant's experience of the mother. By her careful examination of the experience of the infant, Jacobson demonstrated the complex interplay of instinct, object relations, and the structures of id, ego, and superego. The nuances and complexity of her approach, however, exclude any overly neat summary of her thought. Jacobson attempted to explain the gradual but dramatic transition of the screaming baby into the polite, well-behaved young person.

This chapter's presentation of Jacobson highlights her integration of object relations with concepts of instincts and structures of id, ego, and superego. I will examine the following elements of her work: key concepts, psychological structure formation and instincts and object relations, developmental stages, and pathology of depression. A case study and an assessment and critique of her work then follow.

Key Concepts

Self, Ego, and Self Representation

Jacobson criticized Melanie Klein for Klein's confusing terminology, especially for failing to distinguish objects, object representations, and introjected objects from one another (Jacobson, 1964, p. 48). Jacobson, by contrast, carefully defined terms and pointedly distinguished the concepts of self from ego and from self representation. Such distinctions are important because of the central place that self, objects, and the relationship between them have in her theory.

Jacobson used the term *self* in the same way Heinz Hartmann (1964) does, referring to the whole person, including the body as well as the psyche. The self is a term distinguishing a person as subject in distinction to the world of objects (Jacobson, 1964, p. 6). Self is only a descriptive term, unlike the use of self as an active agency by the later self theorist Heinz Kohut.

Ego refers to a structure, a mental system that has various functions. This usage agrees with traditional Freudian use. Jacobson differed, however, with the traditional understanding of the ego's origin. She believed the ego begins as a fused self-image and object image, which requires the presence of a relationship to supply the object image. By contrast, Freud thought the ego evolved from an undifferentiated form or matrix of id and ego.

A *self representation* is an unconscious, preconscious, or conscious representation within the ego of the physical and mental self (Jacobson, 1964, p. 19). A self representation is an image of the self that begins with memory traces of pleasurable and nonpleasurable sensations. Emotions color these mental representations. In the beginning, they are not firm units (Jacobson, 1964, p. 20) but are gradually built up. As development proceeds, they are more unified, realistic, and organized. A realistic image of the self is "one that correctly mirrors the state and the characteristics, the potentialities and abilities, the assets and the limits of our bodily and mental self" (Jacobson, 1964, p. 22).

Self, ego, and self representation occupy different levels of an individual's experience and abstraction. A few sentences might illustrate some of the differences. "I" have an image of "myself," but my "self" is more than my "ego," which is just a term for a number of conscious processes. No one has ever seen or felt an ego; what I see in the mirror is my body, which contributes to my inner image of myself. I do experience my "self." I am my "self."

From Undifferentiation to Differentiation

Jacobson saw growth as moving from undifferentiated, rudimentary forms toward differentiated, clearly distinguishable forms. Thus, she saw the id and ego as differentiating from each other. The instinctual drives differentiate into the sexual and aggressive drives. The early self–object representation separates into a self representation and an object representation.

An *object representation* is an image of a person or part of a person. The earliest object representations are usually fused with images of the self in a single image of self and object, with no mental boundaries between them. Only with time do these early self-images that are fused with images of objects differentiate into representations of the self and representations of the object.

It is difficult for an adult to imagine the preverbal experience of a fused, self–object representation. It is primarily a felt experience of me having feelings that I cannot separate apart from the image and presence of my mother. One experience that might suggest this early, primal experience is adult sexual union in which a lover feels him or herself merged in pleasure with the partner.

Drives and Representations of Self and Object

Jacobson linked drives and object relations by associating the representations of self and object with the drives or feelings obtained from the drives (drive derivatives). She made this radical linkage in her redefinition of narcissism and masochism.

Jacobson saw the self as having contact with the environment in a way Freud did not envision. Freud understood that at the beginning of life, narcissism was an investment of psychic energy "within" rather than toward the "outside." Coming before any libidinal investment in an object in the environment, this conceptually isolates the infant because there are no links to anybody. Object relations theorists, by contrast, believe the infant is essentially related to the people in the environment. Jacobson radically closed the gap between Freudian theory and the object relations position by theorizing that at the beginning of life, the drives are undifferentiated and are invested in a fused self–object representation. A relationship must furnish the object for the object representation. A fused self–object representation is, for example, an image of me and my mother with a sense of warm, pleasant feelings.

By carefully distinguishing between ego and self representation, Jacobson changed Freud's concept of narcissism. Freud called narcissism a cathexis (or emotional investment) of the ego by libido (positive sexual energy), and masochism a cathexis of ego by aggression (cf. Blanck & Blanck, 1974, p. 63). Jacobson saw narcissism as a cathexis or investment of energy in the self representation. She retained the term *primary narcissism* for the earliest infantile period, when undifferentiated libido and aggression invest the undifferentiated, fused self–object representation. Secondary narcissism and masochism occur later, during the period of ego formation, when libido and aggression become differentiated from each other and when self and object representations are differentiating. The representation of the self within the developing ego becomes related to libido and becomes "good" or "loved." When the representation of the self becomes related to aggression, it becomes "bad" or "hated." This extraordinary clarification of narcissism and masochism brings drives into a closer synthesis with object relations.

Psychological Structure and Instincts and Object Relations

Jacobson retained the traditional structures of id, ego, and superego but solidly placed them in a relational or object relations context. In other words, she held onto drive theory but saw how a mother and father foster the development of ego and superego by the way they interact with their child.

The ego develops out of the infant's relationship with the mother but under the influence of the drives (Jacobson, 1964, p. 37). As the drives differentiate into libido and aggression, they become fused and neutralized and invested in the ego and superego (Jacobson, 1964, p. 15). Through gratifying and frustrating experiences with the mother, the infant's ego builds up images of both a gratified and a deprived self. At this period, as the infant is discovering the object world, the dawning distinction between the world and the self contributes to the establishment of the ego as separate from objects.

The infant "borrows" the mother's ego. The mother supports and modifies her child's experiences in such a way that she serves as an external ego. With the support of this external ego, the child's ego controls and partly inhibits the child's drives as well as meets its needs. The mother moderates what happens to her child and assists the child in getting what he or she needs. Her service as a buffer against excessively strong experiences is important, because too much gratification or frustration can make the child regress defensively to an earlier re-fusion of self representation and object representation. These regressive re-fusions can delay establishment of firm boundaries between the object representations and the self representations, and this, of course, retards the formation of ego and superego.

In addition to the help that parents give, drives contribute to the ego's development by being invested in objects and in the child's self. The parents foster this establishment of stable libidinal investment in objects and in the self. By calling attention to the role of parental love in forming healthy love relations and lasting identifications, Jacobson significantly differed from Freud's emphasis on fear during the Oedipal period (cf. Blanck & Blanck, 1974, p. 70; Jacobson, 1964, p. 55). The paren-tal influence helps the child grow beyond early infantile magical expec-tations of total wish fulfillment.

Experiencing frustrations and disappointments, the child has ambivalent feelings: the growing ego at first wants to ascribe to the self what is pleasant and to the outside object what is unpleasant. That is, the child turns aggression toward frustrating objects and libido toward the self. This greatly aids in the differentiation of self and objects. Ag-gression, especially in oedipal envy and rivalry with brothers and sisters and the same-sex parent, also greatly aids in this process of differentia-tion and the discovery of identity. Some of the bickering and fighting of siblings thus serves to sharpen their sense of who they are.

Identifications play a role in building up the ego. Early, primitive identifications, based on introjection and projection, involve fusions of images of the self and objects. Introjection and projection are psychic processes by which self-images assume characteristics of object images and vice versa. These processes begin in early infantile incorporation and ejection phantasies (Jacobson, 1964, p. 46) and are an archaic form of taking on traits of objects in the environment. As the ego matures and establishes boundaries between the self and objects, there are fewer fu-sions with objects or fewer re-fusions of self representations and object representations. Only "by becoming enduring, selective, and consistent can identifications gradually become integrated, become part of the ego, [and] permanently modify its structure" (Jacobson, 1964, p. 68). This ad-vances ego formation and identity formation to the point where the child becomes aware of having a coherent self that remains the same despite external changes.

Growth of the ego involves developing a sense of identity. When the infant is about three months old, there is the awareness of the "not-I," but it is only in the second year that the child has advanced enough to make the startling discovery of his or her own identity, the experience of "I am I" (Jacobson, 1964, p. 59). The discovery of identity is in rela-tion to the child's first love objects, and only gradually does the child build up a concept of self as an entity. Identity formation is "a process that builds up the ability to preserve the whole psychic organization—despite its growing structuralization, differentiation and complexity—as a highly individualized but coherent entity which has direction and continuity at any stage of human development" (Jacobson, 1964, p. 26).

Formation of the Superego

Jacobson worked out the "most comprehensive exploration of the superego in psychoanalytic literature" (Kernberg, 1980, p. 98). Jacobson believed the superego is a structure that forms in reaction to the child's intense sexual and destructive strivings and modifies the libidinal and aggressive cathexis of the self representation. From roughly the child's second through seventh years, the superego forms a consolidated system from many disconnected components and processes. The components are the various forerunners or precursors of the preoedipal period, when many processes are taking place at the same time.

The superego forms from three broad layers of these early processes and components. The first involves primitive, punitive images; the second involves the ego ideal; and the third involves realistic, moderate identifications. During formation of the superego, more moderate and realistic functions replace crude fears and the archaic mechanisms that are the precursors of the superego. In other words, the growing presence of a superego enables a child, who in the preschool years had intense feelings of both a sexual and aggressive nature, to moderate his or her intense reactions and become the well-behaved child of the early school years.

The first and deepest layer of superego formation, roughly during the end of the first year and the start of the second year of life, involves sadistic, archaic images and punitive object representations. These primitive forerunners of the superego occur while self representations and object representations are still not clearly distinct from each other. Due to the lack of distinction and differentiation, these representations can easily re-fuse with each other. This lack of boundaries between self and object enables the child to experience him or herself as an extension of the parent. When the parent disappoints the child, the child feels rage and aggression toward the love object. Because of the fused state of self and object representations and because of primitive projection and introjection, aggressive energies can move back and forth from self-image to object image. The rage felt for the frustrating object is also experienced against the self.

Not enough emphasis can be given to this flow of feelings back and forth between the child's images of self and object. To illustrate, let us look at a small child 2 or 3 years old. Such a child has cruel wishes and aggressive feelings, but because of the lack of clear boundaries between self and object, and because of projection and introjection, the child can easily ascribe its own fears and aggression to its parents and sometimes see them as threatening. The child then fears for its own bodily safety since the parents, who may frustrate the child, seem, in the child's magical inner world, to punish and to retaliate harshly. The child cannot see that his castration fears actually originate in his own sadomasochistic wishes. Ultimately, the superego, as the heir of the successful resolution of oedipal conflicts, will take over the function of self-criticism and by self-criticism give direction to prevent retaliatory punishment from outside. The fear of the superego in the form of guilt feelings gradually will modify and replace the ferocious, unmodified fears of early childhood (Jacobson, 1964, p. 121).

During this first layer of early superego formation, the mechanism of reaction formation plays a part. *Reaction formation* is a process that turns a child's aggression from its love object to itself. This process changes the child's attitudes toward its own instinctual strivings, toward the child itself, and toward objects in the child's world (Jacobson, 1954, p. 107). During toilet training, reaction formation shows up in this way: the idea that feces are dirty expands to the idea that children who soil are dirty and bad. Reaction formation expands the feelings of disgust for feces to feelings of shame in oneself for any loss of control and feelings of pride in oneself for cleanliness. Reaction formation, therefore, by establishing a limited sense of what is valuable and what is worthless, changes the child's attitudes toward his or her forbidden pregenital and genital wishes and destructive impulses (Jacobson, 1954, p. 109).

During this early period, the child gets angry at frustrations and disappointments. Anger and aggression for the frustrating love object also attack the self because the child still cannot distinguish between the self and the object. This anger at and devaluing of the self play an important role in self-esteem and depression. A person is depressed and has low self-esteem if there is a turning of anger toward the self representation (which the child still cannot regularly distinguish from the object representation). More accurately, self-esteem goes up or down depending on the degree of neutralized libidinal and aggressive cathexis of the self representation. In addition, the discrepancy or harmony between the self representation and the wishful concepts of the self also shape self-esteem (Jacobson, 1954, p. 123).

Object relations change and mature. They become more realistic, more affectionate, less archaic, and less partial. The child increasingly sees the parents as human, whole objects that are less magical. Libidinal and aggressive energy, however, still vacillates between the self and object representations. The child feels ambivalences so that the child both builds up an *ego ideal* composed of idealized parental and self-images as well as realistic self and object representations. The self representation rests on a reasonably accurate representation of the self, while the ego ideal rests on the wished-for potential self it would like to be in the future. The idealization helps object relations by protecting the child from the child's own devaluation of his or her parents. On the other hand, the growing ego adjusts to the reality principle, fostering a more realistic and moderate stance toward the parents and the self. The ego ideal is set up as part of the superego, as a "pilot and guide for the ego" (Jacobson, 1954, p. 116). The ego ideal compensates for the lost merger phantasies.

This marks the second level of superego formation. The ego ideal forms as the child gradually gives up its magical preoedipal phantasies about fusing with its love objects. But if the child is disappointed or disillusioned and becomes fixated or stuck, he or she may deny reality and cling to the magic, infantile convictions in a distorted way. The "good" love objects, those omnipotent gods, may turn into "bad," worthless, empty, inferior objects, and because of the lack of differentiation, the self-image will also be degraded and fearful of annihilation (Jacobson, 1954, p. 115).

According to Jacobson, superego formation also involves various levels of internalization (1964, p. 123). The first internalizations are of primitive, aggressive, idealized parental images as well as the commands and standards of parents. Gradually, the internalizations become more realistic and toned down, and this marks the third level of superego formation. The ego matures and makes gains in reality-testing and develops a greater capacity for realistic perceptions of the parents. The more mature identifications involve the advance from trying *to be* the parents to trying *to be like* the parents. Building up inner superego standards requires that the ego have the capacity to take on certain characteristics and traits of the parents. As the child internalizes moral codes and more realistic demands, it fosters the development of effective defenses in the ego and greater control over instincts.

All of these processes come together and produce the superego at the end of the oedipal period, about the sixth or seventh year of life. Self and object representations become more realistic. The child has internalized moral and behavioral codes as well as ideals and standards for self-criticism. Drives become increasingly neutralized as infantile sexual demands lessen. As the normal superego gains control of discharge processes, there is a noticeable difference in the child's moods, self-esteem, and expression of feeling (Jacobson, 1954, p. 123), as those parents who have compared the emotional maturities of kindergartners and third graders well know. The final maturation of the ego and superego occurs, however, only after the taming of adolescent conflicts and when youthful idealism and illusions are modified as reasonable goals are established (Jacobson, 1954, p. 125; 1964, p. 133).

Developmental Stages

Jacobson kept the essential ideas of the classical drive tradition but revised and expanded that tradition in such a way as to comprise a comprehensive object relations theory. Her understanding of development places objects within both drive and relational contexts. Her theme is that normal development rests on evolving images of the self and others (objects).

Jacobson studied the infant's experience at the earliest stage of life when it is a primal, undifferentiated self. At this stage, id and ego are as yet undifferentiated; so, too, are the drives. The undifferentiated drives, during this period when the infant spends most of the time sleeping or half-awake, discharge to the inside. In other words, with such limited contact with the outside world, the physiological discharge of psychic energy toward the self is the earliest infantile form of drive discharge (Jacobson, 1964, pp. 7–9). Jacobson said that "psychic life originates in physiological processes which are independent of external sensory stimulations" (1964, p. 11).

External stimulation, such as from the hands of the mother or the sight of her face, gradually leads the infant to biologically determined reactions and to the differentiation of undetermined drives into libidinal and aggressive drives. These drives endow the id. As they separate out, fuse, and become partly neutralized, the ego begins to take on some of their functions. Further, the infant has various experiences of pleasure and displeasure before it has any awareness of the source of these experiences or the mother as a person.

The infant reacts to the mother's care and stimulation and has experiences of pleasurable gratification and unpleasant frustration. These experiences constitute the first and most important bridge to the mother (Jacobson, 1964, p. 35). There are memory traces of stimulation, gratifying experiences, and visual images of the mother. From these memories and images, images of the self as gratified or deprived are built.

The infant also uses its mouth and hands to discover the object world and its own bodily self (Jacobson, 1964, p. 36). Gradually, images of objects build up. The mother serves as the infant's external ego. She kisses, feeds, holds, and prepares the infant for sitting, crawling, and walking. This fosters the growth of the ego.

Positive identification with the mother builds up a positive feeling about the self. During the earliest period of development, when the mother and infant are a unit, the infant cannot discriminate between its own pleasure and the object from which the pleasure is derived. But with repeated experiences of pleasure and frustration and separation, phantasies of incorporating the gratifying object gradually develop. These are wishful phantasies of being one with the mother or her breast. This infantile experience seems to be essentially the same as that described by Margaret Mahler as occurring during the "symbiotic period" (Mahler, 1958). In sexual experiences of adults, the whole self can seem to merge with the partner, and the pleasure of the sex act may partly be from the sense of emotionally restoring the lost original union with the mother (Jacobson, 1964, p. 39).

These early longings for physical merging with the mother, longings for food and phantasies of being one with the mother, are the precursors of future object relations and the foundation on which all object relations are based.

These longings and phantasies of merger are also the origin of the first primitive identifications. At about three months, the infant can begin to perceive that the love object or part objects are different from the self. When the infant is gratified by its mother, its images of the self and the love object are merged. The increase of instinctual needs and experiences of hunger and frustration arouse aggression, and the phantasy of merger stops. The image of self and the image of object separate. The primitive identification is achieved by the re-fusion of the self-image and the object image.

Up to about the age of 3, it is normal for images of the self and object to rapidly merge and separate, and it is typical for symbiotic interactions to have these phantasies of fusion with the loved object. As the child grows, it develops a more active type of identification as it tries to imitate the love objects. Observations of young children show how they imitate the gestures, voice, and mannerisms of their mothers. The expanding motor and perceptual skills allow for playful imitations of parents, and these are the forerunners of true ego identifications. (*True ego identifications* will involve the development within the ego of ego attitudes and traits taken over from the parents [Jacobson, 1964, p. 43].) During this period of imitation, the magical phantasies of becoming the mother indicate how much the child wants to maintain her as part of itself and keep merged with her without distinction (Jacobson, 1964, p. 43). The child still has grandiose ideas and a sense of magical participation in parental omnipotence.

The child continues to expand its images of self and its images of objects. At this stage, there still is only a weak boundary between the self-image and the object image. The child can be part of the object by pretending or behaving as if he or she were a part of the parent—by imitating the parent, for instance (Jacobson, 1964, p. 46). With regard to the drives, libido and aggression invest these images. There can be a shift of energy from self to object or back again. These processes of investing energy are manifested in the child's introjections and projections, which are based on the child's phantasies of incorporating or ejecting the love object. What this means is that the child vacillates from attitudes of helpless dependency on the omnipotent mother to aggressive strivings for powerful control over the love objects. This vacillation and contradictory swing from passive-submissive to active-aggressive behavior during the preoedipal and early oedipal periods parallels the child's emotional fluctuations of loving its omnipotent parents and being disappointed and depreciating its love objects. Jacobson said that it is to this stage that the psychotic ego regresses.

Gradually, the child begins to make distinctions between self representations and object representations as the ego matures and functions more independently. As ego functions of perception and reality-testing develop, there is a decrease in projection and introjection, and the self representations and object representations become more realistic. As the child becomes more individuated, the desire to make itself part of its love objects or the love object part of itself will recede, replaced by the more realistic wish to be like them. The ego becomes modified as it takes on certain characteristics of the admired object. This leads to further distinctions between wishful self-images and more realistic self-images. The more realistic self-images or representations contain traits taken over from the object of identification. The likeness with and distinction between the self-image and the object image become better established. The more realistic self-image is the basis for establishment of ego ideals, ego goals, and feelings of identity.

When firm boundaries separate the realistic, well-defined self representation from realistic images of objects, true object relations begin. This contrasts with the precursors of earlier object relations, when the child has phantasies of fusion with the love object by either making it a part of self or becoming a part of the object.

Jacobson said that, at first, drives as instinctual conflicts will be manifested in aggression, which finds expression in competitive struggles with powerful love objects and the child's sibling and oedipal rivals. The resolution of the oedipal conflict accompanies the formation of the superego. The superego along with the developing ego fosters the increasing fusion and neutralization of sexual and aggressive drives. The ego establishes better emotional and instinctual control and object relations develop. Libido becomes invested in objects and the self in more enduring and stable ways. In addition, the ego forms a concept of the self as an entity that has continuity and direction (Jacobson, 1964, p. 53). In other words, there is the discovery of identity as drives are neutralized and used in the service of the ego and the ego's higher level functions.

Pathology of Depression

Jacobson provided an explanation of depression. She understood it as involving four elements: the distinction between the self representation and the object representation, identification, the drives, and self-esteem.

Jacobson assumed (1971, p. 244) that in the normal adult, self representation and object representation are distinct from each other; self and object have clearly established boundaries. She explained, however, that during the early preoedipal stage these representations are not distinct, the boundary between them is not firm, and the child has narcissistic phantasies of sharing in the glory of the omnipotent, idealized mother. Jacobson also pointed out that during this preoedipal period, these images or representations could merge and split and remerge.

Early, primitive identifications involve phantasies of being one with the loved object, of merging the self representation and the object representation. These primitive, magical identifications disregard reality and find a refuge in the ego ideal and superego. The ego ideal "is composed of idealized images of the parents blended with archaic, aggrandized images of the self" (Jacobson, 1971, p. 246). This process helps the child transform archaic images of "bad," aggressive, dirty parents into "good," idealized model figures.

Growth brings more mature identifications, which are increasingly realistic. As the child's ego develops additional skills and increased reality perception, its self representation more accurately mirrors what the child is, and the self representation and object representations become more realistic. Growth enables the ego to assume some of the traits of the love object. More realistic ego identifications allow for a partial blending of self representations and object representations (Jacobson, 1971, p. 245).

As for the drives, libidinal and aggressive energies can magically infuse the early self-image and object image so that they can become "good" and "bad." Thus, when the libido attached to the image of the love object, the object image was good; because the image of the self and object are not distinguished from each other at this early period, the self is also good by primitive identification. This magical phantasy of possible fusion with the love object also is true when that image is attached to aggression, so that the love object is a "bad" object. Self-esteem involves having the self representation infused with good, libidinal energy. Moods also are related to the drives and the regulation of the drives by the superego (Jacobson, 1971, chap. 3). The depressed mood depends on the intensity of the aggression and anger and the severity of the disappointment that provoked the anger.

Many situations can cause depression, but the most common cause involves some experience of frustration by loss of, or disillusionment with, a loved object. This triggers a reaction of rage, hostility, and aggression. The hostility, however does not enable the child or the adult to regain gratification of libido. The disappointment causes the child or adult to devalue the love object. At the same time, the child or adult experiences a devaluing of the self, a loss of self-esteem (Jacobson, 1971, p. 183).

Because of the close connection between the self-image and the object image, aggression turned against the object image also turns against the self-image. The aggressive devaluation of the object becomes a degradation of the self, a deflation of self-esteem. This loss of self-esteem expresses the narcissistic conflict underlying depression: a conflict between the wishful self-image and the image of the deflated, failing self. The wishful, magical self-image hopes for the omnipotent gratification of the preoedipal period; the punishing superego, which retains the wishful ego ideal, rages against the deflated, worthless self. The worthless self-image, rather than participating in the admired and omnipotent object, participates in the disappointing, frustrating object image.

Jacobson gave an example of this kind of depressive identification. A woman who loses a husband could take over his business, which might become the leading pursuit of her life. If she turns into an efficient businesswoman who emulates the husband's methods and interest and attitudes, she has identified with him in a healthy, normal way. This contrasts with the depressive identification, in which she would become depressed after the husband's death and instead of taking over his ideals would blame herself for her inability to carry on his business. She is unaware that her self-reproaches unconsciously refer to her husband. Her hostility toward him prevents her from responding to his death in a positive and more healthy manner. Instead of achieving a realistic likeness with him, she treats herself pathologically "as if" she were the "bad" husband (Jacobson, 1971, p. 243). She treats herself as if she were the love object.

Serious depression and psychosis involve severe regressions. In serious regressions, normal realistic object relations disintegrate as do normal ego identifications. Preoedipal, magical identifications replace the healthy normal object relations and identifications. These magical identifications involve the preoedipal phantasies of being one with the object. The primitive object may take the form of a superego forerunner; that is, a "bad," punishing parent image. The aggression toward the self involves this primitive, unrealistic, terrifying aggression.

Case Study

Jacobson (1971, pp. 204–227) described a depressed and fearful client who sought treatment. Peggy was a 24-year-old teacher who was tall and attractive. She felt her depression was in reaction to difficulties in her love and sex life. After various unhappy relationships, she started a sexual relationship with Sidney, another teacher. Foreseeing the inevitable end of this relationship, she became depressed and her work deteriorated.

Peggy remembered her father as a cold, aggressive man. Her brother was born when she was 3½ years old, and from this period on, the father was depressed and unable to work. Peggy's mother, warm but domineering, always babied her and protected her from the aggressive father.

The birth of the brother and disappointments with both parents precipitated an infantile depression. This was approximately at the beginning of Peggy's oedipal period. Up to this time, she was a well-balanced child, loved by her parents. She recalls taking walks with her father. As she was advancing from preoedipal to oedipal issues, her mother returned home with the infant brother. Peggy felt that "everything was over and gone, and I had lost everything" (Jacobson, 1971, p. 210). The mother neglected Peggy to take care of the baby. The father, in a bad mood, withdrew and was unavailable.

Peggy became depressed and had hostile and sexual phantasies about her brother. She recalls him nursing at the breast while she had to eat alone at her table. She experienced abandonment by her parents, disillusionment, and frustration. Such hostility during this preoedipal period, when the boundary between self-image and object image is not firm, can lead to serious disturbances in object relations and moods.

Her mother strictly trained Peggy in toilet functions, and she achieved control at the end of the first year. Someone forcibly stopped her from thumbsucking and from masturbating. During therapy, memories of this strict training shed light on her emotional detachment. As a girl she had not been allowed to show her feelings and had to hold them back like excretory functions and to deny they existed. She resembled her father in her emotional coldness. He, like her lovers, did not accept what she offered in her feelings.

She began to be overly obedient and sweet to gain her mother's favor over her brother, who was greedy, aggressive, and a bed wetter. She received enemas from the mother, which had a sexual overtone so that the relationship with the mother had a secret, homosexual tone. In the later relationship with the female therapist and other mother substitutes, there were also homosexual wishes.

During adolescence, Peggy envied her aggressive and uninhibited brother. She was sexually very controlled and clung to her mother. When she was 17 years old, Peggy tried to free herself from her family, but this caused her to become depressed and fearful. At 24, after some disappointing romantic experiences, she underwent a change in attitude toward her mother. She began her first sexual relationship with Sidney, but she did not reach orgasm. She developed an almost paranoid hostility toward the previously adored mother, whom she blamed for her sexual failures because she had made her so dependent and weak. She moved out of her parents' home.

Peggy failed in her romantic relationships with men. When she doubted Sidney's love, she became depressed. At this point, she went to Dr. Jacobson for therapy. Sidney left for a while, and when he returned to her, she could not express her feelings and could only passively comply. He finally left her for another woman, and in her depression, she felt that all women took men away from her.

After several weeks of depression, Peggy suddenly became elated and started another love affair, which soon broke up, followed by depression. This pattern repeated itself several times during the course of her therapy. In an elated condition she would start an affair and throw herself into a new bondage. There was the same change from being hopeful, with exaggerated expectations, to deep disappointment and despair. Her behavior changed each partner's attitude; after a few dates, she would become jealous and depressed, and her coldness and detachment would repel the man.

In therapy, the transference with the therapist repeated experiences of her childhood. When the therapist was ill for several weeks and had to miss sessions, she requested a male therapist to meet with Peggy and convey this information. Peggy phantasized that this man was the therapist's husband. Her phantasies made her jealous of the therapist. She felt disappointed and abandoned by the therapist and imagined how she might take this man from the therapist. Her disappointment grew when she could not meet the substitute therapist anymore, and she began to depreciate him as being cold and detached like her father. She looked forward again to seeing her regular therapist.

Peggy established a pattern of starting love affairs whenever she felt disappointed in the therapist. The unhappy endings of the affairs would turn her love demands back to the therapist. When she felt disappointed and deserted by the therapist, Peggy devalued the therapist and reanimated a glorified and idealized father image that she attached to the current lover. As this paternal image collapsed, she would return to the maternal ideal represented by the female therapist.

As a child, Peggy had tried to cure herself of depression by a narcissistic withdrawal; that is, deaden her need for love and try to be independent. Her narcissistic withdrawal from the deflated love objects on whom she depended, however, threatened her own immature self-image with collapse. She had to reanimate the powerful parental image and set it up within herself. She lavished love on herself and indulged in wishful phantasies of independence. But she was too young to resolve her intense ambivalences. Peggy's attempt to be independent had the opposite effect, with the result that she became regressively dependent on her love object. This regression impeded the development and differentiation of her self and object representations. Narcissistic libido partly transformed into libido available for investment in an object; that is, she reached out again for her mother.

Because conflict disrupted her oedipal development, her fragile object relations even as an adult retained the characteristics of early object relations. That is, Peggy idealized and overvalued objects, and her expectations of herself and love objects could never be fulfilled. She attached her love demands intensely to persons, male or female, on whom she could depend. Her submissiveness did not protect her sufficiently from underlying jealousy and hostile feelings toward men and women. Peggy projected her high standards onto friends and lovers whose quality she saw as a measure for her own value. She put each on a pedestal and they represented glorified parental images with whom she identified through participation in their superiority.

Thus, Peggy's self-esteem depended on the high value of her love objects. Disappointments caused their devaluation and consequent narcissistic injury to herself. Peggy spontaneously tried to repair her narcissistic hurts by seeking a different person whom she endowed with idealized characteristics only to be disappointed again. In other words, she tried to relieve her narcissistic hurts by introjecting glorified, omnipotent images to replace deflated images of love objects. By this she hoped to gain back love and praise from the punitive, godlike parents or parent substitutes. But such attempts at restitution tend to fail, and the terrible hostility turned toward the self can lead to suicidal feelings. New disappointments shattered relationships and debased the idealized love objects in which her self-image participated. Hers was the basic depressive position.

Jacobson conceived of a double introjection in depression: the introjection of the deflated, bad, worthless parent into the self-image, and the introjection of the inflated, good, or bad punishing parent image into the superego. Such boundless hostility in the superego turned toward the self can lead to intense self-hate and suicidal feelings (Jacobson, 1971, p. 226).

When Peggy's disillusionment reached its peak, she would feel deserted by both parent representations and would fall into a deep, regressive depression. Her triangular love situation prompted the surfacing of destructive impulses. She feared that the power she ascribed to the therapist would vanish and she would be helpless. Frantically trying to build up the image of the therapist again, Peggy clung to the therapist as to an omnipotent goddess who would protect her from the archaic superego that persecuted her with fears of destruction. Her inner conflicts caused her to regress, and for brief periods her relationship with the therapist disintegrated.

She felt there was one way to get rid of the threat of her inner danger and that was to "put out what is inside me" (Jacobson, 1971, p. 220). She "might stand up to those inside dangers, kill and throw them out or be overpowered and die" (Jacobson, 1971, p. 220). When she came close to the desired but terrifying outburst, she was frightened of becoming insane, of killing someone, or of killing herself. Coitus and other situations where she felt either strong libidinal or aggressive tension produced these danger points. Then she would suddenly stop and deny emotion. Anticipating destruction, she pretended she herself or her object world was dead, and by this means avoided her psychic and physical destruction. This defense, the magical and infantile mechanism of denial, caused her detachment and coldness toward her lovers, a lack of sensation in intercourse, and periods of depression. Her feelings of inner death and depression felt like a generalized disillusionment with life that did not fulfill her unrealistic expectations.

Assessment and Critique of Jacobson

Jacobson constructed a model that views the development of the child as a complex balancing of forces. She tracked the interaction of drives, reality influences, and object relationships. Kernberg praises her model for including "the only comprehensive psychoanalytic object relations theory that links . . . object relations, early defensive mechanisms, and vicissitudes of early instinctual development with the structural model of the tripartite psychic apparatus" (Kernberg, 1980, p. 101).

Jacobson's contribution lies in the construction of an encompassing and integrative model that finds a basic link between traditional psychoanalytic notions of drive and object relations theory. She stretched and revised traditional concepts, but her model remains "the most satisfying drive/structural model after Freud" (Greenberg & Mitchell, 1983, p. 306). Critics have praised her for the "comprehensive" (Mendelson, 1960) and "encompassing and integrative" quality of her model (Tuttman, 1981, p. 100). With regard to her work on depression, she was probably "the most influential . . . contributor to the psychodynamics of depression" (Becker, 1977, p. 40).

Jacobson's flaws proceed from her effort to make precise distinctions, with the result that her language and presentation are often abstract and dense. While she may have been revisionist with regard to some classical psychoanalytic notions, she is truly a significant figure influencing many key modern writers. Kernberg acknowledges how much he derives from her unique contribution (1980, p. 103). Other figures, like Kohut, while not openly acknowledging her influence or always agreeing with her, profit from her understanding of narcissism and her crucial distinction between self and the inner representation of self.

References

Becker, J. (1977). *Affective disorders.* Morristown, NJ: General Learning Press.

Blanck, G., & Blanck, R. (1974). The contributions of Edith Jacobson. In *Ego psychology: Theory and practice* (pp. 61–73). New York: Columbia University Press.

Greenberg, J. R., & Mitchell, S. A. (1983). *Object relations in psychoanalytic theory.* Cambridge: Harvard University Press.

Hartmann, H. (1964). *Essays on ego psychology.* New York: International Universities Press.

Jacobson, E. (1954). The self and the object world. *Psychoanalytic Study of the Child, 9,* 75–127.

Jacobson, E. (1964). *The self and the object world.* New York: International Universities Press.

Jacobson, E. (1971). *Depression.* New York: International Universities Press.

Kernberg, O. (1980). The contributions of Edith Jacobson. In *Internal world and external reality* (pp. 85–104). New York: Aronson.

Mahler, M. (1958). Autism and symbiosis: Two extreme disturbances of identity. *International Journal of Psycho-Analysis, 39,* 77–83.

Mendelson, M. (1960). Jacobson. In *Psychoanalytic concepts of depression* (pp. 56–72). Springfield, IL: Charles C Thomas.

Tuttman, S. (1981). The significance of Edith Jacobson's *self and object world* in contemporary relations theory. In S. Tuttman, C. Kaye, & M. Zimmerman (Eds.), *Object and self: A developmental approach. Essays in honor of Edith Jacobson* (pp. 81–102). New York: International Universities Press.

Chapter Seven

Margaret S. Mahler: The Psychological Birth of the Individual

Introduction

Margaret S. Mahler, a physician and psychoanalyst, began her career as a children's analyst in Vienna during the 1930s. In 1938, she left Vienna and moved to New York to become a consultant to the Children's Service of the New York State Psychiatric Institute. During the 1950s, Mahler established her observational studies at the Masters Children's Center in New York City.

Mahler set out on the pioneering task of conceptualizing childhood psychosis from a psychoanalytic viewpoint. She later broadened her scope to include observations of normal babies and their mothers (Mahler & Furer, 1968, p. 13). Her methodology rested on observations of the interactions of mothers and their babies. From these observations of repeated, overt behaviors in child-mother interactions, Mahler inferred the preverbal psychological processes taking place within the child. Her descriptions and formulations about the intrapsychic events of the first three years of life have provided a major contribution to the study of development and of object relations.

Conceptually, Mahler carefully linked her work to the traditional instinct model as well as to the work of Melanie Klein, D. W. Winnicott, René Spitz, and others. Despite her links with other psychoanalytic writers, ranging from traditional instinct theorists to ego psychologists, Mahler herself does not fall into a convenient category. Perhaps she might best be described as a developmentalist because she and her fellow researchers (Mahler, Pine, & Bergman, 1975, pp. 5, 6) have used object relations concepts to focus on the psychological birth of the person.

Psychological birth differs from biological birth. Biological birth is visible and dramatic, while psychological birth unfolds gradually and involves psychic processes only partly manifested in observable behavior (Mahler et al., 1975, p. 3). Psychological birth is the process by which an infant becomes an individual by separating from the mother and individuating. This separation and individuation process runs approximately from 4 or 5 months of age to 30 or 36 months.

Although she was nourished in orthodox psychiatric and psychoanalytic theory, Mahler's model of development differs from the traditional Freudian instinct model of development. She views the progressive organization of the self through processes of symbiosis, separation, and differentiation. Mahler believes the human personality begins in a state of psychological fusion with another human being and works through to a gradual psychological process of separation. Mahler's model has appeal in that it implies that the state of earliest human existence is one of connectedness, attachment, and affiliation. In this way, however, her model differs from the work of Daniel Stern (1985) and other attachment theorists (see Ainsworth & Bowlby, 1991; Ainsworth et al., 1978; Bowlby, 1980) who see achievement of the sense of human connectedness as the end point of infant developmental processes, not the starting point as Mahler implies.

Mahler suggests that the unfinished crises and residues of the early symbiotic state as well as the process of separation and becoming individuated can influence relationships over a lifetime. Mahler's focus on these clinical issues as predictive of later adult psychopathology, however, can sometimes obscure the purely developmental issues.

This chapter focuses on Mahler's use of terms and concepts, her theories on developmental phases and subphases, and pathology and therapy. A case study and an assessment from the viewpoint of Daniel Stern (1985) conclude the chapter.

Key Concepts

Symbiosis

Symbiosis is a term Mahler borrowed from biology and used metaphorically to refer to an infant's intrapsychic experience of being undifferentiated from the mother. On a primitive cognitive and emotional level, the infant has an experience of fusion with the mother as well as images of oneness with her (Mahler et al., 1975, p. 8).

Separation and Individuation

Separation refers to the child's achievement of an intrapsychic sense of separateness from the mother. This sense of separateness involves a clear psychic representation of the self as distinguished from representations of the object world and objects.

Individuation is different from but related to identity. A full sense of identity comes later, after the child succeeds in the earlier processes of separation and individuation. To be individuated is a feeling that *I am*—an early awareness of a sense of being, of entity—while identity is the later awareness of *who I am* (Mahler et al., 1975, p. 8).

Separation and individuation have two intertwined and complementary tracks. The track of individuation involves the evolution of intrapsychic autonomy, by which the child assumes the characteristics of being his or her own individual. The track of separation involves the child's emergence from the symbiotic fusion with mother, and therefore a differentiation and disengagement from her. Both separation and individuation culminate in establishment of clearly differentiated self representations as distinct from object representations (Mahler et al., 1975, p. 63). Outward behaviors and interactions manifest these inward developments.

Individuation and identity formation presuppose structuralization of the ego and the neutralization of the drives. Stimuli must not be so overwhelming as to prevent the formation of structure. In the absence of an inner organizer, the mother has to serve as a buffer against inner and outer stimuli.

Structuralization is promoted by a sequence of gratification and frustration. The mother serves as the auxiliary ego for the infant by providing gratifications of needs and preventing excessive frustration. Her various holding behaviors keep tension and frustration from becoming too great and prevent the infant from prematurely developing its own resources. Premature ego development occurs when the infant actually takes over functions that the mother was performing; the result might be a false self in D. W. Winnicott's sense or "as if" mechanisms (Mahler & Furer, 1968, pp. 11, 16). When needs are not so imperative and the infant can hold tension in abeyance to some extent, and when the infant is able to wait for and confidently expect satisfaction, the process of structural formation of an ego occurs. In brief, some manageable frustration helps development while too much hinders it.

Object Relationships

Object relationships normally mean, in the Freudian sense, "one person endowing another human being with object libido" (Mahler & Furer, 1968, p. 52). With this meaning, object relationship is the most reliable means to assess mental health on the one hand and potential for therapy on the other. Opposed to this meaning of object relationship is the narcissistic relationship, where investment is in the self and there is no true relationship with another person.

Psychotic object relationships refer to interactions that Winnicott also described. The optimal use of transitional, inanimate objects facilitates the autonomy of the child's ego, while too rigid use of transitional objects in place of human relationships may be a reliable sign of later disturbance. Psychotics, blurring and failing to distinguish between the human object world and the inanimate world, de-animate the human object world and animate the inanimate world (Mahler, 1960, p. 548; Mahler & Furer, 1968, p. 54).

Mutual Cuing

Mutual cuing is a form of mother-child interaction and develops into mutual verbal communication. The infant gives cues to needs, pleasures, and tensions, and the mother responds selectively to only some of these cues. The infant gradually alters behavior in response to the mother's selective response. The unconscious needs of the mother activate out of the infant's potential those characteristics that make the infant the unique child of this particular mother (Mahler & Furer, 1968, p. 19). The mother conveys a mirroring frame of reference to which the primitive self of the infant adjusts. From these circular interactions emerge the characteristics of the child's personality (Mahler & Furer, 1968, p. 18). If the mother's mirroring is unpredictable or hostile, then the child has an unreliable frame of reference to check back to. This can disturb the child's self-esteem.

Developmental Stages

Mahler described three developmental phases: normal autism, normal symbiosis, and separation and individuation. During separation and individuation, there are four subphases. During these different stages of development, considerable overlapping occurs, and no one phase is completely replaced by a following phase.

Normal Autism

The period of *normal autism* begins at birth and lasts about a month. During this period, the infant spends most of its time sleeping, seemingly in a state of primitive, hallucinatory disorientation. Mahler used the image of a bird's egg as a model of the infant's closed psychological system. The task of this phase is for the newborn to achieve balance, a homeostatic equilibrium of the organism outside the womb (Mahler et al., 1975, p. 43). In this early phase, the infant cannot differentiate between its own attempts to reduce tension (by urinating, regurgitating, squirming) and the actions of the mother to reduce hunger and other tensions and needs (Mahler & Furer, 1968, p. 7). This is truly a stage of undifferentiation (Mahler et al., 1975, p. 48).

In terms of object relations, this first stage is objectless. Mahler retained the Freudian concept of primary narcissism, and the normal autistic period is one of absolute primary narcissism. The infant gradually attains a dim awareness that satisfaction of needs cannot be accomplished by itself, but must come from somewhere outside the self.

Normal Symbiosis

Around the second month of life, the autistic shell begins to crack and a different, positive kind of psychological shell or membrane begins to form. This protective membrane psychologically encloses the symbiotic orbit of mother and child as a dual entity. From the second month on, the infant has a dim awareness of the need-satisfying object, and this is the beginning of *normal symbiosis*, during which period the infant functions and behaves as though the infant and the mother were an omnipotent system, a dual unity (Mahler & Furer, 1968, p. 35; Mahler et al., 1975, p. 44). Within the common boundary, the infant likely has a sense of boundless oceanic feeling, and this state would resemble the archaic state of early narcissism described by Kohut and others.

The essential feature of symbiosis is the hallucinatory or delusional omnipotent fusion with the representation of the mother, and, in particular, the delusion of a common boundary of the two. It is to this mental state of fusion that severely disturbed children regress (Mahler & Furer, 1968, p. 9).

Good mothering pulls the infant from the tendency toward negative regression to an increased sensory awareness of the environment (Mahler & Furer, 1968, p. 10). There is a shift of libidinal cathexis from inside the body, especially the abdominal organs, to the periphery (Mahler et al., 1975, p. 52). This shift from inside the body (where the experience of tension is discharged by urinating, vomiting, and so forth) to the periphery of the body (with a greater tactile, near-visual, and auditory awareness) takes place about the third or fourth week of life (Mahler et al., 1975, pp. 291–292).

The infant gradually differentiates between pleasure and good experiences and painful and bad experiences. The first orientation to life outside the womb is good-pleasurable versus bad-painful stimuli. The young infant is exposed to a rhythmic pattern of need, tension, and hunger. These inner needs cannot be relieved beyond a limited degree unless there is relief from something outside the self. It is the repeated experience of a need-satisfying, good outside source that eventually conveys a vague affective discrimination between self and nonself. To the "bad" stimuli coming from outside or inside, the infant reacts with aggression and by ridding and ejective mechanisms.

To "good" stimuli coming from inside or outside, the baby reacts with bliss and reaching out (Mahler & Furer, 1968, p. 45). At this level of differentiation, the predominantly good memory islands or foci become allocated to the self, and predominantly bad memory segments get allocated to the nonself—although it is not easy to demonstrate this. Qualities of pleasure-giving or pain-inflicting become linked to the mother. Also, primitive memory islands formed through pleasurable and unpleasurable sensations from within the infant's own body serve as scattered part images of the object and part images of the body self (Mahler & Furer, 1968, p. 44; Mahler & Gosliner, 1955, p. 198). At this period of development, the infant tends to take into its mouth and to engulf as much of the outside object as possible, alternating with ejective, ridding tendencies.

Images of the love object and images of the bodily and psychic self emerge from ever-increasing memory traces of pleasurable (good) and unpleasurable (bad) instinctual and emotional experiences (Mahler & Gosliner, 1955; Mahler et al., 1975, p. 48). The infant gradually develops a body image and the inner sensations form the core of the self. These feelings remain the crystallization point of the feeling of self, around which a sense of identity will be formed (Mahler & Furer, 1968, p. 11). The switch from the biological to the psychobiological probably occurs by the third month when the existence of memory traces allows for the beginnings of psychological forms of learning rather than merely conditioning.

During this early period, there is no differentiation yet of inner and outer self and other. The "I" is not yet differentiated from the "not-I." The level of object relations is "preobject," but the investment in the mother within the vague dual unity is the crucial point from which all subsequent human relationships form; vestiges of this stage remain with us throughout the life cycle (Mahler et al., 1975, p. 48).

Smiling as a response to mother is a crucial sign that the specific bond between the mother and child has been established. In the second half of the first year, it is no longer possible for the infant to interchange the symbiotic partner because the infant has established a specific symbiotic relationship with its mother (Mahler & Furer, 1968, p. 13; Mahler et al., 1975, p. 52).

If the infant has an optimal experience of the symbiotic union with the mother, then the infant can make a smooth psychological differentiation from the mother to a further psychological expansion beyond the symbiotic state.

Separation and Individuation

There are two simultaneous paths of development, one being the developmental track of *individuation*, which means evolving intrapsychic autonomy. The other track is *separation*, which involves psychological differentiation, distancing, and disengagement from the mother (Mahler et al., 1975, p. 63).

The process of separating and individuating involves the child's achievement of separate functioning in the presence of and with the emotional availability of the mother. The pleasure that the child gets in separate functioning enables the child to overcome the separation anxiety that might arise with new steps of separate functioning (Mahler & Furer, 1968, p. 20). The task of this period for the infant is to increase its awareness of separateness of the self and the other, which coincides with the origin of a sense of self, of true object relationships, and of awareness of the reality of the outside world. The ego emerges as a rudimentary structure during this process (Mahler et al., 1975, p. 48).

Four Developmental Subphases

First Subphase: Differentiation and Body Image

At about four or five months of age, at the peak of symbiosis, the infant exhibits behaviors that appear to indicate the beginning of the separation-individuation process. During this first phase, a baby will distance its body slightly from the mother's and begin breaking away from her by developing motor skills to slide down from her lap and play close to her feet.

From about seven to eight months, the baby shows a pattern of visually "checking back" to the mother as a point of orientation, an important sign of beginning body and psychic differentiation from the mother. The baby seems visually to scan others and compare mother with others, the familiar with the unfamiliar. The baby examines what belongs and what does not belong to the mother's body, such as eyeglasses, brooch, clothing, and so on (Mahler et al., 1975, p. 55).

Mahler used the term *hatching* to describe the shift from inward-directed attention to outward-directed attention and alertness (Mahler & Furer, 1968, p. 16; Mahler et al., 1975, p. 54). Hatching can be delayed or premature. If a child has an intense but uncomfortable symbiosis, the child might hatch early, moving rapidly into differentiation as a way to get out of the uncomfortable symbiotic relationship (Mahler et al., 1975, p. 59). Mahler described a little boy who did not get sufficient symbiotic emotional supplies, and who seemed to be able to prolong the symbiotic relationship to give himself and his mother time to catch up. If the symbiotic period is too smothering or too intrusive, then differentiation can show varying forms of disturbance. One boy who found his mother symbiotically too enveloping seemed to push away from her more vigorously and seemed to actively distance himself from her earlier than did other children (Mahler et al., 1975, p. 60).

Second Subphase: Practicing

The *practicing* period overlaps differentiation and is a peak point of hatching. The early practicing period is marked by the infant's ability to move physically away from the mother by crawling and standing up but while still holding on. The practicing period proper begins with free, upright walking.

The child increasingly ventures away from the mother and, very absorbed in his or her own activities, seems oblivious to the mother's presence. There will be periodic returns to her for emotional "refueling," a physical or emotional contact. Some mothers and their children seem to value independent functioning and can refuel at a distance; that is, they maintain contact through verbal means (Mahler et al., 1975, p. 68).

If the mother has been able to provide optimally for the infant's needs, the child will be able to hatch from the symbiotic orbit without straining its resources. The child will be better equipped to separate out and differentiate the self representation from the previously fused self-object representation (Mahler & Furer, 1968, p. 18). But the self representation is not yet firmly established and integrated as a whole self representation.

The ability to crawl and then walk, to physically move away from mother, plays a crucial role in the clear psychic representation of the "I." The physical ability to separate from mother may not be matched by emotional readiness for psychological separation (Mahler & Furer, 1968, p. 41). Some children who are unable to function separately from their symbiotic partner may try to reenter the delusional phantasy of oneness with the omnipotent mother and compel her to serve as an extension of the self (Mahler & Furer, 1968, p. 42).

The practicing period culminates in free walking about the middle of the second year. Toddlers at this period seem to be at the peak of belief in their own omnipotence, which is derived from their sense of sharing in their mother's magical powers (Mahler & Furer, 1968, p. 20). The period from 16 to 18 months is a nodal point of development when the toddler is at the peak of an idealized state of self. The affective representation of self and mother in symbiotic dual unity provides an inflated sense of omnipotence, as the toddler feels his or her own magic powers, the result of developing autonomous functions (Mahler & Furer, 1968, p. 22).

Walking upright and unaided is the greatest single step in human individuation. The upright position gives the child a whole new perspective on the world and the period roughly from 10 to 18 months is a precious period in a child's personal history. The child has a love affair with the world and seems intoxicated. Narcissism is at a peak but is vulnerable to deflation. Characteristic of children during this period is the narcissistic investment in their functioning, in exploring their expanding world, in their imperviousness to falls (Mahler & Gosliner, 1955, p. 71). Elation also comes from the escape from fusion and engulfment with mother. Running off and being swooped up seems to be the toddler's way of working out autonomy and a way to get reassurance that mother will still want to catch the child.

The negativistic phase, the "no" period, is the accompanying behavioral reaction of the process of individuation or disengagement from the mother-child symbiosis. The fear of reengulfment threatens the barely started differentiation (Mahler & Furer, 1968, p. 42; Mahler & Gosliner, 1955). The less satisfying or more parasitic the symbiotic phase, the more exaggerated will be the negativistic reaction, the declaration of independence.

Mother's varying reactions

A mother's attitude plays an important role in helping the normal child to feel encouragement and to gradually exchange the magic omnipotence for pleasure in separateness and autonomy. This period is good for children who have an intense but uncomfortable symbiotic relationship. Some mothers, however, who like the closeness of symbiosis now that it is over, would like their children to be already grown up. Children of these mothers find it hard to grow apart and actively demand closeness with their mothers (Mahler et al., 1975, p. 66). Some mothers see in their toddler's walking proof that "he's grown up now," even though the child intrapsychically is not yet hatched. Some fail their children by abandoning them to their own devices prematurely, while others may find it hard to give up their symbiotic holding behavior (Mahler & Furer, 1968, p. 22). Other mothers fail their fledgling toddlers because they find it difficult to balance giving support and merely watching from a distance. The mother of a boy named Mark seemed to avoid close physical contact with him, and then at times interrupted him in his activities to hug him and hold him—when she needed it, not when he did (Mahler et al., 1975, p. 70).

Third Subphase: Rapprochement

During the second half of the second year, the toddler's maturing ego recognizes both its separateness from mother as well as its inability to really be alone without her. The decline in its sense of omnipotence and the increased sense of dependency cause the toddler to turn back to mother.

The toddler becomes more aware of physical separateness from the mother, along with a lessening of imperviousness to frustration and a lessening of the child's previous obliviousness, during the practicing period, to her presence. The toddler now turns back to the mother (Mahler & Furer, 1968, p. 23). Having experienced a growth in cognitive skills and a differentiation in emotional life, the toddler now experiences increased separation anxiety. Arriving at an awareness of his or her separate self, the child once again has an increased need to seek closeness with the mother, a need for closeness that was held in abeyance during the practicing subphase (Mahler, 1971, p. 410). Mahler called this new period *rapprochement.*

The rapprochement subphase is a time when the toddler wants the mother to share each newly acquired skill and experience (Mahler et al., 1975, pp. 76, 77). During this period, an observer notices a toddler continually bringing things to the mother, putting objects in her lap, with the emotionally important issue being the child's need to share them with her. The toddler is aware of his or her need for mother's love. At the same time, the child desires expanded autonomy but protects this autonomy by negativism toward mother. The toddler may reach out to the father, who is not fully outside the symbiotic union but not fully a part of it either (Mahler et al., 1975, p. 91).

Early rapprochement culminates at about 17 or 18 months with an acceptance of physical separation and pleasure in sharing activities with the mother. The awareness of separateness brings the pleasures of autonomy, the discovery that the child could ask to have his or her wish gratified ("cookie"), that the child could command mother's attention ("Look, Mommy"), or that the child could find others and express delight in seeing them ("Hi") (Mahler et al., 1975, p. 94). But toddlers face an important emotional turning point as the painful aspects of separateness begin to dawn on them.

Toddlers experience the obstacles to their conquest of the world in a way they did not during the height of the exuberant practicing period. Increasingly they sense their helplessness and feel small and separate (Mahler & Furer, 1968). Just feeling a need is not sufficient to command relief. There are blows to the child's omnipotence and self-esteem. Wooing of the mother and fear of losing the love of the object (as distinguished from fear of object loss) increasingly become evident. Intrapsychically, the representation of the object becomes more clearly differentiated from the representation of the self.

Rapprochement crisis refers to rapprochement conflicts in which toddlers work out their increased need for the mother while protecting their own autonomy. On one hand is the gradual and painful relinquishing of the delusion of their own grandeur. On the other hand is the child's continued sense of individuality and separateness. The inner tension often gets expressed in fights with mother. The conflict is expressed by a clamoring for omnipotent control, by occasional periods of extreme separation anxiety, by a dizzying—for the adult—alteration of demands for closeness and for autonomy.

Shadowing and darting behavior becomes noticeable. Toddlers shadow their mothers and incessantly watch and follow their every move. They dart away from her with the expectation of being chased and swept into her arms. These patterns indicate the wish for reunion with the love object and fear of reengulfment by it. Toddlers of this age continue to protect their autonomy by their use of "no" as well as by the increased aggression and negativism of the anal phase (Mahler, 1971, p. 411).

The rapprochement crises occur roughly from 18 to 24 months. Children of this age do not want to be reminded that they cannot manage on their own. They are caught in the conflict between their own separateness, grandiosity, and autonomy and their wish for mother to magically fulfill their wants without the need to acknowledge that help. Some children can become fixated at this stage and cling to splitting mechanisms. The child will sometimes use the mother as an extension of the self, such as impersonally using the mother's hand to get something (Mahler et al., 1975, p. 95).

The rapprochement period is marked by anxious reactions to strangers, indecisiveness manifested in conflicting wishes, increased problems with the parents' departure, and clinging to mother. The child will create various ways to deal with mother's absences, such as through the use of transitional objects and processes of internalization and ego identification with the parents (Mahler et al., 1975, pp. 92, 100).

From 19 to 36 months, the ideal state of the self must become gradually divested of its delusional and omnipotent elements. So the second 18 months of a child's life are a period of vulnerability, a time when the child's self-esteem may suffer deflation as the child gradually divests the self of some of the delusional overestimation of his or her own omnipotence. During this period of vulnerability, the mother's emotional availability is very important for the child, for it allows the child's autonomous ego to attain its best functioning. The mother's availability allows for the child's imitation and identification with her. The child internalizes the good mother-toddler relationship, and this allows for a lessening of magical omnipotence. The mother's availability must be balanced by her willingness to let the child go. Like the mother bird, she needs to give her toddler a gentle push, encouragement toward independence (Mahler et al., 1975, p. 79).

As they struggle to find individual solutions to developmental challenges, children often develop transient development deviations, probably as attempts to correct a developmental imbalance in one area or phase by overdeveloping other behaviors. Thus, an especially acute awareness of separateness can make a child excessively concerned with mother's whereabouts, and the child may cling to the mother or manifest strong separation anxiety. The case of Barney, a boy who precociously developed walking skills during the practicing period, illustrated individuation lagging behind separation. Walking at 9 months, he would often fall and hurt himself, but he reacted with imperviousness. He could not properly evaluate the potential dangers of his physical feats. But by the end of the 11th month, he became visibly perplexed to find that his mother was not always nearby to rescue him. As the boy cognitively became aware of his separateness from his mother, his calm acceptance of falls disappeared. He began to manifest dangerous and exaggerated darting away behavior during the rapprochement period, with the expectation that his mother would sweep him up in her arms and thereby undo the physical separateness. His precocious physical maturation during the practicing subphase seemed to have resulted in excessive darting behavior during the rapprochement phase as a developmental corrective; other facets of his rapprochement period were normal. He would frequently fill her lap with toys or stand near her and do jigsaw puzzles (Mahler et al., 1975, pp. 80–81).

Mother's reactions

Some mothers cannot accept the child's demandingness during this period. By contrast, others are unable to face the child's gradual separateness, the fact that the child is becoming increasingly independent of them. Anxious because of their own symbiotic and parasitic needs, some mothers hover over and shadow the child. This closeness may drive the child to more determined efforts at separateness.

Maternal unavailability can make practicing and exploratory activities brief and subdued. A child preoccupied with mother's availability is unable to invest energy in his or her environment and in the development of other important skills and often returns to her in efforts to engage her (Mahler et al., 1975, pp. 80, 81). The child can become insistent and even desperate in attempts to woo her. This desperation depletes energy from the ego and the child may revert to earlier splitting mechanisms; serious developmental arrest can result in pathological narcissism and borderline phenomena.

Fourth Subphase: Emotional Object Constancy and Individuality

This fourth subphase of the separation-individuation period occupies mainly the third year of life without a distinct ending point. The two main tasks in this period are to attain some degree of object constancy and to consolidate individuality (Mahler et al., 1975, p. 109).

The establishment of emotional object constancy depends on the internalization of a positive inner image of the mother that supplies comfort to the child in the mother's physical absence and that allows the child to function separately (Mahler et al., 1975, pp. 109, 118). The emotional or affective object constancy described by Mahler differs from Jean Piaget's object permanency, which takes place at about 18 to 20 months. The object Mahler spoke of is specifically the mother who is cathected by the child with positive emotional energy, as opposed to the inanimate object, such as a rattle, which is only transiently cathected but which Piaget believed was the permanent object (Mahler et al., 1975, p. 111). The image of the mother is the result of a long process of gradual unification of "good" and "bad" aspects of the object into an inner whole representation. Along with a whole object representation, the child continues to develop a unified self-image based on true ego identification.

This object constancy subphase also witnesses the unfolding of complex cognitive functions, and verbal communication slowly replaces other modes of communication. Superego precursors begin, and there is considerable development of the ego and its functions. One of the most important tasks of the evolving ego is learning to cope with the aggressive drive. The reality principle gradually replaces the pleasure principle, and the ego is capable of increased reality testing (Mahler et al., 1975, p. 226). As for zonal development, the child is still mainly in the anal and early phallic phases of development (Mahler et al., 1975, p. 116).

Some children more actively seek after their fathers, possibly out of fear of the mother reengulfing them. The process of intrapsychic separation from the mother continues, and whatever negativism is present seems necessary for the continued development of the child's sense of identity.

Pathology and Therapy

Mahler's view of psychological disturbance and therapeutic response rested on her understanding of developmental tasks. Each developmental stage has certain tasks, challenges, and risks. To be traumatized during a developmental phase or to leave some tasks uncompleted can result in serious psychological disturbance. Developmental disturbance almost invariably involves the relationship between child and parent or parent substitute. During early developmental phases, especially the autistic and symbiotic phases, normal children require a libidinally available mother who allows for the unfolding of innate potentials. Disruption of the parent-child relationship during the autistic, symbiotic, or separation-individuation phases results in varying degrees of serious pathology. Therapy offers a corrective for developmental failure, with the therapist being the substitute parent and auxiliary ego, performing certain functions for the disturbed child or adult.

If, during the most vulnerable autistic and symbiotic periods, some serious trauma occurs, then psychosis is possible (Mahler & Furer, 1968, p. 48). In infantile psychosis, symbiosis is distorted or missing. The core of the disturbance seems to involve a deficiency or defect in the child's intrapsychic use of the mother during the symbiotic phase. Because the child cannot internalize the mother, the child is unable to differentiate the self from fusion with the part object. So, psychosis usually means faulty or failed individuation, with psychotic children not achieving a sense of individual identity (Mahler & Furer, 1968, pp. 32, 35).

Borderline and narcissistic disorders seem to result from traumas and disturbance of developmental processes during the separation-individuation phase. Some of the symptoms of narcissism and borderline pathology that involve omnipotence, splitting, and grandiosity are behavioral manifestations of developmental tasks that were disturbed or not completed.

Some conflicts are specific to a particular developmental phase, and Mahler emphasizes the psychological vulnerability of the practicing and rapprochement subphases. At the height of the practicing period, when children are at the peak of delusion about their own omnipotence, normal narcissism is extremely vulnerable to the danger of deflation (Mahler et al., 1975, p. 228). During the rapprochement subphase, children become increasingly aware of their own separateness and use various mechanisms to deny this separateness. They give up delusions of grandiosity and the belief in the omnipotence of their parents, which results in increased separation anxiety. Children's rapidly maturing egos recognize separateness, but they are not yet able to stand alone (Mahler et al., 1975, p. 229).

Clinicians and theorists are increasingly employing Mahler's developmental categories in seeking to understand serious disturbance. Althea Horner (1979, p. 282) sees the narcissistically disturbed personality as emerging from the junction of the practicing period (the grandiose self) and the rapprochement subphase (the helpless self). For some children, the rapprochement crisis leads to great ambivalence and the splitting of objects into "good" and "bad." Otto Kernberg (1980, p. 24), in agreement with Mahler, attributes to rapprochement the lack of integration and the splitting mechanisms that are characteristic of the borderline personality. With this emphasis on the importance of the rapprochement subphase in understanding borderline phenomena, some caution is needed against a too simplistic linking of precise subphases with particular disturbances.

Therapy

Therapy, according to Mahler, must be based on the developmental needs of the patient, whether child or adult. Thus, by enabling a patient to reexperience the early stages of development, therapy can help the patient reach higher levels of object relationships (Mahler & Furer, 1968, p. 167, n. 3). A child patient needs to progress through the missed periods of development, with the therapist serving as substitute mother (Mahler & Furer, 1968, p. 184). The therapist also serves as an auxiliary ego that provides those ego functions the child has not yet attained. Such functions might include being a stimulus barrier that protects the child from inner or outer overstimulation (Mahler & Furer, 1968, p. 174). Some child patients are not able to communicate, but a therapist can assist in translating primary process experiences into words. The therapist can also foster processes of integration and synthesis and the establishment of boundaries between the self and the external world. With time and therapeutic effort, the child will gradually take over these substitute ego functions.

In autistic psychotic disorders, in which a child seemingly never establishes symbiotic bonds to the mother or anyone else, further human development is impossible without the symbiotic experience. Treatment for the autistic psychotic child involves contact with a human love object (Mahler & Furer, 1968, p. 166). The therapist must "lure" the child out of the autistic shell with music and rhythmic activities, because the child is intolerant of direct human contact (Mahler & Furer, 1968, p. 168).

By contrast, the symbiotic psychotic child is unable to resolve separation and individuation and regresses to a symbiotic panic state (Mahler & Furer, 1968, p. 166). The symbiotic psychotic child responds with panic to any realization of separateness and dreads the loss of self through symbiotic parasitic fusion. This panic is intolerable, so the child regresses to an autistic state. Therapy must supply a corrective symbiotic experience (Mahler & Furer, 1968, p. 167). This corrective early experience demands time and patience of the therapist, who must allow the child to proceed at the child's own pace. For example, some symbiotic psychotic children who have been toilet trained before attaining the anal phase never experience libidinal gratification and feelings of mastery. The therapist encourages a living through and working through of the missed phase of development by means of suitable substitute experiences, such as playing in clay or with finger paints (Mahler & Furer, 1968, pp. 171, 174).

Case Study

The following is a summary of an extended account of the development of a normal child named Donna (Mahler et al., 1975, pp. 138–152). This case illustrates that even though there are clear overall patterns of phases of development, there are an infinite number of individual variations within the larger patterns.

Donna was a gifted child with a mother, Mrs. D., who was very attentive, patient, and available. Mahler and her co-workers expected that with such a good environment Donna would make a smooth transition through the different developmental tasks. Donna, however, encountered problems during the separation-individuation period.

At 4 and 5 months of age, the height of symbiosis, Donna seemed to be a calm, contented infant. Mrs. D. seemed well-attuned to her daughter. Donna babbled happily in her playpen and was held in her mother's lap when she was tired.

When she started crawling, Donna did not seem to manifest the excitement and enjoyment that other children did. Mrs. D. did not seem to give the "gentle push" to her fledgling during this active distancing and early practicing period. Donna may have sensed her mother's unconscious doubt that Donna could manage alone. Donna seems to have had a greater dependency on her mother's approval and disapproval, a form of early superego precursors.

At 6 months, Donna showed mild stranger reaction, suggesting she had some early awareness of differentness. By 8 months, at times Donna often displayed a low-key energy when her mother was out of the room, but exuberance when reunited with her. Mrs. D. clearly was the center of Donna's life. When held by others, Donna avoided looking at their faces, and displayed stranger anxiety.

At 9 and 10 months, the period of early practicing, Donna played happily and independently of her mother. She learned to walk at 11½ months, but, unlike her peers, was cautious in her motor activities. At the peak of the practicing period, she experienced a love affair with the world, a characteristic of this subphase.

At 13 and 14 months, Donna's widening activities led to greater frustration and even anger. When she did not get her way she often screamed. Mrs. D. rarely opposed Donna and manifested much patience. As a result, there was little confrontation between mother and daughter, although some observers felt Donna's mother should have intervened more to prevent Donna from being too rough with other children.

At 14 and 15 months, Donna was the most aggressive, assertive, and alert of all the children in the Masters Children Center. She was an active, happy child who enjoyed climbing and other activities. Exuberant and independent, she always knew what she wanted, and observers found her an impressive child.

At about this period, observers noticed a change in Donna's interactions with her mother. Donna started to share pleasurable activities with her. This seemed to be the start of the rapprochement period. Donna would start crying as soon as her mother left the room but could be distracted by others and reengaged in activities. She had some anxious anticipation of her mother leaving but seemed to cope with this separation anxiety by actively practicing for it by saying "bye-bye" frequently. It then became difficult to distract Donna from crying when her mother left. Less tolerant of frustration and now more aggressive, Donna began to react to her mother's exits from the toddler room by crying immediately.

At about 16 months, Donna showed signs of rapprochement crisis. She became increasingly aware of her mother as separate, and she wanted to be close to her. Donna did not like her mother's attention to other children, was jealous of her brother, and began to use the word "no" more frequently. Mrs. D. reported that Donna provocatively darted away from her in the playground and manifested fears that she had not previously had. Donna began to become aware of sex differences; she would pull up her dress and look at her tummy and touch her genitals.

From 16 to 18 months, Donna seemed to gain some temporary resolution of rapprochement crisis by identifying with her mother. She played mother for her dolls. At this period, Donna manifested precocious ego development by knowing the names of all the other children and being able to identify persons in some photographs. She had excellent frustration tolerance.

Within a month, the rapprochement crisis reappeared. She again showed concern for her mother's whereabouts. Previously, Donna had gone to the toddler room by herself from the time she could walk; now she would go only if accompanied by her mother. Donna appeared very distressed when her mother left the room.

About this time, Donna got sick and needed an antibiotic injection. Observers speculated that this shook Donna's wavering belief in her mother's magical powers; she rejected her mother's efforts to comfort her and began asking for her father. Donna manifested increasing signs of a conflict between wanting to be independent and needing to be close to mother. She constantly needed to know where mother was. When she encountered even slight frustrations, she wanted to go to her mother. But she was also negativistic and stubborn, insisting on doing things for herself and resisted being dressed, changed, or put to bed. Her clinging behavior alternated with more adventurous and independent behavior.

This period of rapprochement crisis seems to have been made even more poignant and difficult for Donna by the presence of some of the main anxieties of childhood: fear of abandonment (object loss), fear of loss of love, and castration concerns. On one occasion during this period, for example, Mrs. D. had to stay briefly in the hospital with Donna's sick brother.

During the final period of the second year, Donna continued to show the exaggerated behaviors of the rapprochement subphase. She needed to be close to her mother or, after some separation from her mother, was with her at a regressed level by touching and feeling her mother rather than by just seeing her and knowing she was present. She also manifested a great ambivalence in this period.

Mahler and her colleagues confessed to being puzzled how such a well-endowed child with a competent mother such as Mrs. D. would have difficulties resolving this subphase. One would expect a smoother resolution and transition toward the establishment of object constancy during the third year. But Donna continued to be a somewhat troubled child. She clung to her mother and did not respond to efforts to engage her in play. As soon as her mother did leave the room, Donna would do fine in her play and other activities. During this early part of the third year, she manifested anxiety over castration, sex difference, and toilet activities. She avoided looking at boys who were without pants, and after seeing one boy urinate, she said that he was a girl. She manifested fears and phantasies of being a boy and turned to boys as playmates. Once, when she fell down, she said her mother had pushed her, as if her mother had become a dangerous person now that she was separated from her. Donna regressed to her previous level of toilet training.

Mrs. D. needed to comfort Donna as one would a baby. She regressed, sucking her fingers. Her father became more important for her. When she resisted doing what her mother wanted, such as getting ready for bed, she would more readily accommodate her father. At times now, she would kiss her father and not her mother.

By the second half of the third year, Donna began to be freer in her activities, and often she imitated the play of boys. She seems to have had ongoing concerns about her body and harm coming to it. Her mother reported that at times Donna liked to go around without her pants and would frequently touch her genitals.

By the end of the third year, Donna still fluctuated between independent behavior and babyish behavior. Her maturity was in areas where she identified with her mother, such as mothering dolls or toileting herself. But she still drank from a bottle and manifested stranger anxiety by pulling at her clothes. By now, the normally patient Mrs. D. responded to her daughter with more impatience and irritation.

Mahler commented that Donna was a very well-endowed girl with a good mother and family life but that she had difficulties resolving some of the separation-individuation subphases, especially rapprochement. Mahler was confident that Donna would not be disturbed in the future and that her troubles in resolving separation-individuation issues fell within the normal range of development.

Assessment and Critique of Mahler

Mahler believes the individual begins life in a state of undifferentiated fusion with the mother. Gradually, the infant psychologically emerges from this symbiotic union to begin developing a separate, differentiated self. Mahler further believes that the object relations of later life build on the early mother-child relationship and the child's search for a reconnection with the mother once the child is separate from her. This model of early development has strongly influenced psychoanalytic thinking for several decades.

Mahler and her co-workers sought to illuminate the preoedipal period of development by an observational methodology that allowed for replication and that was different from psychoanalytic reconstruction. Her studies were grounded in the psychoanalytic tradition, and she sought a conceptual and experimental base for the causes of psychological disturbances, such as different forms of childhood psychosis and various borderline and narcissistic phenomena.

Mahler's concepts of symbiosis, separation, and individuation are organizing clinical ideas for early phases of personality development. Her ideas of an early undifferentiated phase are somewhat similar to other object relations and self psychology theories. Although some self psychologists (Shane & Shane, 1980) seek to establish a close link between Mahler's work and Heinz Kohut's, Kohut himself emphasizes the difference between his methodology and that of Mahler's. Kohut (1980, p. 452) stresses that he reconstructs the inner life of childhood from the transference revival of early childhood experiences, while Mahler directly observed childhood behavior. He does not deny similarities but does not try to build links with Mahler's work.

A compelling critique of Mahler's work comes from experimental findings articulated by Daniel Stern (1985, p. 13*ff.*). Stern considers both the "observed infant" (the realm of observable behavior and experimental studies) and the "clinical infant" (the subjective world of the infant's experience and speculation about the origins of adult pathology). Stern maintains a dialogue between these two approaches, using the structuring of the infant's experience of the sense of self and others as an organizing principle of development. This results in different senses of the self (emergent self, core self, subjective self, and verbal self) that are not successive phases but continue to function and be active throughout life once they are formed. Stern (p. 10) questions the notion of phases of development that are specifically devoted to such "clinical issues" as symbiosis, autonomy, and trust. While Mahler and others see such clinical issues to be the developmental tasks for age-specific periods, Stern sees clinical issues like these operating at essentially the same levels over the whole of the lifespan, at all points in development. Further, Stern (p. 23) maintains that no longitudinal studies support the predictions of later-occurring psychopathology, as psychoanalysis has always hoped to do.

Stern argues that Mahler's developmental sequences are too concerned with specific time frames during which basic clinical issues of life get their own separate turn, such as a period for symbiosis, a period for separation, and so forth. It is more accurate to say clinical issues are being negotiated all the time, and the relative prominence of a particular clinical issue, such as symbiosis, is either illusory or due to cultural pressure or some theoretical or methodological bias. To pick out one basic life issue and devote a developmental approach to its decisive resolution, Stern believes, is to provide a distorted picture of developmental processes. Stern (1985, p. 23) is convinced that there are no grounds in observations of infants for considering basic clinical issues as adequate definers of phases or stages of development.

Therefore, for Stern (p. 240), the idea of a period of undifferentiation that is subjectively experienced by the infant as a form of merger and dual-unity with the mother—Mahler's symbiotic period—is very problematic. But Stern does grant, from the point of view of core-relatedness, that pervasive feelings of connectedness and interpersonal well-being do occur during the period from the second month to the seventh month of the infant's life, the period of Mahler's symbiosis. Stern also accepts that these feelings do serve as an emotional reservoir of human connectedness. Stern differs from Mahler in that he believes the infant is not passive during these early processes but is actively constructing representations of interactions with self-regulating others. Stern suggests that the developmental tasks of Mahler's phase of normal symbiosis and the first phase of separation and individuation are occurring simultaneously during what he calls core-relatedness.

Stern's notion of the sense of the core self moving in the developmental direction of intersubjective relatedness differs from Mahler's ideas. He shares with attachment theory the perspective that early psychic development makes the achievement of a basic sense of human connectedness the end point, not the starting point, of a long, active development that involves the interplay of predesigned and acquired behaviors. Stern summarizes: "For Mahler, connectedness is the result of a failure in differentiation; for [Stern] it is a success of psychic functioning" (1985, p. 241).

As for the effect of infant research on Mahler's notion of normal autism, Stern clarifies that infants are not "autistic" in the sense of lacking interest in and registering stimuli. "Infants are deeply engaged in and related to social stimuli" (Stern, p. 234). Through empirical studies on the direction, for example, of an infant's gaze, Stern (pp. 21–22) suggests that infants are active at a surprisingly early stage and are able to distinguish themselves from other significant people. The phase of development that Mahler calls normal autism might better be described as an "awakening" or an "emergence" (Stern, 1985, p. 235).

Stern's findings would seem to undermine the assumptions of Mahler's centerpiece idea that psychological birth occurs gradually out of the symbiotic merger with the mother. Fred Pine (1986, 1990), a collaborator of Mahler, concedes that it might be hard to substantiate the concept of symbiosis as a global phase, and he proposes that the infant has *moments* of boundarilessness or merger—moments being a substitution for the idea of weeks or months of symbiotic merger. Mitchell (1993, p. 239 n. 8) suggests that perhaps the merger experience, even if it does not occupy the infant all the time, may still be the primary shaper of the infant's experience.

Emanuel Peterfreund (1978) warns of Mahler's tendency toward the "adultomorphization" of the experience of infants; that is, looking at the infant's world of experience from an adult standpoint. Peterfreund is also concerned that many of the terms used to describe infantile experiences, such as *fusion, without boundaries, undifferentiated,* are applied to states that are normal for infants but pathological for adults.

References

Ainsworth, M. D. S., Blehar, M. C., Waters, E., & Wall, S. (1978). *Patterns of attachment.* Hillsdale, NJ: Erlbaum.

Ainsworth, M. D. S., & Bowlby, J. (1991). An ethological approach to personality development, *American Psychologist, 46,* 333–341.

Bowlby, J. (1980). *Attachment and loss.* New York: Basic Books.

Horner, A. J. (1979). *Object relations and the developing ego in therapy.* New York: Aronson.

Kernberg, O. (1980). Developmental theory, structural organization and psychoanalytic technique. In R. R. Lax, S. Black, & J. A. Burland (Eds.), *Rapprochement: The critical subphases of separation-individuation* (pp. 23–28). New York: Aronson.

Kohut, H. (1980). From a letter to a colleague. In A. Goldberg (Ed.), *Advances in self psychology* (pp. 456–469). New York: International Universities Press.

Mahler, M. S. (1960). Symposium on psychotic object relationships: III. Perceptual de-differentiation and psychotic "object relationship." *International Journal of Psycho-Analysis, 41,* 548–553.

Mahler, M. S. (1971). A study of the separation-individuation process and its possible application to borderline phenomena in the psychoanalytic situation. *Psychoanalytic Study of the Child, 26,* 403–422.

Mahler, M. S., & Furer, M. (1968). *On human symbiosis and the vicissitudes of individuation.* New York: International Universities Press.

Mahler, M. S., & Gosliner, B. J. (1955). On symbiotic child psychosis. *Psychoanalytic Study of the Child, 10,* 195–212.

Mahler, M. S., Pine, F., & Bergman, A. (1975). *The psychological birth of the human infant.* New York: Basic Books.

Mitchell, S. A. (1993). *Hope and dread in psychoanalysis.* New York: Basic Books.

Peterfreund, E. (1978). Some critical comments on psychoanalytic conceptualizations of infancy. *International Journal of Psycho-Analysis, 59,* 427–441.

Pine, F. (1986). The "symbiotic phase" in the light of current infancy research. *Bulletin of the Menninger Clinic, 50,* 564–569.

Pine, F. (1990). *Drive, ego, object & self: A synthesis for clinical work.* New York: Basic Books.

Shane, M., & Shane, E. (1980). Psychoanalytic developmental theories of the self: An integration. In A. Goldberg (Ed.), *Advances in self psychology* (pp. 23–46). New York: International Universities Press.

Stern, D. N. (1985). *The interpersonal world of the infant: A view from psychoanalysis and developmental psychology.* New York: Basic Books.

⊚ Chapter Eight

Otto Kernberg:
A Synthesis

Introduction

Otto Kernberg was born in Austria in 1928, educated in Chile, and received further psychiatric training at the Menninger Clinic in Topeka, Kansas. The New York area serves as his base for clinical and research activities, but he travels widely to lecture. He is probably the most influential yet controversial proponent of object relations theory in the United States (cf. Brody, 1982).

Kernberg set out to accomplish two theoretical goals: (1) to integrate object relations theory with psychoanalytic instinct theory, and (2) to understand the borderline conditions (and a subgroup of the borderline condition, the narcissistic personality) by using a conceptual model that integrates object relations and instinct theory (Kernberg, 1975, p. 3; 1976, p. 131).

Kernberg's first goal, an ambitious synthesis of classical Freudian impulse theory and object relations theory, is an attempt to reconcile the traditional instinctual and tripartite model of id, ego, and superego with object relations theory. Some critics view his synthesis as revisionist and not completely successful (Calef & Weinshel, 1979; Klein & Tribich, 1981). Most theorists agree, however, that Kernberg has succeeded in his second goal by providing a significant contribution to the understanding of borderline pathology. In the same way that Freud's theory stemmed from his clinical experience with neurotics and Fairbairn's work flows from his work with schizoid personalities, Kernberg's work revolves largely around his therapy with borderline patients. This clinical work nourished his efforts to construct a model that integrates and synthesizes traditional psychoanalysis and object relations theory.

Reading Kernberg's writings presents several difficulties. His three books (1975, 1976, 1980) are collections of papers that are not always related to each other. His writing is dense and technical, and his terms are the same as those used in the instinctual model but often differ from traditional meanings.

This chapter summarizes the major ideas of Kernberg's synthesis and indicates his contributions as well as his drawbacks. Topics treated in this chapter are Kernberg's key concepts; theory of psychic structure and developmental stages; analysis of pathology, especially borderlines; use of therapy; a case study; and an assessment and critique of his work.

Key Concepts

Object Relations Theory

Kernberg very generally defines object relations theory as the psychoanalytic study of interpersonal relations and how intrapsychic structures grow from internalized past relationships with others (1976, p. 56). He examines this general definition from broad to more narrow usage.

Broadly, object relations theory could refer to a general theory of the structures of the mind influenced by interpersonal experiences. In such a broad definition, psychoanalysis, as a general theory, would constitute an object relations theory; thus, no distinct object relations theory would be necessary.

More narrowly, object relations theory is a more circumspect approach within psychoanalysis, stressing the construction of structures from internal objects; that is, self representations linked with object representations. Kernberg would include Melanie Klein, Edith Jacobson, Margaret Mahler, John Bowlby, Erik Erikson, W. R. D. Fairbairn, and himself in this narrower approach. Kernberg prefers this partially restricted definition because it focuses on what is specific to object relations theory within psychoanalytic theory at large. This approach includes a common unit (the unit of self representation and object representation) that allows for a comparison of the work of different writers.

The most restricted definition of object relations theory limits the term to the British School, which includes Klein, Fairbairn, Winnicott, and Harry Guntrip.

Kernberg values object relations theory because it helps explain disorders that are more serious than neuroses. It sheds light on structural issues and provides new insights into the clinical issues of small groups and marital difficulties.

Object

When Kernberg uses the term *object,* he is usually referring to the human object, and thus object is a mental image of a person, a mental image colored with feelings. He uses mental image and mental representation interchangeably.

Kernberg's work examines the formation of structures within the intrapsychic world of the individual. Structures—that is, enduring psychological patterns—result from the child's internalizing early relationships with people in the environment, principally that with the mother. This relationship is internalized as an object relationship or *internalized object relation.* This internalized object relationship expands externally and internally. Externally, it expands to more complex relationships with people outside the self, and internally, it develops into the traditional structures of id, ego, and superego.

The relationship with the mother, an interaction with a person in the environment, is taken within as the internalized object relation and is a unit with three parts: an image of the object in the environment, an image of the self in interaction with the object, and a feeling that colors the object image and the self-image under the influence of whatever drive was present at the time of the interaction (Kernberg, 1976, p. 29). More simply, the units of internalized object relation are a self-image, an object image, and a feeling or *affect disposition* linking the two images (Kernberg, 1980, p. 17). These units are the substructures of the very earliest developmental stages. Out of these substructures will develop and differentiate the traditional structures of id, ego, and superego, according to Kernberg.

Freud understood the ego as emerging because of the repression of the drives of the id, and classical psychoanalysis has viewed structure formation as evolving out of the transformation of drives. In contrast, Kernberg sees affectively charged *relational* experiences as the basic building blocks of psychic structures (Greenberg & Mitchell, 1983, p. 337). Through his concept of units of internalized object relations, Kernberg attempts a synthesis of drive theory and object relations theory. By means of these units, he expresses the internalization of emotional interpersonal experiences (Kernberg, 1976, p. 31). That is, he mixes the drive model and the object relations model by having the self representation and the object representation build up under the influence of libidinal and aggressive drives or drive derivatives. (By *drive derivatives,* Kernberg does not mean pure drives but any result or aspects of drives that filter into experience [Greenberg & Mitchell, 1983, p. 336].)

But Kernberg does not merely say that these units of object relations serve as building blocks for psychic structures. He makes the unexpected claim that they also help build up the drives. He accomplishes this by some ambiguity in his use of the terms "good" and "bad." Good and bad can mean pleasurable or unpleasurable as well as some level of libidinal or aggressive drive. Good affective experiences accumulate and are the basis for libidinal drives, and bad affective experiences serve as the basis for aggressive drives. In other words, the object-directed feelings of love and hate precede and build up the drives (Kernberg, 1976, p. 87). This notion of object relations units building up the drives is very different from Freud's view of the drives as innate. Kernberg's model thus ultimately makes the person innately responsive and relational rather than innately sexual or aggressive (Greenberg & Mitchell, 1983, pp. 338, 339). By implying that the person's object relations can build up the drives, Kernberg's model is compatible with an object relations theorist like Fairbairn. By including drives in his theory, Kernberg supports traditional psychoanalytic theorists, but by making the person innately responsive and relational, Kernberg falls into the object relations camp.

Splitting

Splitting is both a defensive activity and a normal function that occurs during development. It is an activity by which the ego sees differences within the self and within objects or between the self and its objects. A defensive measure, splitting involves an unconscious phantasy by which the ego splits off unwanted aspects of the self or splits threatening objects into more manageable aspects (Grotstein, 1981, p. 3). In more extreme cases, one thinks of Dr. Jekyll splitting off and repressing Mr. Hyde, the threatening aspect of his own personality. Less extreme might be the tendency to see persons in terms of all good or all bad characteristics without seeing both aspects as being present in the same person. Kernberg uses the concept of splitting to help understand the formation of distinctions between good and bad self representations and object representations in early development. He also understands splitting as a characteristic mechanism in borderline personalities (Grotstein, 1981, p. 57).

Kernberg's style of writing can make it difficult for the reader to follow his thought. It helps to keep in mind that Kernberg is trying to explain the infant's early experiences as fragmented and uncoordinated. Good experiences produce islands of good feelings that link up and become organized in increasingly complex ways so that they help form the structures called ego and superego. Bad experiences, on the other hand, continue to produce frustrated feelings. Defenses of splitting keep the bad feelings apart from each other, so that in this fragmented inner world, anxiety cannot contaminate all the child's experiences and ruin those islands of good feelings, which are linking together. Too much anxiety hinders the processes that organize and coordinate the formation of psychic structures so that the person will grow up with key parts of the personality isolated from other parts. The inner world of such a person will be a world easily fragmented into different islands of experience, different ego states, and different subselves.

Psychic Structure

Structure is built through a continuous process of internalizing object relations. The units of object relations, as discussed previously, are made up of a self representation, an object representation, and a feeling (an affect disposition). By the process of internalization, these units become integrated and gradually consolidated into the structures of ego, id, and superego (Kernberg, 1972; 1976, p. 33).

The process of internalization (or taking in relationships from the environment) has three levels: introjection, identification, and ego identity.

Introjection

Introjection is the earliest stage of the process that builds the personality and its structures of ego, id, and superego. The infant interacts with the environment and, by processes of perception and memory, takes in an interaction with someone in the environment. In these earliest introjected units, the self representation and object representation are not yet differentiated from each other. They are fused, and the feelings are primitive and intense. These units of self and object representation gradually become differentiated and crystallized into clear components. Splitting helps in the process of differentiation.

The feelings, or *affective disposition*, are important. If the child has a pleasant oral experience of sucking, such as occurs in a loving mother-child interaction and feeding, then there is instinctual gratification with a positive libidinal feeling attached to the child's self-image and the object image of the mother. The whole fused unit (self-mother-good feeling) is introjected as a good internal object. If frustration or aggression is present in the interaction, the introject (self-mother-bad feeling) is taken in as a bad internal object. In discussing the internalization of both the good and bad objects, Kernberg differs significantly from Fairbairn, who says that there is no need to take in the good object— only the bad object is internalized.

The intensity and kind of feeling during the process of introjection influences the fusion of the self-images and object images as well as the later organization of personality structures. Introjects of positive or negative feelings are kept apart or split at this level of development because they happen separately and because the ego is too immature to integrate feelings that are dissimilar. Splitting or keeping apart dissimilar affective experiences helps modify the intensity of feelings and anxiety. Later, the maturing ego uses this mechanism of splitting more actively for defensive purposes.

Introjection plays a key role in when and how the ego is formed. Kernberg believes some ego functions, such as perception and memory, exist from the beginning of life. Because the child can see and remember, the child can introject object relations, which as forerunners of the ego serve as early psychic structures. These object relations units of self-image, object image, and affective charge are the "precipitates" around which "ego nuclei" consolidate. Introjects with hostile feelings are kept defensively split off from each other, while positive, libidinal introjects come together into a primitive ego core. The good internal objects are positive introjections with undifferentiated and fused self-images and object images (Kernberg, 1976, pp. 36, 38). There are fusions, dissolutions, and re-fusions of similar, positively charged units or "good objects," which consolidate into multiple "egos"; these, in turn, become integrated into the emerging ego. As the ego becomes consolidated and integrated, it takes on additional functions, especially defensive functions.

Kernberg's position on psychic structure contrasts with Freudian concepts of ego. Freud explained the emergence and differentiation of the ego from the id by processes of repression, while Kernberg believes the ego is built and organized from the process of internalization of interpersonal relationships. Kernberg disagrees with Klein and Fairbairn, who hold that the ego exists from birth, although Kernberg suggests the presence of forerunners of the ego; that is, various functions, such as perception and memory traces.

Identification

Identification is a second level and higher form of internalization than introjection. This process appears late in the child's first year and continues during the second year. Identification, the taking in of social roles, appears only when the child has matured enough perceptually and cognitively to recognize the role aspects in interactions with people. The notion of role suggests the presence of a socially recognized function that is being carried out by the object or by both participants in an interaction (Kernberg, 1976, p. 30). For example, when a mother helps a child get dressed, she is both initiating and actualizing the role of parent—to help, to teach, and so on.

Identification presupposes an actual object relation in which the individual experiences him or herself as the subject interacting with another person. The affective coloring of the interaction, which is of a libidinal or aggressive nature and links the subject and object, is the primary reason for the internalization of this relationship (Kernberg, 1976, p. 76).

Ego Identity

Ego identity is the third and highest level in the internalization processes. Ego identity refers to the ego in its synthetic function as organizing its identifications and introjects.

The ego organizing at this stage results in a consolidation of ego structures so that the child has a sense of the continuity of the self, the self being the self-image that is organized from introjections and identifications (Kernberg, 1976, p. 32). At this stage, internalized object relations, according to Kernberg, are also organized into the representational world, which internally represents the external world. This internal world of object representations, ranging from unconscious to conscious phantasies, does not perfectly correspond to the actual world of real people. It is an approximation, strongly colored by earlier object images. Primitive object images remain repressed and unmodified in the unconscious, while most object images are integrated into higher level ego and superego structures, such as the ego ideal and autonomous ego functions (Kernberg, 1976, p. 33).

Identity formation means that early primitive identifications are replaced over time by selective identifications in which only those aspects of the object relation that are in harmony with individual identity formation are internalized. These partial identifications are of people who are loved and admired in a realistic way.

Developmental Stages

Kernberg believes that internal object relations develop into structures of id, ego, and superego, as outlined above. Kernberg also views structure formation as a series of developmental stages. Failures in normal development can result in various forms of mental illness or psychopathology.

Stage One

The earliest stage of development covers the first month of life. Very little occurs during this period that influences the building up of personality structures. Then begins the gradual formation of undifferentiated self representations and object representations (Kernberg, 1976, p. 60). Undifferentiated means that the self representations and object representations are fused with each other, that there is no sense of distinction between the self and any objects. Problems at this stage would show up in the lack of development of the self and object representations and the consequent inability to establish a normal symbiotic relationship with the mother. Such inability to establish a close relationship with the mother is very serious and is called an *autistic psychosis.*

Stage Two

The second stage runs from the infant's second month to approximately the sixth or eighth month. Characteristic of this stage is building up and consolidating "good" units of self-object representations. Pleasurable, gratifying experiences that the infant has with its mother during this stage construct images of self that are fused with images of the object (mother), and these images are linked by feelings of pleasure. These are "good," undifferentiated self-object units around which the ego will form.

At the same time that pleasurable experiences build up good self-object representations, frustrating experiences build up "bad" self-object representations with painful, frustrating, and angry feelings. At this stage, the "good" representations and the "bad" representations are kept apart from each other by primitive mechanisms of splitting.

Stage two ends when the self-image becomes differentiated from the object image within the "good" self-object representation. That is, these self-object images differentiate into an image of self that is separate from the image of object; they occasionally re-fuse into a self-object image and then again differentiate. The "bad" self-object units do not yet differentiate at this stage, and the infant pushes them to the periphery of psychological experience where they are the first sense of an "out there," or a world "outside the self."

This second stage of Kernberg's developmental stages overlaps part of Margaret Mahler's symbiotic stage.

Stage Three

The third stage, roughly covering the same period as the separation and individuation stage as described by Margaret Mahler, begins between 6 and 8 months and reaches its completion between 18 and 36 months. This stage starts when the self representation finishes differentiating from the object representation within the core "good" self-object representation and includes the start of the differentiation of the self representation from the object representation within the core "bad" self-object representation (Kernberg, 1976, p. 64). In short, this stage is marked by the differentiation of self from object representations, of delimiting self from nonself.

The "good" and "bad" self representations and object representations coexist separately at first and then gradually integrate. Stage three ends with the eventual integration of "good" and "bad" self representations into an integrated self-concept. The integration of "good" and "bad" object representations into a "total" object representation also occurs, which is the achievement of object constancy.

The use of splitting, keeping separate the "good" from the "bad," is normal at this stage. This is the way the child protects the ideal, good relationship with the mother from contamination with the frustrating and bad. There is a gradual lessening in the use of splitting by the normal child, whereas borderline personalities continue to make use of splitting to protect their weak egos from disorganizing anxiety.

The differentiation of self-image from object image contributes to the establishment of stable ego boundaries, which continue to be fragile and fluctuating. There is not yet an integrated and full sense of self or an integrated concept of other persons, so this is still a stage of partial object relations. Fixation at this stage or a pathological regression to it determines the borderline personality organization.

Stage Four

Stage four (Kernberg, 1976, p. 67) begins in the latter part of the third year and lasts through the oedipal period, which ends approximately in the sixth year. This stage overlaps Mahler's practicing, rapprochement, and object constancy subphases.

Characteristic of this stage is the integration of partial images into whole images. "Good" images of the child's self with pleasurable feelings and "bad" images of the self with aggressive feelings coalesce into a whole self system. Similarly, "bad" representations of the object with angry feelings come together with "good" images of the object (the mother) with pleasurable feelings; the child now has a whole and more realistic representation of the mother.

The ego, superego, and id are consolidated as intrapsychic structures during this period. Ego identity—the overall organization of identifications and introjects—is established during the fourth stage. The inner world of object representations becomes more organized and understood; the world of brothers and sisters and aunts and uncles begins to make some sense to the child.

The mechanism of repression now becomes mainly a defensive operation of the ego. From this point on, repression separates the id from the ego, and Kernberg has said that the id as a psychic structure comes into existence only at this stage. This formulation implies a common matrix or source from which ego and id develop (Kernberg, 1976, p. 69). For Kernberg, then, the structure of the ego seems to precede the structure of the id, which radically reverses the classical psychoanalytic sequence of the id existing prior to the ego. Kernberg's reversal of this sequence comes from his emphasis on object relations and the importance of the environment for the formation of the structure of the ego. Some ego functioning needs to be present to relate to objects in the environment.

As repression becomes more common and the id becomes more organized, the primitive elements that once had access to the child's consciousness are repressed and kept in the unconscious part of the id. Thus, the intense feelings (possibly uncontrolled temper tantrums and primitive clinging feelings), as well as unacceptable internalized object relations, are repressed, and this further contributes to the integration of the id. These disturbing units of self-image and object image, with their disruptive feelings, remain in the id or the unconscious unless they return to consciousness during a profound regression or a collapse of the psychic structures, such as in a "nervous breakdown."

Also during stage four comes the integration of the superego as an independent intrapsychic structure. Kernberg follows Jacobson in proposing a three-level schema for the development of the superego. The earliest superego structures derive from the internalization of hostile, unrealistic object images. These sadistic forerunners of the superego correspond to Klein's primitive, sadistic superego and Fairbairn's anti-libidinal object. If a child has experienced intense early frustration and aggression, the child will have more intense and more sadistic superego forerunners (Kernberg, 1976, p. 71). A second layer of superego structures is from the ego's ideal self and ideal object representations. The child's superego has to integrate these wishful, magical, pleasurable representations with the more aggressive, sadistic forerunners. This integration modifies and tones down these absolute, phantastic primitive ideals and the sadistic forerunners. It parallels the process that the ego has already begun of modifying and integrating the primitive libidinal and aggressive qualities of internalized object relations. The third level of superego formation is the internalization and integration of the more realistic demands and prohibitions of parents during the oedipal period.

Stage Five

Kernberg's fifth stage starts in later childhood with the completion of the integration of the superego (Kernberg, 1976, p. 72). The opposition or conflict between the superego and ego lessens. As the superego becomes integrated, it fosters further integration and consolidation of ego identity. Ego identity continues to evolve by a process of reshaping experiences with external objects in light of internal object representations, and these internal object representations are reshaped in light of experiences with actual persons. These experiences further reshape the self-concept.

Pathology, Including Borderline Disorders

Making use of his concepts of structure and development, Kernberg proposes a classification of character pathology with three levels of severity. Psychic organization can be at a higher, intermediate, or lower level. At each level Kernberg looks at drives, structures, object relations, and developmental progress.

Kernberg builds his classification on several assumptions. He assumes that drives have three possible levels of instinctual fixation: higher, intermediate, and lower levels. The higher level implies that the person has normal sexual feelings, while at the lower level the person has pregenital sadistic and masochistic feelings (Kernberg, 1976, p. 141). As for the structure of the superego, Kernberg assumes that the superego can be at higher, intermediate, and lower levels of organization. At the intermediate and lower levels, the superego is harsh and excessively strict. As for object relations, again Kernberg assumes there are three levels—higher and intermediate levels, and a lower level where internalized object relations are pathological. Object relations at this lower level are partial rather than total. This means that the person will relate only to partial aspects of other people and that relationships will have an intense all-or-nothing quality.

At the *higher level*, a typical individual has a well-integrated but punishing superego. Although sexual and aggressive drives are at an appropriate developmental level, they are partly inhibited. An individual at this level typically has an integrated ego with a stable self-concept. Defenses tend to be repressive in nature. As for object relations, stable object representations with a variety of feelings allow for deep involvement with others. Among the disturbances falling under this category are hysterical, depressive-masochistic, and obsessive-compulsive characters.

Individuals at an *intermediate level* of character organization have reached a genital level of libidinal development, but pregenital and oral conflicts tend to emerge. Patients usually have harsh superegos, and mood swings result from the poor regulation of the ego by the superego. Contradictory demands on the ego result from the poor integration of the superego. Defenses are less inhibitory, although repression is still the main defense. Object relations allow for relationships with people, and there is the ability to tolerate the ambivalences and conflicts that usually occur in relationships. Some narcissistic and sadomasochistic personalities and personalities who have stable sexual deviations can be found at this level.

The *lower level* of character pathology includes, among others, antisocial personalities, chaotic and impulsive character disorders, and some borderline and prepsychotic personalities. Individuals at this level have sadistic superegos with impaired capacity for feeling concern and guilt. Such individuals may lack good boundaries between ego and superego and tend to be impulsive, often failing at work and relationships because of ego weakness and a lack of integration. Splitting and dissociative defenses are characteristic. The lack of a solid self-concept allows for an inner world peopled with caricatures of the good or horrible aspects of other people. Individuals may have an inner view of themselves as a chaotic mixture of shameful and exalted images, resulting in a confused identity. Excessive pregenital aggression impairs such individuals' abilities to integrate contradictory good and bad self-images and object images. Their sexual feelings are often mixed with pregenital sadistic and masochistic needs. Their need to get close to someone or have sex with someone is mixed with cruel phantasies or feelings of wanting to be punished.

In this lower level, Kernberg includes infantile and antisocial personalities, chaotic and impulsive character disorders, patients with multiple sexual deviations, prepsychotic and schizoid personalities, and borderline disorders. Borderline personalities have the ability to differentiate between self and object representations, and in this way differ from psychotics, who are unable to perceive reality accurately, a skill that depends on the ability to differentiate between self and object representations (Kernberg, 1976, p. 148).

Borderline Disorders

Kernberg describes the *borderline personality organization* as belonging to individuals who have a stable but disturbed form of ego structure. The disturbed characteristics of this group differ from the less serious pathology of the neuroses and the more serious pathology of the psychoses. Thus, this group of individuals occupies a borderline area between neurosis and psychosis (Kernberg, 1975, p. 3).

Kernberg distinguishes the borderline personality organization from borderline states, "as if" personalities, and transitory psychotic states. He uses *borderline* to identify a stable organization of disturbed characteristics. In his clarification of these characteristics, Kernberg lists: (1) specific patterns of symptoms, (2) typical causes and dynamics,

(3) stable structural issues determined only by careful analysis, (4) typical disturbances of internal object relations, and (5) typical defenses.

Specific Patterns of Symptoms

Borderline personalities present symptoms similar to many neuroses and character disorders. For example, the borderline personality may show such signs of ego weakness as chronic, diffuse anxiety and the lack of impulse control. These eruptions of impulses make the borderline person uncomfortable outside the impulsive episodes, but he or she is acceptable and even pleasant during the impulsive episode. The borderline may exhibit multiple neurotic signs, such as irrational fears and obsessive-compulsive thoughts and feelings. These patients may present sexual deviations in which several sexually perverse trends coexist, such as promiscuity coexisting with sadistic urges. Classical prepsychotic personality features, such as schizoid behavior or paranoid ways of thinking, may also be present.

Causes and Dynamics

Borderline personalities usually have a history of extreme frustration and intense aggression during the first few years of life (Kernberg, 1975, p. 41). When a young child has to endure frustrations that then make the child intensely angry and aggressive, the child tries to protect itself by projecting this aggression back onto the parents, distorting the child's image of his or her parents. The mother is seen as potentially dangerous and threatening, and so the child hates and fears her and often the father as well. This distortion produces two related results: first, a mother-father image that is threatening and dangerous, and second, later sexual relationships that are viewed as dangerous.

When a young child still at a preoedipal level (2 to 5 years old) struggles with intense aggression and hate, it influences the instinctual struggles of the child. The presence of early aggression prompts the premature emergence of oedipal or heterosexual strivings as an attempted solution. But this solution usually fails, and a compromise solution that usually involves disturbed sexual patterns and poor interpersonal relationships often develops.

In other words, the child tries to cope with its rage and fears by premature sexual and oedipal strivings. In boys, the premature strivings take the form of attempts to overcome dependency, but such attempts usually fail because of fear and the prohibitions against sexual feelings for the mother. The boy may develop an image of a dangerous, castrating mother. Some males may develop homosexuality as a solution for gratifying their needs and dependency without involving such women as their mothers. Other males attempt to gratify their needs by unconsciously adapting a narcissistic and promiscuous lifestyle in which they get revenge on their frustrating mothers through shallow relationships with women.

Some girls, whose early dependency needs have been frustrated by their "dangerous" mothers, may develop premature genital strivings for their fathers. As substitute gratifications, these attempts fail because the father's image may be contaminated by aggression from the mother and from rage projected by the child onto the father. Such a girl attempts a heterosexual defense against her own dependency and so flies into shallow promiscuity as a way of denying her needs, dependency, and guilt over oedipal strivings (Kernberg, 1975, p. 42). Some girls' solutions involve becoming emotional victims, since they are reinforcing the masochism that comes from internalized mother images making inner, punishing demands.

Others seek a solution that involves a renunciation of heterosexuality. In other words, seeking gratification of needs from an idealized mother image that is split off from the dangerous mother image, they seek gratification from female relationships where there is the presence of this idealized "partial" mother figure.

Disturbed Object Relations

In borderline personality organizations, early internalized object relationships persist in a "nonmetabolized" or nonintegrated form. These fragmented or undigested object relationships resemble split-off aspects of the self. These dissociated parts of the self result from a failure of the synthesizing process, which modifies and integrates early contradictory feelings. Each dissociated ego segment is a unit of self-image, object image, and a feeling that was active when that particular internalization took place (Kernberg, 1975, p. 34). What kept normal integration from taking place during childhood was the presence of intense feelings of aggression or frustration.

Borderline personalities fail to integrate loving and hateful images of self and objects because of the presence of this intense early aggression. Unable to synthesize contradictory self-image and object image, this type of personality cannot integrate self-concept and establish whole object relations and object constancy around a solid core of an ego. As a result, they have part object relationships; that is, relationships that are intense and changeable. The "good" representations struggle with the "all bad" representations of self and object, and these persons make use of splitting and other primitive defense mechanisms to preserve their weak and poorly organized egos. This helps explain the intense and distorting nature of borderline transferences in therapy (Kernberg, 1976, p. 162).

Structural Issues

For diagnostic purposes, Kernberg analyzes the personality structures of his patients. He considers the ego as an overall structure that integrates substructures and functions, Kernberg is particularly looking for evidence of primitive ways of relating and signs of ego weakness in his patients. From the point of view of structure, the borderline exhibits ego weaknesses in the form of a lack of anxiety tolerance, a lack of impulse control, and a lack in ability to sublimate impulses. The borderline manifests primary process thinking, especially in unstructured situations where primary process appears in the form of primitive phantasies (Kernberg, 1975, p. 24). The borderline's part object relations, with "all good" and "all bad" self-image and object image, interfere with superego integration because these representations evoke phantastic ideals of perfection rather than realistic goals and moderate ego ideals.

Defenses

The characteristic defense of the borderline is splitting. The clinical manifestation of splitting may be the alternate expression of opposite sides of a conflict with a blank denial and lack of concern for the contradictions in behavior and internal experience. Another manifestation of splitting might be the selective lack of impulse control in critical situations where primitive impulses break through. Thus, feelings about a particular person may swing from "all good" to "all bad" and then abruptly reverse. The oscillation between contradictory self-concepts is also due to splitting.

Splitting appears in combination with primitive idealization (that is, seeing external objects as totally good) and early forms of projection. For example, in projective identification the projection of an individual's own impulse or aggression onto another occurs, followed by the attempt to control the threatening object and keep it from attacking. This happens because of a lack of differentiation between self-image and object image.

Therapy

On the basis of his theoretical framework, Kernberg makes specific suggestions for treating borderline personality disorders.

Kernberg uses the term *borderline personality organization* because he feels that these patients present a stable pathological personality organization rather than mere transitory states between neurosis and psychosis. He finds that supportive therapy with these patients often fails and that their characteristic defenses prevent establishment of a good working relationship with them.

Kernberg's treatment modifies standard psychoanalytic techniques and necessitates that the therapist be actively involved in several areas of treatment. Kernberg proposes that the therapist: (1) investigate and point out the negative transference that the patient has toward the therapist, which hinders the working relationship with the therapist; (2) confront the patient's pathological defenses that weaken the ego and reduce reality-testing; and (3) structure the therapeutic situation in such a way as to stop the patient's acting out of transference feelings (Kernberg, 1975, p. 71).

In particular, Kernberg calls attention to the development of the transference psychosis, which he believes is a characteristic problem in working with borderline patients. A *transference psychosis* is the premature activation in the transference of very early conflict-laden object relations. This implies different ego states that are dissociated from each other, with each ego state representing an intense and usually troubled relationship. The transference psychosis is the reproduction of unconscious and disturbed object relationships and conflicts from childhood along with elaborate defenses to protect the self from the threatening past interpersonal relationships (Kernberg, 1975, p. 89).

In therapy, the typical neurotic only gradually regresses and slowly develops a transference that causes only a slight distortion of the actual relationship with the therapist. By contrast, the borderline patient tends to rapidly develop a transference that often seems chaotic and is predominantly negative. The regression of therapy causes a rapid activation of nonintegrated, primitive object relations.

One aspect of this negative transference is *projective identification*, a primitive form of projection where the patient externalizes aggressive self-image and object image and continues to relate to the object in an effort to control the object that is now feared because of this projection (Kernberg, 1975, p. 80). In the negative transference, projective identification is typically manifested as an intense distrust and fear of the therapist, who is experienced as attacking the patient. The patient might try to control the therapist in a sadistic or overpowering way. The patient may be aware of his or her own hostility but more likely feels that he or she is just responding to the aggression of the therapist. The patient's aggression evokes a countertransference aggression in the therapist. "It is as if the patient were pressing the aggressive part of himself onto the therapist and as if the countertransference represented the emergence of this part of the patient from within the therapist" (Kernberg, 1975, p. 80).

From an object relations framework, what seems to be occurring in the transference of the borderline is the activation of primitive object relations units. What is projected onto the therapist is a primitive, sadistic parent image, and the patient experiences him or herself as a frightened, attacked child. Moments later, this may shift so that the patient might experience him or herself as the stern, sadistic parent and the therapist as the guilty, frightened child (Kernberg, 1975, p. 81).

The intense aggression of the patient, the distortions of reality in the relationship with the therapist, the countertransference—all make it hard to establish a working relationship between therapist and patient. (A working relationship or therapeutic alliance occurs when the observing ego of the patient can be pulled into the process of cooperating in the therapeutic work on the troubled aspects of the self.) Kernberg argues for directly dealing with the negative transference of its projections for the sake of enlarging the scope of the observing ego and for the sake of broadening the conflict-free sphere of the ego. Part of the therapist's task is to call attention to the discrepancy between the patient's view of the therapist as an archaic phantasy object and the therapist as a real object (Kernberg, 1975, p. 82).

What further makes the transference difficult in the borderline patient is the weakness of the ego and occasional problems in differentiating self from object. This produces a confusion in the patient as to what is within him or herself and what is outside or belonging to another. The patient can experience a strong enough breakdown of ego boundaries and a subsequent loss of reality-testing to make the patient feel as if he or she and the therapist were interchanging personalities. This would be the terrifying transference psychosis in which the patient cannot distinguish phantasy from reality, the past from the present. "Clinically, this appears as the patient experiencing something such as, 'Yes, you are right in thinking that I see you as I saw my mother, and that is because she and you are really identical'" (Kernberg, 1975, p. 84).

In the transference psychosis, where the transference object and the therapist become identical to the patient, and where there may be delusions or hallucinations, the patient continues to be able to function unimpaired outside the treatment setting. Within treatment, the patient indeed sees the therapist as the father or mother or some dissociated self representation.

Along with active interventions in the negative transference and in pathological defenses such as projective identification, the therapist also has to control the patient's acting out transference feelings in the treatment setting. *Acting out transference feelings* means that the patient puts feelings for the therapist into behavior rather than words. Thus, a patient might yell at a therapist and gratify aggressive needs that would actually be a form of resistance. The therapist must establish firm structures in the therapeutic situation, and thus help block acting out, which aids the patient in differentiating self from the therapist.

Case Study

Kernberg's description of therapy with one of his patients illustrates some of his theoretical and treatment insights (1980, pp. 158–162). He believes that treatment involves structural intrapsychic change in a context of working through primitive transference paradigms (1980, p. 206). These transference paradigms manifest themselves in a patient relating to the therapist as a partial object, perhaps, or as some figure from the past. Part of the resistance to therapeutic change involves shifting and reversing roles to avoid integrating feelings and ego states. An ego state is a way of relating to someone along with the feelings relevant to that way of relating.

Kernberg's patient in this case study was a white, middle-aged male who was experiencing marital difficulties and problems in his work. The patient was occasionally impotent, and in his occasional dealings with prostitutes, he acted out sadistic sexual behavior. The patient's father was a powerful figure whom the patient feared. His mother was submissive, complained often, and evoked guilt.

In therapy, Kernberg was able to explore the patient's submission to his wife and his fear of displeasing her. He described how she set domestic rules, demanded quiet, and interfered with his work. The patient began to see how his resentment of his wife was displaced into his sadistic behavior with prostitutes. He came to understand that his sadistic relations with these prostitutes represented an identification with his sadistic father. It is likely that his submission to his wife was also a playing out of his partial identification of his submissive mother in her relationship with the patient's father.

In sessions with Kernberg, the patient was verbally aggressive and often reacted to Kernberg's therapeutic interpretation with put-downs that made Kernberg feel impotent and insecure. When this happened, Kernberg at times felt himself to be in an insecure role, similar to the one the patient felt with his nagging wife (and his powerful father). Kernberg suggested that the patient was repeating with Kernberg the relationship with his wife, only with a reversal of roles so that the patient was the demanding and interfering one. The patient changed his mood and moved into a different ego state, one of fear and vivid associations. He remembered how Kernberg had once blown his nose forcefully in a session and this struck the patient as "brutally uninhibited." The patient felt that Kernberg would be powerful and able to stand up to the nagging wife and the patient's boss very effectively, while the patient always played the nice, compliant boy. Kernberg notes how he experienced a shift in feelings in himself so that he felt powerful in contrast to the insecure helplessness he had felt in previous sessions. It was as if he now represented the patient's powerful father forcing the patient into submission, and that the patient was engaged in pathetic efforts to be like Kernberg, to be as powerful and ruthless as when he was engaged in his sadistic relations with prostitutes.

This case study suggests some of the rapid shifts experienced in therapy by both the patient and the therapist. As the patient plays out his internal object relationship with the therapist, the therapist will often experience some of the feelings of this relationship as the patient projects an object representation onto the therapist. There may be rapid shifts as a patient alternates between identifying with the self representation and the object representation. In this case, the patient sometimes felt like the helpless boy and projected onto Kernberg the representation of being the powerful, nagging object; at other times the roles were reversed.

Object relations theory can yield insight into clinical situations where there are primitive object relations in the transference, especially with borderline personalities. The patient can shift or regress rapidly from one level of relationship to another. The task of the therapist is to help the patient work through these primitive ways of relating so that ultimately the patient can begin dealing with the therapist as a real object and not merely as a transference object.

Assessment and Critique of Kernberg

Drawing upon Freud, Klein, Jacobson, and Fairbairn, Otto Kernberg has attempted to integrate into one theoretical framework ideas drawn from object relations theory, developmental theory, and traditional Freudian instinct theory. His synthesis is consistent within itself, is exciting for its lavish comprehensiveness, and is influential in current discussions of borderline and narcissistic pathology, although his complex program for delineating the borderline personality organization implies diagnostic certitude and clarity of categorization that is not very often attainable (cf. Masterson, 1981; Meissner, 1984).

At its core, however, Kernberg's theory is not a synthesis of drive theory and object relations theory. Although he claims to be a drive theorist, an understanding of his writings indicates his differences with this theory and how he often reshapes drive theory to fit his own notions. Kernberg uses the traditional terms but believes the object precedes the drive. Essentially, he sees people as social by nature rather than primarily instinctual, as Freud suggested by his emphasis on the id. The importance that Kernberg gives to object relations alters the structural model so that ego is primary and processes such as splitting take on more importance than repression. Kernberg believes structure is formed from relational experiences and not from the id's efforts to deal with reality. It is no surprise, then, that traditional Freudian theorists regard him as revisionist, as radically altering the drive model by retreating from an emphasis on instincts and the centrality of the oedipal conflict (Calef & Weinshel, 1979; Heimann, 1966; Klein & Tribich, 1981; Sternbach, 1983). Freudian theorists see Kernberg's ambitious efforts to conceptualize the early building blocks of personality as a departure from the traditional structural model as well as too speculative and too often based on inferences rather than careful research in preverbal developmental periods.

References

Brody, S. (1982). Psychoanalytic theories of infant development and its disturbances: A critical evaluation. *Psychoanalytic Quarterly, 51*, 526–597.

Calef, V., & Weinshel, M. (1979). The new psychoanalysis and psychoanalytic revisionism: Book review essay on *Borderline conditions and pathological narcissism. Psychoanalytic Quarterly, 48*, 470–491.

Greenberg, J. R., & Mitchell, S. A. (1983). *Object relations in psychoanalytic theory.* Cambridge: Harvard University Press.

Grotstein, J. (1981). *Splitting and projective identification.* New York: Aronson.

Heimann, P. (1966). Comment on Dr. Kernberg's paper. *International Journal of Psycho-Analysis, 47*, 254–260.

Horner, A. J. (1979). *Object relations and the developing ego in therapy.* New York: Aronson.

Kernberg, O. (1972). Early ego integration and object relations. *Annales of the New York Academy of Science, 193*, 233–314.

Kernberg, O. (1975). *Borderline conditions and pathological narcissism.* New York: Aronson.

Kernberg, O. (1976). *Object relations theory and clinical psychoanalysis.* New York: Aronson.

Kernberg, O. (1980). *Internal world and external reality.* New York: Aronson.

Klein, M., & Tribich, D. (1981). Kernberg's object-relations theory: A critical evaluation. *International Journal of Psycho-Analysis, 62*, 27–43.

Masterson, J. F. (1981). *The narcissistic and borderline disorders.* New York: Brunner/Mazel.

Meissner, W. W. (1984). *The borderline spectrum: Differential diagnosis and developmental issues.* New York: Aronson.

Sternbach, O. (1983). Critical comments on object relations theory. *Psychoanalytic Review, 70*, 403–422.

© *Chapter Nine*

Heinz Kohut:
Self Psychology
and Narcissism

Introduction

Heinz Kohut, born in 1913 in Vienna, received his medical degree in 1938 from the University of Vienna. He came to the United States and spent most of his active professional life at the Chicago Institute for Psychoanalysis, where he was a training analyst and teacher. He served as president of the American Psychoanalytic Association from 1964 to 1965. Despite these orthodox analytic credentials, Kohut's later writings aroused intense reactions and criticism from the psychoanalytic community as his theories moved beyond the traditional psychoanalytic drive model.

With many similarities to the work of Fairbairn, Winnicott, and Mahler, Kohut's work shares with object relations theories an emphasis on relationship and a retreat from the Freudian drive model. This retreat from the drive model and his ideas about the self aroused protests from more traditional writers. His psychology of the self stakes out new theoretical and clinical ground, different from the object relations theories, and points psychoanalysis in a major new direction. Kohut developed his ideas about the self over a long period of time and continuously revised his theories. By 1977, he no longer spoke of libido at all and only infrequently referred to ego and superego.

Although in disagreement with many aspects of classical psychoanalytic theory, Kohut did not reject the theory outright but favored its use within clearly defined areas, such as the neurotic conflicts of intact personalities. Because of the changing styles of family interactions, however, he felt that new problems had arisen and that many areas of the psyche were not illuminated by the classical model

(1977, pp. xviii, 269). His psychology of the self explains certain phenomena unexplained by the classical drive model, especially—and foremost for Kohut—the area of narcissism. His contribution to the study of narcissism has been significant. Like Otto Kernberg, Kohut widened the scope of psychoanalysis by applying its understanding to areas broader than neurosis (cf. London, 1985, p. 96).

Rather than replacing the classical psychoanalytic drive model, however, Kohut proposed *two* models. The first proposed a broad psychology of the self, putting the self at the center. His substantial contribution was here. More narrowly, he proposed a second approach that retained the basic traditional model but with slight extensions, with the self a structure contained in the ego (Kohut, 1977, p. xv), similar to the model developed by Edith Jacobson and similar to concepts accepted by contemporary American classical psychoanalytic theory.

This chapter will contrast Kohut's models with the classical model; define his key concepts; examine his theories on normal development of the cohesive self, pathology of the self, and therapy; present a case study and an assessment and critique of Kohut.

Kohut and the Classical Drive Model

Kohut's formulations proceeded largely from his analytic work with patients with narcissistic personality disorders. As a scientific method, he used observations based on an introspective and empathic immersion in the inner life of his patients. Because the subject matter of psychoanalysis is complex mental states, Kohut said its scientific methodology could not be coldly objective and far from the experience of the patient. Kohut therefore formulated his theories to explain the data gained from an empathic, active involvement with his patients' experiences.

The classical drive model views the neurotic patient as having an intact structure, with structure understood in terms of id, ego, and superego with all their various adaptive and defensive functions. Neurosis is a conflict between relatively intact structures. Thus, the classical Freudian drive model understands pathology in terms of repressed, unresolved conflicts of an oedipal nature. Successful therapy means achieving relative freedom from conflict over instinctual involvements (Kohut, 1977, p. 2).

In contrast, narcissism and disorders of the self imply that the very central structures of the personality are defective. Kohut explained narcissism as involving childhood-acquired defects in the psychological structure of the self and with the buildup of secondary defensive or compensatory structures (1977, p. 3). Successful therapy involves healing the deficits by acquiring new structures. If drive experiences and instincts are problematic, they tend to occur as the self disintegrates when it is unsupported.

Key Concepts

Narcissism

Freud (1914/1957) described narcissism from the point of view of the drive model and libido. Narcissism thus involves a withdrawal of instinctual energy from external objects and an investment of libido in the ego. This investment in the ego implies that the person is unable to love or relate with others and is self-absorbed. The classical psychoanalytic model regards persons with narcissistic disorders as nonanalyzable because they are unable to invest in a relationship, especially a therapeutic one. The establishment, interpretation, and resolution of transferences in the analytic situation constitutes traditional psychoanalytic treatment.

Freud (1914/1957, p. 109) compared narcissism to a sleeping or ill person who withdraws all emotional investment from external things, with the result that such a person is indifferent to all that is outside him or herself, since all the energy and attention is focused on the self.

Freud's model, a drive and object model, essentially sees narcissism as pathological, with the exception of primary narcissism when the ego has an early sense of omnipotence which the growing child gradually transforms into object love by cathecting an object. The person who has the self as a love object is narcissistic.

Heinz Hartmann (1964, p. 127) changed the definition of narcissism so the self rather than the ego was the target or object of libido. Thus, Hartmann's definition of normal narcissism is the libidinal investment of the self. This preserved the drive model but raised more problems by introducing the concept of self. Edith Jacobson (1964, p. 19), building from Hartmann, spoke of narcissism as a libidinal investment of the *representation* of the self.

Kohut altered Hartmann's definition by changing the notion of libido. He said that narcissism is defined not by the *target* of the instinctual or libidinal investment but by the *nature* or *quality* of the instinctual or libidinal charge (1971, p. 26). Self-aggrandizement and idealization characterize narcissistic libido. By 1977, Kohut no longer spoke of libido and replaced the traditional instinctual understanding of narcissism with a new theoretical understanding.

Persons who invest others with narcissistic libido, Kohut said, are experiencing those others *narcissistically*—that is, as selfobjects. To a narcissistic person, a selfobject is an object or person undifferentiated from the individual who serves the needs of the self. The narcissistic person has phantasized a control over others similar to the way an adult has control over his or her own body (Kohut, 1971, p. 27). Kohut's theories help explain the phenomena of narcissistic patients who do not necessarily withdraw interest from objects in the external world but are unable to rely on their own inner resources and have therefore created intense attachments with others (Teicholz, 1978, p. 836).

While Kohut's work in the early 1970s still used the traditional terms of the drive model, by 1977 he had explicitly moved beyond the drive model, which he now claimed was inadequate to explain certain clinical phenomena (1977, pp. 128, 224).

While traditional psychoanalysis has looked upon narcissism as pathological, Kohut (1980b, p. 453) reformulated the concept of narcissism in such a way as to see how it played a role in psychological health. Freud regarded narcissism as the precursor to object love, which then replaced narcissism. Kohut believed that narcissism has its own line of development so that ultimately no individual becomes independent of selfobjects, but rather requires throughout life a milieu of empathically responding selfobjects in order to function (Kohut, 1980b, p. 454; 1980c, p. 477).

Self

Self is a difficult term to define and conceptualize, in part because many disciplines—theology, psychology, philosophy—approach it from different levels of experience and viewpoints. The particular method used by theorists to view and observe individuals gives a different vantage point and suggests a different way of defining the self (Shane & Shane, 1980, p. 27). Thus, an objective self would be derived from the data of systematic observation, such as in Margaret Mahler's studies. But Kohut (1980b, p. 452) found Mahler's formulations unsatisfactory because the mode of observation is objective and distant from the experience of the child. Kohut felt that a different self, one closer to experience, is revealed within the framework of the psychoanalytic situation because the method of observation is an empathic immersion in the person's inner life. He stressed a methodology of introspection and empathy by which an analyst obtains the data on which to base formulations about the self.

Psychoanalytic literature, however, has tried to clarify the self and which level of consciousness and experience the term refers to. For example, Hartmann (1964, p. 127) distinguished between the self as one's own person and the ego as one of the substructures of the personality. This allowed Edith Jacobson to further distinguish between the self as the person and the self as a self representation or an intrapsychic structure that originates from the ego and is clearly embedded in the ego" (1982, p. 900). This means that the libidinal investment of the self is the libidinal investment of the self representation. Kohut altered this use of terms in his discussion. He defined self narrowly and broadly, with the broad definition being used in his psychology of the self.

Only in Kohut's *narrow sense* of the term did he adhere to the traditional use of self, understanding it as a specific structure of the mind or personality; that is, as a self representation in the ego. The more common use of the term by Kohut was in a *broad sense*: "as the center of the individual's psychological universe" (1977, p. 311). This self cannot be known in its essence, only by means of introspection and by the empathic observation of psychological manifestations in other persons. The self, for Kohut, was not a concept, and he broadly defined the self more in terms of awareness and experience as "a unit, cohesive in space and enduring in time, which is the center of initiative and a recipient of impressions" (Kohut, 1977, p. 99). This makes the self the locus of relationships and an active agent performing functions that were traditionally ascribed to the ego. Kohut's concept of self allowed him to make less reference to the ego.

Kohut's theory describes how a rudimentary self emerges from relatedness with others in the environment, becoming a cohesive self. The rudimentary self has both an *object*, which is the idealized parent image, and a *subject*, the grandiose self. Gradually, the grandiose self becomes tamed and merged into an intact, cohesive personality. The maturing self of the child allows it to begin to see the idealized object as a separate object, and aspects of the idealized parent image become introjected as the superego (cf. 1971, p. 33).

Selfobject

Kohut (1971, p. xiv) defined selfobjects as those persons or objects that are experienced as part of the self or that are used in the service of the self to provide a function for the self. The child's rudimentary self merges with the selfobject, participates in its well-organized experience, and has its needs satisfied by the actions of the selfobject (Kohut, 1977, p. 87). The term *selfobject* only has meaning with regard to the experiencing person; it is not an objective person or a *true object* or a *whole object*.

Kohut's use of the term *object* differed from the standard psychoanalytic use, the difference resting on two bases: his developmental model, which emphasized normal narcissism rather than instincts, and his methodology, which strived to get close to experience by means of introspection and empathic observation rather than by distant objective observation. He used *selfobject* and *true object* to express the experiential qualities of object relations rather than the standard terms *part object* and *whole object* (Ornstein, 1978, p. 67). When the object is cathected with narcissistic libido—rather than object libido—it means that it is perceived or experienced as relating to the self as part of the self or in the service of the self, thus functioning as a selfobject (Ornstein, 1978, p. 68).

Transmuting Internalizations

Psychoanalysis usually struggles with the question of how psychic structures are built by using the concept of internalization. Object relations theorists, for example, speak of building up and organizing the inner world by taking in aspects of relationships in the form of psychic representations of the object (cf. Meissner, 1980).

Kohut spoke of a similar process of internalization, called *transmuting internalization*, by which aspects of the selfobject are absorbed into the child's self. Normal parents will occasionally fall short of or delay gratification of a child's needs, but the frustration is tolerable, not traumatic, and gratification is not overindulgent. This optimal frustration compels a child to take in aspects of the selfobject in the form of specific functions. The child withdraws some of its magical, narcissistic expectation from the selfobject and gains some particle of inner structure. The inner structure of the child then performs some function that the object previously performed for the child, such as comforting, mirroring, controlling tension, and the like (Kohut, 1971, pp. 50, 64). The transmuting part of transmuting internalization refers to the depersonalizing shift from the personality of the object, which performs the function, to the function itself.

Normal Development of the Cohesive Self

Kohut viewed development in terms of the self in relationship to selfobjects, not as a progressive sequence of steps. Not all elements of his theory, however, were fully worked out in a coherent way.

Kohut viewed development in terms of the self forming in a relationship, neither in isolation nor from drives. An infant is born into a human environment. The child does not yet have a self, but the parents act and respond to the child as if it already had a self. The child's self arises as a result of the relationship; that is, the interplay between the infant's innate potentials and the responsiveness of the adult selves or selfobjects. It is not totally unlike the intake of foreign proteins to build your own proteins (Kohut & Wolf, 1978, p. 416). A nuclear or core self is formed through the responsiveness of the selfobjects, similar to D. W. Winnicott's holding environment and the good-enough mother.

There are two main constituents of a nuclear self. One is the grandiose-exhibitionistic self that becomes established by relating to a selfobject that empathically responds to the child by approving and mirroring this grandiose self. The other constituent of the nuclear self is the child's idealized parental *imago*. This becomes established by relating to a selfobject that empathically responds to the child, by permitting and enjoying the child's idealization of the parent (Kohut, 1977, p. 185). Both constituents involve some form of ecstatic merging experience with the selfobject.

The grandiose self refers to the child's self-centered view of the world and its exuberant delight in being admired. (Kohut used *grandiose self* to replace a term he had previously used: *narcissistic self*.) The experience might be summarized as, "I am terrific, perfect; look at me!" The idealized parental imago is antithetical or contradictory to the grandiose self in that it implies someone else is perfect. But the child is cognitively too immature to notice and also experiences a merger with that idealized object. The experience of the idealized image might be expressed this way: "You are perfect, but I am a part of you."

The expectations of the environment, in the form of the parents, channel the emerging self into specific directions. Through countless repetitions, the selfobject empathically responds to the child's mirroring needs and idealizing needs; that is, aspects of the grandiose self that the child exhibits and aspects of the idealized image the child admires. The grandiose self responds to the acceptance and pleasure that the mirroring selfobject or parent provides.

Kohut implied two phases of this formation of the self. The first phase involves the formation of a rudimentary self by the processes of inclusion and exclusion of psychological structures. That is, the nuclear or core self experiences some archaic mental contents as belonging to the self, and other contents or experiences are assigned to the nonself and excluded. The next phase involves organizing and strengthening the increasingly cohesive self. This involves strengthening and ensuring the boundaries of the self. Failures on the part of the selfobject to mirror the growing self and to foster idealization can lead to the fragmentation of the self or the loss of vitality by the immature self (Tolpin, 1978, p. 174).

The primary factors contributing to the emergence of the self are the inborn potentials of the child and the empathic relationship between parent and child. The infant starts with no self but has its innate potential and the hopes and projections of the parents. The parents or selfobjects respond to the child's mirroring and idealizing needs. Nontraumatic failures in parental responsiveness give a push to the emergence of the nuclear self. The nuclear self emerges through a process of transmuting internalizations by which the selfobjects and their functions are replaced by a self and its functions (Kohut & Wolf, 1978, p. 416).

This self increases in its cohesiveness and integration, and gradually the risk of fragmentation recedes. In the healthy personality, the grandiosity of the self becomes modified and channeled into realistic pursuits. The transformed and integrated grandiosity supplies energy, ambition, and self-esteem (Kohut, 1971, p. 107). As the child regards the idealized object with increasing realism, the child withdraws the idealizing, narcissistic investment from the parental object. The idealized object or parental imago is introjected as an idealized superego, taking over the functions previously performed by the idealized object (Kohut, 1968/1978b, pp. 86, 89).

If childhood traumas and deprivations prevent the cohesive, narcissistic self from integrating into a healthy personality, then the grandiose self and the idealized object continue in an unaltered form and strive for the fulfillment of their archaic needs (Kohut, 1968/1978b, p. 87). The grandiose self and the idealized object can remain isolated from the rest of the growing psyche and cause disturbance by their archaic needs.

What is the timing of these developmental processes? The precursors of the self become organized into a cohesive self sometime during the latter part of the first year or the early part of the second year. The grandiose self and the idealized parental image are developmental phases that "probably correspond predominantly to the transitional period between a late part of the stage of symbiosis and an early part of the stages of individuation in Mahler's sense" (Kohut, 1971, p. 220). Once the cohesive self has emerged, there are the further relations with the self-object whereby the child strengthens the boundaries of the self by confronting the selfobject, by demarcating its self from the environment, by the "no" period, and so on (Wolf, 1980, pp. 123, 125).

Frustration and Psychic Structure

Frustration plays a central role in the building up of self structures. During the period of primary narcissism, the earliest developmental stage, the infant has a sense of omnipotence and perfection because of being merged with the mother. The mother's shortcomings, however, disturb the serenity and equilibrium of the child's narcissistic perfection. In response to the frustration of this narcissistic perfection, and preserve a part of the original experience of perfection, the child establishes a grandiose and exhibitionistic image of him or herself: the grandiose self. The child further attributes the perfection of the narcissistic period to an admired, omnipotent selfobject: the idealized parental image.

The grandiose self is a stage in development where everything pleasant and good is regarded as part of the infant, and all badness and imperfection is outside of the infant. The child attempts to maintain the original perfection, bliss, and omnipotence by assigning to the adult absolute power and perfection; that is, by forming an idealized parent imago (a psychic representation) (Kohut, 1966/1978a, p. 430).

But things cannot stay the same, blissful and undisturbed. Time and growth bring about minor, nontraumatic failures in the responsiveness of the parents, the mirroring and idealized selfobjects. Optimal failures imply a close, empathic bond that is the necessary context for the nontraumatic failures. The mother's attentions are imperfect or delayed. The child's psychic organization attempts to deal with the disturbance of narcissistic equilibrium by building up new structures, and gradually replacing the selfobject by means of inner structures that perform the functions that the selfobject once did (Kohut, 1966/1978c, p. 416). This process of structure formation is called transmuting internalization.

What is internalized is an aspect of the mature psychological structure of the adult selfobject. Born into an empathic and responsive human environment of selfobjects, the child's beginning self magically expects this environment to be in tune with his or her psychological needs and wishes. (Winnicott's good-enough mother, who is in tune with her child, comes to mind.) When the child becomes tense, the parent, serving as the selfobject, seems to respond in two steps. First, there is the merger response, and second, some action taken to satisfy the child's need. The adult serving as the selfobject assesses the child's need and situation, includes the child in its own adult psychological organization, and then takes action to restore the child's homeostatic balance. The child's needs threaten its own disintegration, and the selfobject responds by talking to the child, picking up the child, and creating a situation in which the child experiences a merger with the omnipotent selfobject. The child's rudimentary psyche shares in the more mature psychic organization of the selfobject as if it were the child's own. Gradually, bit by bit, the child takes on the comforting, tension-reducing tasks that had been done for the child. It is this type of optimal failure that leads to structure building by means of the transmuting internalization (Kohut, 1977, p. 86).

The two psychic configurations, the grandiose self and the idealized parental image, although antithetical to each other, coexist from their beginnings as mechanisms to preserve the primary narcissistic experience. Gradually, in normal conditions, the exhibitionism and grandiosity of the grandiose self become tamed and, once integrated into the structure of the personality, fill the emotional "tank" with resultant good feelings about the self, about the child's ambitions and enjoyment of activities (Kohut, 1971, p. 28). The idealized parental image also becomes integrated into the child's personality as the idealized superego, where it serves as a structure to regulate tension and provide idealism (Kohut, 1971, p. 28).

Bipolar Self

Kohut refers to two forms into which narcissism becomes differentiated: the grandiose self (healthy self-assertiveness vis-à-vis the mirroring selfobject) and the idealized parental image (healthy admiration for the idealized selfobject). It is as if there were a tension arc between these two poles, with ambitions clustering around the grandiose self and ideals clustering around the idealized image. The tension and psychological energy between the two poles of the self promote action, with the person being *driven* by his or her ambitions and *led* by his or her ideals (Kohut, 1977, p. 180).

These two basic constituents of the nuclear self that the child attempts to build have divergent aims, but the strength of the one can offset the weakness of the other (Kohut, 1977, p. 186). That is, children have two choices as they move toward the consolidation of the self. On the one hand, the child establishes his or her cohesive, grandiose-exhibitionistic self by the relation to the selfobject, which mirrors and approvingly responds to the child. On the other hand, the child establishes his or her cohesive, idealized parent imago by the relation to the selfobject parent, who responds empathically and permits and enjoys the child's idealization and merger. Often the development in the boy proceeds from the mother as the mirroring selfobject to the father as selfobject, providing the function of being idealized by the child. Of course, it often happens, especially in girls, that the child's developmental needs for selfobject are directed toward the same parent, such as the mother (Kohut, 1977, p. 185).

A Narcissistic Line of Development

Kohut argued for a line of development separate from Freud's conception of libidinal development (1971, p. 220). Freud understood libido to develop from autoeroticism via narcissism to object love. Kohut's independent line of development proceeded from autoeroticism vis narcissism to higher forms and transformations of narcissism. This fundamentally changed Freud's notion of narcissism by viewing narcissism in terms of different levels of maturity.

Normal adults have narcissistic needs and continue to need the mirroring of the self by selfobjects throughout life. The ongoing importance of selfobjects can be briefly illustrated by referring to the difficulties of dealing with a nonresponsive person. If we make efforts on behalf of someone who is indifferent and nonresponsive to us, we feel helpless and empty, with a lowered self-esteem and a narcissistic rage (cf. Kohut, 1971, p. 187n). We can also conceptualize adult love in terms of a person who serves as a selfobject, for love involves mutual mirroring and idealization, which enhances the self-esteem of both persons involved (Kohut, 1977, p. 122n).

Narcissism, then, continues throughout life, being transformed into various forms. Healthy narcissism is manifested in adulthood in such forms as creativity, humor, and empathy (Kohut, 1966/1978a, p. 446). It is the interplay of the narcissistic self (the grandiose-exhibitionistic self), the ego, and the superego (with its internalized ideals) that determines the characteristic flavor of a person's personality (Kohut, 1966/1978a, p. 443).

Development, in Kohut's view, involves more than drives. Kohut's developmental model shifts the emphasis from drives to the self. The traditional psychoanalytic emphasis on drives does not sufficiently explain why a child might be orally or anally fixated, for example. Kohut believed drives emerge when the fragile self is not responded to and begins to lose its cohesiveness and begins to fragment. Consider the child's self of the oral and anal periods. The need for food or the interest in feces are not primary. What the child needs is a selfobject who gives food, a selfobject who receives the fecal gift. The mother responds, not so much to a child's drives as to a self that is forming and is seeking confirmation through giving and receiving from the mirroring selfobject. The child experiences the mother's pride or rejection as the acceptance or rejection of his or her active self—not merely an acceptance or rejection of a drive (Kohut, 1977, pp. 76, 81).

Pathology of the Self

The Experience of Narcissism

Kohut was interested in staying close to a patient's subjective experience, and his model seeks to explicitly explain the narcissistic experience. The narcissistic perception of reality involves an omniscient, perfect selfobject and an archaic self that has unlimited power, grandiosity, and knowledge. In the narcissistic world, in which everyone and everything is an extension of the self or exists to serve the self, if there is any setback, it is experienced as a flaw in this perfect world. This flaw or narcissistic injury arouses an insatiable rage that cannot recognize the offender as separate from the self. The offender or enemy is experienced as a recalcitrant part of this extended self over which the narcissistic person had expected to have full control (Kohut, 1966/1978c, p. 644).

The narcissistic rage, then, responds to a self or object that does not measure up to the unrealistic expectations of the narcissistic person.

If the phantasy of absolute control is disturbed, such narcissistic persons experience intense shame and violent rage. Their self-esteem, their very self, depends on the unconditional availability of the mirroring self-object or idealized object that permits merger (Kohut, 1966/1978c, p. 645).

Narcissism is a stage of development, and the narcissistic tantrums of infants or young children are not inappropriate to their stage of development. But if the person gets stuck at this stage and the self becomes unmirrored and unintegrated with the rest of the growing self, certain experiences and behaviors become increasingly inappropriate and pathological. Let us look at some commonly occurring patterns of these pathological experiences (Kohut & Wolf, 1978, pp. 418–419).

The understimulated self, because of a lack of responsiveness to the self, lacks vitality. This person is boring and listless. A child might try to combat painful feelings of deadness by head-banging or compulsive masturbation. An adult might try to stimulate the self and cover the empty depression by promiscuous sex, gambling, or some other compulsive activity. The fragmenting self might manifest itself mildly in the normally well-dressed patient who arrives disheveled. To fragment is another way of speaking of structural regression, a shift to more archaic levels of mental organization. More serious fragmentation is experienced as a sense of coming apart, a loss of continuity in the self or loss of cohesiveness that might show up in a hypochondriacal brooding. The overstimulated self, because of inappropriate mirroring in the form of overstimulation or inappropriate stimulation, is flooded with unrealistic phantasies of greatness and power.

A person with an unmirrored, archaic self might be described as a mirror-hungry personality yearning for someone who will serve as a selfobject to confirm and feed the famished self. *Archaic* refers to normal preoedipal or preverbal behaviors that persist in an adult (London, 1985, p. 96). Such mirror-hungry persons are compelled to display themselves to attract the attention of others and to counteract their inner lack of self-esteem. Some narcissistic personalities may be ideal-hungry, searching for people they can admire for their power or beauty. These personalities experience themselves as worthwhile only if they are with such selfobjects. Because the inner void cannot be easily filled, narcissistic personalities continue their restless search. Kohut and Wolf (1978, p. 421) describe the alter ego personality as one who needs a relationship with someone who has the same appearance and values as themselves because they need such a selfobject to confirm the reality and existence of the self. Merger-hungry personalities, because of their impoverished selves and the fluid boundaries of the self, have trouble distinguishing their own thoughts and feelings from those of the person serving as their selfobject. Merger-hungry personalities demand the presence of the other person because they experience the other as their own self (Kohut & Wolf, 1978, p. 422). The reverse of this pattern is the contact-shunning personality who avoids social contact to deny an intense need of others.

Narcissistic and Self Disorders

Usually, patients with narcissistic personality disturbances initially present ill-defined symptoms. They may complain vaguely of problems at work, perverse sexual phantasies, or lack of interest in sex. Other presenting symptoms might include problems in forming relationships, hypochondriacal complaints, tendencies toward attacks of rage (Kohut, 1971, pp. 16, 23). As analysis proceeds, however, the most significant diagnostic feature emerges in the form of a narcissistic transference. It is the presence of the narcissistic transference that confirms a diagnosis of narcissistic or self disorder.

The narcissistic transference may be a mirroring transference or an idealizing transference. These transferences are the therapeutic revival or key developmental phases of childhood. The mirroring transference mobilizes the grandiose self. That is, the patient revives that early developmental stage in which a child tries to hold on to a part of primary narcissism by concentrating perfection on a grandiose self and assigning all imperfection to the outside (Kohut, 1968/1978b, p. 96).

The mirroring transference may manifest itself in a variety of ways. In the most primitive manifestation, the self-experience of the patient will include the therapist, almost as if the therapist did not have a separate existence. Kohut referred to this as merger through the extension of the grandiose self (1968/1978b, p. 96). In a less severe form of transference, the patient assumes that the therapist is like the patient himself—a process Kohut referred to as the *twinship* or *alter ego transference* (1968/1978b, p. 96). Kohut used the term *mirror transference* in a narrow sense for a third form of transference in which the patient cognitively knows the therapist is separate, but the therapist has importance only within the context of the patient's needs—that is, only insofar as the therapist fulfills the individual's need for approval and confirmation of the patient's grandiosity and exhibitionism (1971, p. 204).

The other kind of narcissistic transference, *idealizing transference*, mobilizes the idealized parent image. That is, the patient revives that early phase in which the child tries to hold onto global narcissistic perfection by assigning it to an archaic object, the idealized parent image, and by striving to stay merged with this object. To be separated from the perfect object is to be powerless and empty (Kohut, 1968/1978b, p. 88; 1971, p. 37).

Idealizing transferences can be developmentally more archaic or more mature, depending on the developmental place of fixation

(Kohut, 1971, p. 55). Once the idealizing transference is established (that is, when the individual's self-experience includes the idealized therapist), the patient feels powerful, capable, good (Kohut, 1971, p. 90). Any disturbance that seems to rob such patients of the idealized therapist can lessen their self-esteem and make them feel worthless.

The essence of the narcissistic self disorder is a defect in the structure of the self, the result of not completing the process of integrating the grandiose self and idealized object into the reality-oriented structure of the ego. The patient, of course, is not conscious or fully aware of his or her own pathology, which is why he or she initially presents only vague feelings of emptiness or of not being fully alive. The preconscious center of the disorder is the sense of the incomplete reality, foremost, of the self and, secondarily, of the external world (Kohut, 1971, p. 210). There is still an archaic, unmirrored, grandiose self and a narcissistically invested idealized object. These archaic, isolated narcissistic structures can impoverish an adult personality's energy and self-esteem because that energy is still invested in the unintegrated archaic self structures. These archaic structures can also manifest themselves in a different way, by making infantile demands that disrupt the mature functioning of the adult personality (Kohut, 1971, p. 3). These demands can show up in a relationship or in expressions of rage that do not match the injury. Only the empathic observer will understand the depth of the wound from the seemingly minor irritant (Kohut, 1966/1978c, p. 645).

Causes of Disturbance

The narcissistic personality disorder consists, then, of the defects in the structure of the self—that is, an unmirrored self that seeks the idealized object. The defects in the structure of the self are due to deficits in childhood. Secondary structures are built up in childhood, either covering or compensating for the defects.

Narcissistic pathology is due to the absence of the parents' empathic response to the child's needs to be mirrored and to find a target for idealization (Kohut, 1977, p. 187). It is not the occasional lapse of the selfobject that causes problems but the chronic incapacity to respond appropriately. This chronic inability is most likely due to the parents' own pathology of the self (Kohut, 1977, p. 187n). Kohut deemphasized the role of traumatic events. Given a healthy milieu, a child can handle the occasionally traumatic event (Kohut, 1971, p. 65; Kohut & Wolf, 1978, p. 417).

More explicitly, pathology results from the disturbance in the empathic merger of the self and the selfobject at the stage of development preceding the firm establishment of the self (Kohut, 1977, pp. 88,

89). Disturbance results when a selfobject's empathic response to the child is absent or seriously dulled or is only selectively aware of the child's experience. The parent may be unable to listen to the child with pride in the child's accomplishment, or the parent may distract attention from the child and not fulfill the child's need for appropriate admiration. The chronic nonresponsiveness deprives the child of the merger with the omnipotent selfobject. Such a deprivation keeps the child from building up the psychic structures capable of dealing with anxiety and so on. The child cannot build up structures that regulate tension and tame affects, or the child builds faulty structures, for example, that tend toward the intensification of affect or toward panic. Drives (sexual and aggressive) become more manifest and there is a sense of disintegration when the self is not supported (Kohut, 1977, p. 171).

Differentiating Narcissism from Other Disorders

While narcissistic personality disorders may share some features with other psychological disturbances, there are critical differences between narcissism and transference neuroses, borderline disorders, and psychoses.

A transference neurosis usually involves a personality with a cohesive self and an intact psychic structure. The disturbance is centered on a conflict with libidinal and aggressive strivings directed toward objects from childhood. These objects are differentiated from the self. The person feels anxious in the face of the neurotic danger—that is, the fear of the instinctual strivings breaking into consciousness (Kohut, 1971, p. 19).

In contrast, the narcissistic personality disturbance centers on the self and archaic selfobjects (which by definition are experienced as not separate from the self). These archaic configurations of grandiose self and idealized object are not integrated into the rest of the personality and so the personality is deprived of self-esteem and healthy narcissistic vitality. The anxiety of the self-disorder proceeds from the awareness of the vulnerability of the self; the discomfort comes from the inability to regulate self-esteem (Kohut, 1971, p. 21).

The borderline and psychotic personalities have not developed a stable, narcissistic configuration; that is, a cohesive self with cohesive, idealized objects. They have trouble holding themselves together, and they use delusions and even hallucinations to protect against intolerable fragmentation and the loss of idealized objects. Their inner objects tend to be harsh and persecuting. This inner disintegration and harshness tend to cause the borderlines and psychotics to have serious relational problems and therefore problems relating to a therapist. Presenting symptoms of borderline and psychotic personalities are usually clear and dramatic in contrast to the initially vague symptoms of those patients with narcissistic personality disorders.

In contrast to borderline and personality disorders, the narcissistic personality has attained a cohesive self and cohesive archaic objects that allow this patient to establish a relationship with a therapist and within the therapeutic situation (Kohut invariably referred to psychoanalysis) to establish stable narcissistic transferences. The transference allows for the reactivation of the early narcissistic structures and the process of working through those structures in therapy (Kohut, 1971, pp. 8, 16). The idealized object tends to be the omnipotent, comforting parent image, which gets activated in the transference, helping to alleviate the feelings of emptiness and depression that were initially present in the narcissistic patient. This contrasts with the therapeutic experience of the borderline, usually an experience of serious emotional swings.

Categories of Self Disturbances

Kohut felt that his self psychology illuminates the reactions of the normal, consolidated self as it responds to the ups and downs of life. Such normal reactions of rage and depression, hope and self-esteem are not, of course, pathological (Kohut, 1977, p. 192).

Focusing on disturbances of the self, Kohut found that some self disorders are not analyzable although some rapport is possible with a therapist. He included here the psychoses (in which there is a fragmentation, enfeeblement, or serious distortion of the self), borderline states (where fragmentation and distortions of the self are covered over by defensive structures), and schizoid and paranoid personalities (where there are defensive organizations that use distancing) (Kohut, 1977, p. 192).

Kohut (1977, p. 193) believed there are two forms of self disorders that are analyzable because they allow for a rapport with a therapist and the emergence of a transference where the therapist can become a therapeutic selfobject. The narcissistic personality disorder and the narcissistic behavioral disorder both represent temporary fragmentations or serious distortions of the self. These disorders of the self have in common a disturbed, unmirrored self covered by defenses that seek a mirroring selfobject's response. The narcissistic behavioral disorder differs from the narcissistic personality disorder primarily in the promiscuous or antisocial *behavior* by which the disturbed, unmirrored self is covered. Thus, a man might sleep with many women and be sadistic to them in a desperate, Don Juan-like attempt to get a satisfying mirroring response to his archaic, unmirrored self. On the other hand, defensive *phantasies* cover the unmirrored self in the narcissistic personality disorder, and such a person will primarily restrict himself to sadistic phantasies rather than actual sadistic behavior.

Therapy

Kohut's self psychology emphasizes an empathic sensitivity to the subjective experience of the patient, especially the patient's experience of the therapist. Self psychology also strives to be alert to variations in the level of ego organization and allots to traditional analysis patients who have reached an oedipal or more intact level of organization. Self psychology focuses on patients with early deficits in the organization of the self and gives special attention to how such patients experience the therapist.

Therapy (Kohut usually spoke of analysis) demands that a patient have an observing segment of the personality that can cooperate with the therapist and take on the work of therapy. The work of psychoanalytic therapy involves a process of working through; that is, the ego must repeatedly get in touch with the repressed strivings of the personality and the defensive response to those childhood strivings. The therapist will provide a realistic ego that helps the patient tolerate delay and anxiety. As the patient internalizes the qualities of the therapist, the patient's realistic ego gradually gains dominance over the childhood strivings (Kohut, 1971, p. 143).

The therapist establishes a situation that encourages the reactivation of original developmental tendencies. For the narcissistic personality, these unfinished developmental tasks are manifested in the narcissistic transferences that confirm the diagnosis for the therapist. The specific developmental task is the need of the unmirrored self for the idealized selfobject's response and affirmation (Kohut, 1977, p. 130).

Thus, the mirroring transference activates the grandiose self that seeks confirming attention from a selfobject as well as the idealizing transference the self seeks to merge with the ideal, omnipotent object. For the narcissistic patient, the task of therapy is to confront the idealizing and mirroring transference, which the patient is initially unaware of. The patient, of course, has no wish to be mirrored but does not function well unless mirroring occurs (London, 1985, p. 98).

The transferences will make themselves known to the therapist by the patient's demands for attention, admiration, and a variety of mirroring and echoing responses to his or her mobilized grandiose self (Kohut, 1971, p. 176). The observing ego of the patient, with the help of the therapist, has to confront and understand the demands of his or her grandiose self and the idealizing of the therapist. Gradually, mastery comes about as the patient internalizes aspects of the therapist and builds new inner structures. Internalizing is fostered by manageable frustrations of the patient's needs for the therapist's personal presence and perfect functioning—almost identical to the process by which the child builds up inner structures by transmuting internalizations. Ultimately, the patient can tame and relinquish the primitive demands (Kohut, 1971, p. 207). Successful therapy results in the establishment of a firmly established, fully functioning rehabilitated self (Kohut, 1977, p. 173).

The patient may defensively retreat from these infantile demands when the therapist in some way fails to empathically respond. When the relationship with the analyst becomes disturbed (by a vacation, for example, or by the therapist's lapses in perceptive and empathic insight), the narcissistic patient starts feeling he or she is not fully real, and the patient's emotions are dulled. These complaints indicate the depletion of the ego because it has to put a wall between itself and the unrealistic demands of the archaic grandiose self or the intense hunger for a powerful external supplier of self-esteem (Kohut, 1971, p. 16). Normally, the healthy ego is able to find emotional supplies within; that is, it long ago integrated the grandiose aspects of the self into its whole.

In narcissistic transferences, the grandiose self has not been integrated with the reality-oriented organization of the ego. The narcissistic patient, as a child, was deprived of the opportunity to free the self from narcissistic enmeshment, a freeing that involved a process of gradual withdrawal of narcissistic cathexis. When this process is interrupted by the parent's pathology or because the parent died or went away, a child may continue to idealize a father, for example, if there is no opportunity to discover his realistic shortcomings and if there is no gradual disillusionment through normal interactions. Such an individual can continue to search for an external omnipotent figure since there is no modification of this need, no integration with the realistic ego (Kohut, 1971, pp. 83, 84).

The same is true of the grandiose self needing affirmation from a selfobject. The unmirrored self of childhood continues its desperate search. The task for the therapist is to point out to the patient how the unmirrored child within still feels the hopeless need. The patient's observing ego begins to see the underlying helplessness and hopelessness as the defenses and repressions become clear as the patient is more empathic with him or herself (Kohut & Wolf, 1978, p. 423).

Although Kohut often describes phenomena that others have noticed, Kohut made new and helpful contributions to treatment techniques. Specifically, therapists have noticed that patients manifest intense idealizations of subject (grandiosity) and object and therapist (idealizing transference). Kohut encouraged a neutral stand toward these rationalizations, rather than regarding them as obstacles to treatment; he also argued that they are the material for analysis. A neutral stance often allows the patient to express these grandiose and idealizing phantasies in ways appropriate for treatment (London, 1985, p. 95). Otto Kernberg, in contrast to Kohut, sees idealization as a pathological projection of the patient's own grandiose self onto the analyst (Kernberg, 1975, p. 278). For example, he regards the mirror transference as a pathological defensive process by which the patient attempts to force the therapist to behave as the patient needs him or her to behave. Since Kernberg sees this as a defense and not the fixation of a normal developmental process as Kohut suggested, Kernberg tends to actively confront this defense.

Vertical Split

The psyche can be split in two ways, according to Kohut. Repression is usually understood as a horizontal split between consciousness and unconsciousness. Sometimes the grandiose self, by means of a horizontal split, remains unintegrated with the reality ego. The reality ego is thus deprived of the narcissistic energy and feels diminished in self-confidence and zest (Kohut, 1971, p. 177). Patients with a horizontal split have symptoms of narcissistic deficiency—vague depression, lack of self-confidence, and the like.

On the other hand, a vertical split involves the side-by-side conscious existence in the psyche of incompatible psychic attitudes (Kohut, 1971, p. 176). Thus, the reality ego may be walled off from the unrealistic narcissistic aspects by means of disavowal or isolation. The unmodified grandiose self is excluded from the realistic area of the psyche by a vertical split, conspicuously intruding into many activities, such as by vain and boastful behavior (Kohut, 1971, p. 178). A vertical split is more common than a horizontal split alone. The horizontal split is present in most narcissistic patients, usually in some combination with the vertical split (Kohut, 1971, p. 240).

Therapy seeks to remobilize the split-off or repressed grandiose and idealizing self by means of the narcissistic transference for the sake of taming the grandiose and exhibitionistic needs and bringing them under the influence of the reality ego (Kohut, 1971, p. 108). *Working through* involves completing processes that were traumatically stopped in childhood.

Case Study

The case of Mr. K, who had a narcissistically disturbed personality, illustrates several themes of Kohut, in particular, the reactivation of the grandiose self in therapy and various forms of the narcissistic transference.

Mr. K was an industrial engineer in his early 40s. The external and presenting pathology, rather than the underlying narcissistic pathology, involved problems in his ability to work consistently and meaningfully at his employment and to commit himself to long-term goals. He did participate very successfully in sports, especially those involving speed and danger. His presenting issues involved him in social conflict, and he also had a sense of depression and inner depletion.

The course of his analysis illustrates the course of his disturbed psychological structure (Kohut, 1971, p. 257). The analysis started with a rapidly established idealizing transference that lasted for some weeks. This manifested itself in expressions of great conscious admiration for the analyst, for his appearance and his capabilities (Kohut, 1971, p. 139). The activation of his grandiose self soon followed, at first in the form of a merger-twinship transference where he felt merged with or experienced the analyst as an alter ego who was just like himself. Replacing the merger-twinship transference was a mirror transference in the narrow sense, where he was able to intensely experience narcissistic needs, especially his exhibitionistic and grandiose needs in the area of physical prowess. When the possibility of separation from the analyst arose because of scheduling problems or vacation, the work of analysis stopped, and Mr. K became emotionally withdrawn and shallow, with lowered self-esteem (Kohut, 1971, p. 243). At these times of separation, he reported dreams that focused on machines, wheels, and wires rather than on people.

What seems to have occurred in the course of analysis is the remobilization of fixation points in normal narcissistic development (Kohut, 1971, p. 258). As a child, Mr. K had a pathologically enmeshed relationship with his mother, who suddenly lost interest in him at the time of the birth of her second child. When he was about 3½ years old, he tried to deal with his intense narcissistic frustration by turning toward his father and setting him up as a wonderful object to whom he could attach himself—that is, to restore his narcissistic equilibrium. The brief idealization of the therapist seems to have revived this childhood attempt to idealize his father. His father was unable to accept what the boy needed him to be and so rejected the boy's attempts to idealize him and attach himself to him (Kohut, 1971, p. 139).

After he failed with his father, the boy made two other attempts to restore his narcissistic equilibrium and enhance his self-esteem. First, he regressed to a reactivation of his grandiose self, which was now a pathological replacement of the normal narcissistic developmental step where he was when his mother turned away from him and toward her second child. This grandiose self, revived in analysis after the initial idealizing transference, took the form of a mirror transference in the narrow sense, with the patient very aware of his needs and demands for approval from the analyst. Mr. K's second childhood attempt to restore his narcissistic balance was more successful. He was able to discharge narcissistic tensions through physical activities that were marginally grandiose and dangerous but which also provided some realistic gratification of his underlying grandiose phantasies and exhibitionism (Kohut, 1971, p. 248). These activities represented the archaic exhibitionism of a body self (precursor to the cohesive grandiose self); some were repressed and others sublimated, continuing on into adulthood as exhibitionistic athletic activities.

When Mr. K was ignored or abandoned as a child, he had narcissistic preoccupations and worries about his body parts. He was able to use mechanical toys and bikes and sleds as means to overcome these narcissistic and autoerotic tensions and worries about his body. In analysis, Mr. K's dreams, which changed from people to machines when he feared separation from his analyst, expressed his regressive preoccupation with body parts; that is, a regression to the archaic, fragmented body self, which is a less differentiated precursor of the cohesive, grandiose self (Kohut, 1971, pp. 244–245). His adult skills and racing abilities as a glider pilot maintained his self-esteem in adulthood and were an important part of his adult self-image. His dreams about machines represented amalgamations and compromises between current and archaic self representations.

The birth of a brother did not actually cause Mr. K's narcissistic disorder. More likely, the pathological relationship with his mother and her withdrawal from him constituted the focus of the narcissistic fixations that shaped his personality and became the nucleus of his transference reactions to the analyst. Even if his brother had not been born, Mr. K would probably have been narcissistically fixated because of his mother's tendency toward overinvolvement (Kohut, 1971, pp. 247, 254).

Assessment and Critique of Kohut

Kohut felt that narcissism is essentially normal and healthy, has its own line of development or transformations, can become fixated at certain points, and thus has its own forms of pathology requiring its own form of treatment. Kohut moved the drives and the traditional ego-id model from the center of the psychic stage. His clinical insights were substantial, and his self psychology made positive contributions to psychoanalysis. The concepts, however, are not always clear or well-defined, such as with the concept of self. But despite its flaws, Kohut's self psychology made considerable advances, although they were not related to the rest of the psychoanalytic tradition.

Otto Kernberg (1980) goes to great lengths to link himself with others in the psychoanalytic tradition, especially Margaret Mahler, Edith Jacobson, W. R. D. Fairbairn, and Melanie Klein. Kohut, by contrast, said that it is not his interest to attempt any integration with other psychoanalytic theorists (1977, p. xx). While he may acknowledge some similarities of his work to that of others, he did not systematically elaborate or acknowledge those similarities.

In a letter to Margaret Mahler, Kohut wrote that they were both digging tunnels into the same mountain from different directions (Kohut, 1980c, p. 477). This comparison of himself with Mahler raised the issue of Kohut's methodology and the validity of his evidence. Kohut's only source of data was adult patients in treatment (cf. Eagle, 1984, p. 50). Kohut's empathic, introspective methodology was in contrast with Mahler's observations of children interacting with parents in a non-therapeutic environment. The question can be asked whether the empathic, introspective methodology of Kohut's psychoanalysis is sufficient for obtaining data for the scientific construction of theory.

Kohut recalled chatting with Kernberg in the late 1960s and summarized his difference with Kernberg by saying that Kernberg looked on narcissism as essentially pathological while he looked on it as healthy (Kohut, 1980c, p. 477). Kernberg and Kohut do have contrasting approaches to narcissism and its disorders. Because Kernberg has tried to maintain a synthesis of object relations and the traditional drive model, he feels it is impossible to discuss and treat narcissistic disorders without including the sexual and aggressive drives and object relations (Kernberg, 1975, p. 271). Kohut left behind the traditional emphasis on drives and only referred to them when the self is fragmented and shattered (Kohut, 1977, pp. xv, 77). In his self psychology, Kohut set the discussion of narcissism within a context other than drives; that is, the separate development of narcissism and its transformations.

Kernberg includes the narcissistic personality within the wider category of borderline personalities, while Kohut did not always clearly differentiate the narcissistic from the borderline. Thus, these two theorists are not always discussing the same group of patients (cf. Kernberg, 1975, p. 334; Meissner, 1984, p. 104). For Kernberg, the difference between narcissistic and borderline personalities involves the presence of an integrated but pathological grandiose self. The crucial difference between Kernberg's notion of narcissistic personality and Kohut's is that Kernberg finds the *presence* of a pathological self, while Kohut found the *absence* of a full self, or more correctly, the presence of an *incomplete* or fixated normal, archaic, cohesive self whose development has been blocked.

Kernberg would agree with Kohut that narcissistic personalities can be helped by analysis, but their different understanding of the nature of narcissism causes each to talk about the treatment process in a different way. Kernberg tends to see Kohut as gratifying or indulging, although Kohut saw his fostering of the mirroring or idealizing transference as leading to a mastery based on insight. Kernberg (1975, p. 285) challenges what he believes are the defenses of the patient and the patient's disappointment.

There is no question that Kohut resembled the object relations theorists in a variety of ways: in moving away from the drive model, in finding an alternate to the id-ego model, in finding pathology in the lack of a sense of self rather than in instinctual conflict. Of central importance is his proposal of a separate line of development for narcissism than for drives. Some theorists find this emphasis on the self over the primacy of the drives a radical overhauling of traditional psychoanalysis and clearly inconsistent with the traditional model, implying a replacement of the id-ego model with a self model (Eagle, 1984, pp. 35, 44, 75). By moving to preoedipal developments, Kohut's self psychology and the object relations theorists have dethroned the oedipal complex from its central position with psychoanalysis.

References

Eagle, M. N. (1984). *Recent developments in psychoanalysis: A critical evaluation*. New York: McGraw-Hill.

Freud, S. (1957). On narcissism. In J. Strachey (Ed. and Trans.), *The standard edition of the complete psychological works of Sigmund Freud* (Vol. 14, pp. 67–102). London: Hogarth Press. (Original work published 1914)

Hartmann, H. (1964). Comments on the psychoanalytic theory of the ego. In *Essays on ego psychology* (pp. 113–141). New York: International Universities Press.

Jacobson, E. (1964). *The self and the object world*. New York: International Universities Press.

Kernberg, O. (1974). Contrasting viewpoints regarding the nature and psychoanalytic treatment of narcissistic personalities: A preliminary communication. *Journal of the American Psychoanalytic Association, 22*, 255–267.

Kernberg, O. (1975). *Borderline conditions and pathological narcissism*. New York: Aronson.

Kernberg, O. (1980). *Internal world and external reality*. New York: Aronson.

Kernberg, O. (1982). Self, ego, affects, and drives. *Journal of the American Psychoanalytic Association, 30*, 893–916.

Kohut, H. (1971). *The analysis of self*. New York: International Universities Press.

Kohut, H. (1977). *The restoration of the self*. New York: International Universities Press.

Kohut, H. (1978a). Forms and transformations of narcissism. In P. Ornstein (Ed.), *The search for the self: Selected writings of Heinz Kohut: 1950–1978* (Vol. 1, pp. 427–460). New York: International Universities Press. (Original work published 1978)

Kohut, H. (1978b). The psychoanalytic treatment of narcissistic personality disorders. In P. Ornstein (Ed.), *The search for the self: Selected writings of Heinz Kohut: 1950–1978* (Vol. 1, pp. 477ff.). New York: International Universities Press. (Original work published 1968)

Kohut, H. (1978c). Thoughts on narcissism and narcissistic rage. In P. Ornstein (Ed.), *The search for the self: Selected writings of Heinz Kohut: 1950–1978* (Vol. 1, pp. 615–658). New York: International Universities Press. (Original work published 1978)

Kohut, H. (1980a). From a letter to a colleague. In A. Goldberg (Ed.), *Advances in self psychology* (pp. 456–469). New York: International Universities Press.

Kohut, H. (1980b). From a letter to one of the participants at the Chicago conference on the psychology of the self. In A. Goldberg (Ed.), *Advances in self psychology* (pp. 449–456). New York: International Universities Press.

Kohut, H. (1980c). Reflections on *Advances in self psychology*. In A. Goldberg (Ed.), *Advances in self psychology* (pp. 473–554). New York: International Universities Press.

Kohut, H., & Wolf, E. S. (1978). The disorders of the self and their treatment: An outline. *International Journal of Psycho-Analysis, 59,* 413–425.

London, N. J. (1985). An appraisal of self psychology. *International Journal of Psycho-Analysis, 66,* 95–107.

Meissner, W. W. (1980). The problem of internalization and structure formation. *International Journal of Psycho-Analysis, 61,* 237–248.

Meissner, W. W. (1984). Differential diagnosis: The narcissistic disorders. In *The borderline spectrum* (pp. 103–136). New York: Aronson.

Ornstein, P. H. (1978). Introduction: The evolution of Heinz Kohut's psychoanalytic psychology of the self. In P. Ornstein (Ed.), *The search for the self: Selected writings of Heinz Kohut: 1950–1978* (Vol. 1, pp. 1–106). New York: International Universities Press.

Shane, M., & Shane, E. (1980). Psychoanalytic developmental theories of the self: An integration. In A. Goldberg (Ed.), *Advances in self psychology* (pp. 23–46). New York: International Universities Press.

Teicholz, J. G. (1978). A selective review of the psychoanalytic literature on theoretical conceptualizations of narcissism. *Journal of the American Psychoanalytic Association, 26,* 831–861.

Tolpin, M. (1978). Self-objects and oedipal objects: A crucial developmental distinction. *Psychoanalytic Study of the Child, 33,* 167–184.

Wolf, E. S. (1980). On the developmental line of selfobject relations. In A. Goldberg (Ed.), *Advances in self psychology* (pp. 117–130). New York: International Universities Press.

Chapter Ten

Stephen A. Mitchell:
The Integrated Relational
Model

Introduction

By now the reader of this text has witnessed the sometimes confusing variety of terminology and concepts used by the theorists outlined in earlier chapters of this book. The diversity and variety of terms and concepts can serve as an opportune starting point for considering the recent work of Stephen A. Mitchell, who seeks an integrative approach to the various relational theories within psychoanalysis.

Mitchell, a training and supervising analyst in New York City and a fine writer, considers that much of the psychoanalytic theorizing of the past several decades is "fragmented, diffuse, and developed by psychoanalytic schools that regard themselves as competing with, rather than complementing, one another . . . [specifically the relational model, and] has never been developed into a coherent, comprehensive theoretical framework" (1988, p. viii). Mitchell and his coauthor Jay Greenberg (Greenberg & Mitchell, 1983), in a careful review of post-Freudian writings, divide psychoanalysis into two broad competing perspectives: Freud's drive theory and the relational model. The relational model includes a cluster of theories: British object relations theory, interpersonal psychoanalysis, and self psychology.

Mitchell feels there has been a revolutionary shift in the past few decades in how psychoanalysis thinks about the person. Rather than seeing the mind as a set of predetermined structures emerging within the individual (the classical drive model), emphasis has now shifted to the relational model, which envisions the individual existing in transactional patterns with internal structures derived from an interactive, interpersonal field (1993a, p. 31). Many of the creative and influential contributions for the past several decades have flowed from this relational model.

Psychoanalysis has become very different from Freud's initial vision, and Mitchell considers the drive theory to be outdated despite its conceptual unity and comprehensiveness. Those analytic theories that consider relations with others, not drives, as the basic stuff of mental life speak with a multiplicity of voices. It is to this fragmented and diffuse relational model that Mitchell turns: "The most pressing questions in contemporary psychoanalytic theory and practice are, What do the vast array of different psychoanalytic schools and traditions have to do with one another? Do they fit together? If so, how? If not, why not?" (1988, p. vii).

The task that Mitchell sets for himself is to explore the various traditions within the relational model and suggest ways in which those traditions can be integrated and developed into a comprehensive perspective. Mitchell's book *Relational Concepts in Psychoanalysis* (1988) aims at developing a coherent and comprehensive framework for examining some major areas of psychoanalytic inquiry, such as sexuality, infantilism, and narcissism, specifically through the lens of the relational matrix.

Obviously, his relational perspective relocates some of the central concerns of psychoanalytic thought, and in *Hope and Dread in Psychoanalysis* (Mitchell, 1993a), Mitchell continues his consideration of key psychoanalytic concerns, such as the self and analytic therapy. He especially calls attention to the interactive aspects of the psychoanalytic relationship, calling psychoanalysis "a process involving . . . the hopes and dreads of two participants, the analyst and the analysand" (1993a, p. 9).* Mitchell's work, largely confined to three books, various essays, and his editorship of *Psychoanalytic Dialogues*, is nuanced and resistant to easy summary.

Mitchell believes "it is essential that psychoanalysis never discard Freud's thought" (1993a, pp. 32, 90), and he insists that he is not constructing a comprehensive alternative to classical Freudian thought. Indeed, he believes it was a mistake for many post-Freudian theorists like Fairbairn, Kernberg, and Kohut to offer their work as an alternative. He seeks a methodology, an approach to integrate different conceptual strategies of the relational models (1993b, p. 462). Nevertheless, Mitchell sees a profound conceptual shift away from the classical model, and in his construction of an integrated relational perspective he omits the concept of drives.

*Mitchell alternatively uses the terms *analyst* and *analysand* in place of *therapist* and *patient*. For consistency and because this text is aimed at a broader audience, the terms *therapist* and *patient* will ordinarily be used.

This chapter will consider some of the key psychoanalytic themes Mitchell has been scrutinizing through the lens of the relational matrix as he seeks a methodology for integrating different conceptual strategies (1993b, p. 462). Although he often points out differences and similarities in different relational theorists' approaches, it will largely be his positions that are emphasized. A summary of his relational model formulations for the self, narcissism, sexuality, and infantilism will be given. He is always interested in the application of the relational perspective to clinical situations.

Key Concepts

Relational Matrix

The relational matrix is an organizing principle and a frame for interpreting clinical data. The content of the relational matrix includes the self, the object, and transactional patterns (Mitchell, 1988, p. 41). As an organizing principle, the relational matrix contrasts with the idea of drives, which serves as the organizing principle of the classical model. Both concepts look at clinical data but arrange that data differently, engage it differently, and consequently interpret it differently.

Drives

Drive, which in the classical model was defined as a "demand made upon the mind for work" (Freud, 1905/1957, p. 168), becomes the motivational energy empowering the whole psychic apparatus. The sexual and aggressive instincts or drives become primary and are the link to the human animal past. One hundred years ago, when Darwinism was new and fresh and Victorianism pervasive, the idea of primitivism—to see humans as essentially animalistic with fragile civilization built precariously on bestial instinct—provided surprising new perspectives on human experience. For vividness and concreteness, Mitchell summarizes this whole view in the phrase "metaphor of the beast" (1988, p. 121).

Interactional Field

Can drives be integrated with the context of the relational matrix? Historically, several ways have been tried to bring the differences of the two models together. Mitchell sees much of post-Freudian psychoanalysis as a series of strategies for dealing with this drives versus relationship dilemma (Greenberg & Mitchell, 1983, p. 380; Mitchell, 1988, p. 52*ff.*). The relational model theories, in leaving behind the drive framework, often deemphasize the clinical importance of sexuality or place it developmentally later—after the preoedipal period—or simply see it in the context of relatedness. Some theorists viewed the relational model as implicit within the concept of drive. Some, like Kernberg, see relational models as natural extensions of drive theory. A third group claims that the relational matrix and the drive model are essentially incompatible.

Mitchell points out that Freud himself struggled with the conceptual problem of including both relationships and innate drives within the same framework but ultimately declined to mix these elements and relied solely on drives as the core motives. Mitchell himself claims the alternate fork of the nonmixing position: "a purely *relational* mode perspective, unmixed with drive-model premises" (1988, p. 54). His strategy is "to develop an integration of the major lines of relational-model psychoanalytic theorizing into a broad, integrative perspective" from which the concept of drive is omitted (1988, p. 60).

To deemphasize drives and put the focus on relational aspects does indeed alter classic psychoanalysis. But Mitchell maintains that giving up theoretical constructs does not mean surrendering the clinical data, including data that led Freud to ideas about instinctual drives. Such data would include the sense of being driven, the experience of pressure and urgency, and self-descriptions using bestial or bodily imagery. Mitchell seeks to retain the clinical contributions of classical psychoanalysis, but he recasts the clinical data within an interactive, relational theory of the human mind.

Mitchell uses the idea of the relational matrix in a broad sense, a paradigm sense. The relational stance finds all meaning to be generated in relation, and nothing is innate in the way held by the classic drive model (1988, p. 61). Mind is composed of relational configurations. Indeed, the very nature of being human is to seek after an infinite variety of connections, whether they are for security, merger, pleasure, or dependency. Humans are formed by and embedded within a matrix of relationships, an *interactional field* within which individuals struggle to make contact, maintain ties, or differentiate themselves. In the relational model, the basic unit of study is not the individual as a separate entity whose desires clash with external reality but the interactional field within which individuals establish and maintain connections with others. Desire, orgasm, bodily experiences—all are considered in the context of relatedness.

Psychoanalysis without the Drive Theory

Mitchell is aware that removing the concept of drive changes psychoanalytic theory fundamentally. To illustrate his vision of the relational model, he looks at several central pillars of psychoanalytic belief through the relational lens. First, let's consider his views on sexuality.

Sexuality

The drive model regards channeling and control of sexual instincts as central. The relational model construes establishment and maintenance of relational patterns as the central structure of experience. Sexuality is interpreted as a response, expression, or action within an interactive context. Both models account for the clinical data but arrange and interpret the data differently.

The classical drive model presumes that the motives and meanings of a person's behavior are derived from instincts and that these drives provide the categories for interpretation. Bodily, sexual, and aggressive themes are found beneath every feature of human experience. For example, aspects of anality are seen in experiences of control, hoarding, and cleanliness.

The relationship model offers different categories for organizing human experiences. For example, to establish strong relationships with others is regarded as primary, whether those connections are real or phantasy. Much attention is paid to the variety of relationships, and an abundance of metaphors exist for the different kinds of relational patterns, such as merger, differentiation, domination, controlling (1988, pp. 90–92).

The drive model loosens the connection between sexuality and its objects (that is, it minimizes the charms of the attractive object in favor of the primacy of innate instincts). The drive model, Mitchell suggests, draws heavily on the metaphor of the beast within us and so locates problems in the nature of sexuality as a prehuman vestige of our animal past. Contrary to this approach, the relational model takes the opposite tack: It strengthens and expands the connections between sexuality and its objects and points out how sexuality provides pathways by which relational configurations get established and maintained (1988, p. 89). The drive model makes the individual's sexuality the centerpiece of personality. Thus psychosexual urges and wishes motive behavior and shape the individual's sense of self or identity. Where libido gets fixated determines certain kinds of character types, such as the oral personality—to reach genital primacy signifies psychological health. On the other hand, the relational model argues that the maintenance of identity and continuity is the central human concern, and sexual experiences only get their meaning and significance as they become involved in this task. Sexuality becomes a realm where relational conflicts get shaped and played out (1988, pp. 66, 92–99).

Sexuality plays a central role in most intimate relationships. Establishment and maintenance of relatedness is fundamental, and the mutual exchange of intense pleasure and emotional responsiveness is perhaps the most powerful medium through which emotional connection and intimacy is sought, established, lost, and regained (1988, p. 107).

Perverse sexuality can be understood as reflecting different types of object ties, alternative routes to the object (1988, p. 92).

Sexuality in all its many forms and variations is an array of different kinds of self organizations and object ties or connections. Indeed, the earliest clinical problems that Freud encountered, the bizarre neurotic symptoms that were disguised aspects of his patients' sexuality, he believed were due to the detachment from the rest of the life of sexuality and the repression of this sexuality, which was then forced to find expression in a circuitous fashion. But these neurotic disturbances are not, according to the relational model, the result of bestial, innate nature but rather the result of splitting, anxiety, and fragmentation in the search for and maintenance of connections with others (1988, p. 65).

The centrality of sexual experience and its key role in psychopathology derive not from its innate properties but from its interactive and relational meanings. Sex, for example, is demanded in the name of love, and the absence of sex is felt as a betrayal and humiliation. Lack of sex is experienced in terms of mounting sexual pressure, which has more to do with anxiety than with arousal. Sexual release is experienced not just in terms of tension reduction but as a desperately sought reassurance against abandonment and betrayal. Even masturbation can be seen in relational terms, such as an escape from dilemmas over fears around reassurance and abandonment. Masturbation is a form of self-gratification, where the self is soothed and the interpersonal message is that I can regulate myself and gratify myself and so am independent of your availability. The pressure driving compulsive masturbation is not innate tension but anxiety about the sense of interpersonal vulnerability experienced in physical terms (1988, pp. 108, 118).

The relational matrix does not detract from the centrality of sex but accounts for that centrality as driven and bestial in a way different from the drive model. The metaphor of the beast in drive theory has appeal because it is vivid and suggests that part of us has escaped the control of society and exists apart from necessary accommodations of interpersonal relationships. But such a reification of metaphor can serve to obscure the manner in which an individual's sexuality expresses significant relational patterns. Like other metaphors that help organize the self, the metaphor and experience of the self as beast arise within the complexity and conflicts of the relational matrix. In summary, Mitchell believes that the importance of sexuality is appreciated more and more accurately understood by seeing it within an interactive relational context (1988, pp. 121–122).

Infantilism

Infantilism, another key area of the psychoanalytic tradition Mitchell rethinks using the relational model lens, refers to the central role that ideas about early development play in shaping an individual; that is, early troubling experiences from infancy are alive in the present struggles of an adult. Mitchell certainly thinks this is important but suggests changes in the way we think about early life experiences.

Psychoanalysis often provides insight into puzzling adult behavior by viewing the *adult as child* and by viewing the adult's behavior in terms of the sexual and aggressive impulses that dominated childhood from birth through the oedipal period. The metaphor of the baby has powerful appeal because it expresses for many patients their experience of their wishes and needs as some infantile longing or, perhaps, as some effort to escape an infantile terror. The baby is an organizing metaphor for psychological experiences, and much insight is gained by seeing how the past underlies the present and continues to exist beneath later psychological processes. But Mitchell urges caution in the use of the baby metaphor, suggesting that an overly concrete use of developmental ideas might be seen as explaining rather than suggesting. Further, overreliance on the baby metaphor might obscure how much the person is embedded in a matrix of relationships and that certain human longings and terrors characterize human experience at all ages, not merely infancy (1988, p. 134). Mitchell worries that theories emphasizing developmental arrest draw too heavily on the metaphor of the baby and consequently view pathology as frozen, aborted development, with infantile deprivation and parental failure underlying adult psychopathology (1993a, p. 172).

Some relational theories fall into what Mitchell calls the developmental-arrest model. This model generally replaces drives or instincts with the relational matrix as the essential motivational framework. Developmental continuity is explained by a kind of stunted growth, and emotional deficiencies and failures often take place early in life and continue on to generate adult psychopathology. These early experiences and needs tend to persist into adulthood and are seen as infantile, preoedipal, or immature. Mitchell takes issue with this "tendency to collapse relational needs into the earliest years" (1988, p. 134). He suggests that a "developmental tilt" has been built by these post-Freudian theorists, such as Winnicott, Kohut, and Mahler. The "tilt" implies that relational issues are tilted or skewed toward infancy and not seen as extending over all stages of the life cycle—even though these tilt models do offer valuable insights in the relational needs and processes of preoedipal experiences (1988, pp. 137–139). Some developmental-tilt models seem to imply that the earliest months of life are the most basic layer of human experience and govern processes that originate chronologically later in life. Mitchell cautions against such a view, which sees early dynamics as necessarily being the deepest and most fundamental of processes. If taken literally, the assumption here is that psychopathology would be neatly predicable from problems and traumas early in life (1988, pp. 140, 144). But early life issues, especially relational issues, tend to be lifelong struggles. The reality is that "later difficulties in living are often *not* direct causal products of earlier deprivation and problems, but a complex combination of the impact of early experiences and reactions to later stresses and conflicts" (1988, p. 145). Certain relational issues, such as fusion and separation and dependence and independence, are common to the human experience through all ages. Although it would be conceptually convenient to see adult psychopathology in terms of early deprivation, with these patients imagined as carrying a damaged inner psychological baby, empirical evidence shows some children from impoverished backgrounds (such as orphaned war refugees or abused children) grow up with minimal observable damage if they can be introduced to normal homes in time (1988, p. 146).

Mitchell does not dispute that there can indeed be aborted developmental processes, but he does not want to put too much causative weight on the earliest years of life. Parental limitations and deprivations are not usually specific to a particular developmental period; problematic parental relational issues most likely continue over longer periods of time. The parent who is not attuned to the infant is probably not going to be very good at engaging the toddler or very involved with the adolescent either (1988, p. 147).

Mitchell summarizes the interactional vision of developmental continuity as reflecting the similarities of problems that humans struggle with at all points in the life cycle. Being a self with others involves a constant dialectic between attachment and self-definition, between connection and differentiation. The interpersonal environment plays a continuous and crucial role in the creation of the self. Earliest experiences are important and meaningful because they are the earliest representation of patterns of family interactions that will be repeated over and over in different ways at different developmental stages. It is not that the past so much lies concealed under the present; rather, to understand the past is to obtain clues as to how and why patients approach the present the way they do.

The Self

Although the self has been a central concept in psychoanalytic writing for the past quarter century, no one needs reminding of the disconcerting variety of meanings and uses of the term *self*. Theorists have variously referred to the self as an idea, a structure in the mind, something we all experience, and something that does or acts. Western thinkers have made the self a central theme for several centuries, with the question ultimately being reduced to "What does it mean to be a person?" In non-Western cultures, the idea of the supraindividual group carries much of the burden for the sense of self.

Mitchell sees two views or ways of thinking about the self in psychoanalytic writings: (1) the self as layered, with a single inner core, with revelation and concealment being under the individual's control; or (2) the self as multiple, woven into reciprocal interactions between the subject and others, a view of self as multiple and embedded in relational contexts (1993a, pp. 96–110).

The self as layered, singular, and continuous is grounded in a spatial metaphor. This metaphor implies that the mind somehow is a place, and the self—composed of parts or structures—is something in that place. For example, a person sometimes is heard to say, "I am not all here today," or perhaps they refer to their "core" or the "deepest" part of themselves. (When theorists use the concept of psychic structures, they are referring not to something substantive but to recurring patterns of experience and behavior over time.)

The second broad model of self is grounded on a temporal metaphor. This metaphor suggests a view of self as multiple and discontinuous, as exemplified in a situation where one might say, "I am not myself today." The self is what an individual does and experiences over time rather than something that exists someplace. Self refers to the subjective organization of meanings an individual creates moving through time, doing things such as having ideas and feelings, including self-reflective ideas and feelings about oneself (1993a, p. 103).

The model of self in object relations theory puts an emphasis on multiplicity and discontinuity, portraying the self as inevitably embedded in particular relational contexts. The object relations approach focuses on self and object units; that is, the kind of person an individual experiences him or herself as being when he or she interacts with other people. These units are understood to derive from how the person felt with a significant other in a particular context. Because we learn to become a person through interactions with different others and different kinds of interactions with the same other, our experience of self is discontinuous, composed of different configurations, different selves with different others. Thus, an individual might experience herself as herself in relation to a significant other, with the experience organized around the image of a solicitous mother caring for a dependent child. At a different time, she might organize her sense of meaning and her experience of herself around the image of another in relation to herself, perhaps around the image of a querulous sibling making demands. The result is many organizations of the self, patterned around different self and object images or representations, derived from different relational contexts. We are all composites of overlapping, multiple organizations and perspectives, and our experience gets smoothed over by a kind of illusory and subjective sense of continuity and unity (1993a, pp. 104–107). Pathology, in this framework, might well be measured by degrees of dissociation of important versions of the self. In other words, if the versions of oneself were so different there could not be a unified self. Where Freud painted conflict as a clash between impulses and the forces of regulatory functions and moral prohibitions, the object relations models primarily locate conflict between the contrasting and often incompatible self organizations and self-other relationships (1993a, p. 105).

If there is a variable "I" that has changeable content, that feels different today from most days, that contains different suborganizations, I am, nevertheless, still able to recognize all these differences as a version of a more or less invariant "self" despite the discontinuities. A sense of self exists that is independent of shifts over time, a sense of self that proves to be continuous from one subjective state to the next, with some self-reflection. I name that enduring sense of self as "myself" and assign it specific content so that I can match up my current experience with previous subjective states and content so as to be able to say "I feel very much myself today" or "I am not myself today" (1993a, pp. 107–108). The continuity of subjective experience forms the core of a sense of self. The qualities of integration and singularity distinguish a normal or average person from a multiple personality where the discontinuities of subjective experience are too great. That is, the multiple personality has no sense of continuity from one self organization to the next—no recognition of a continuous, enduring subjectivity or singularity. All of us constantly create meaning out of the context in which we are operating, and even though the content of the meaning may vary, there is a sense that the "I" that creates meaning today in organizing my experience is a continuation of the "I" that created subjective experiences yesterday and the day before (1993a, pp. 108–109).

At times the self seems as if it were an entity deep within us that can get revealed or hidden from others. We may also speak of self-observation and self-reflection, but many of these private experiences of ourselves, experiences in which we play the role of both subject and object, really harken back to past interactions with others. The categories and language by which we represent ourselves to ourself likely point to past relationships with others, according to Mitchell. Even though we may feel most private and independent, we are deeply connected with others because it was others through whom we learned to become a self. The "self is defined and experienced largely through contrasts and in relations to others" (1993a, p. 113).

When we try to think about the core or center of the self, we should not confuse poetic metaphor for objective thinking. Most of the efforts to think about the true or core self use spatial metaphors and images to locate essential from superficial features of self. That is, thinking about the core or depth of the self is an attempt to get "underneath" the superficial adaptations that the self has made in society. However, thinking of self in temporal terms probably is a more useful way of approaching the important issue that the search for the core was meant to solve; that is, the need to distinguish among degrees of authenticity in one's experience. If the self moves in time rather than space, it has no fixed core but rather has many different ways of operating. In daily life we have different experiences of the self. Some versions of the self seem spontaneous and constructive, some hidden and tortured. Some ways in which I act and express myself feel more authentic, more representative of me. At times I feel more "myself" than others; other times I feel less "myself." This differs from the suggestion of the spatial self as an invariant core, a true self removed from time (1993a, p. 130).

In distinguishing authenticity from inauthenticity, the crucial difference lies not in the specific content of *what* I feel or do but in the *relationship* between what I feel and do. I am authentic when I somehow present my thoughts and feelings in an accurate way and reveal myself spontaneously. What feels "right" somehow suits the interpersonal context and my internal emotional context. Feeling not right or inauthentic refers to feeling contrived—out of sync both interpersonally and internally. "Speaking of authenticity versus inauthenticity or true versus false experience frees us from the spatial metaphor in a way that speaking of a true or false self or a 'core' or 'real' self does not" (1993a, p. 131).

In classical psychoanalysis, the key questions used to be about patterns of gratification and frustration that shaped an individual's life. In contemporary analysis, the key question seems to be about how meaningful and authentic is the individual's experience and expression of self. Richness in living involves the degree of truth and falseness expressed with respect to one's experience. Spontaneous and vital self-expression serves as the ground for authentic experience, while the need for security often leads to a concern with the impact of one's self-presentation on others (1993a, pp. 132–133).

Certain kinds of experience may be hard for some patients to risk sharing with others. These experiences, perhaps previously inaccessible or dissociated, are often expressed through vivid metaphors, such as animals or babies or demons, for instance. The metaphors around which versions of self are organized often come in complementary pairs, such as the needy baby versus the joyless adult, the savage beast versus the civilized adult. Therapy is a collaborative struggle to discover, explore, and name these versions of the self, these states of mind. As the patients experience themselves in richer forms, temporal and spatial dimensions of the self complement each other (1993a, pp. 138–139).

In some areas of activity I may feel more truly and deeply myself. Using both temporal and spatial dimensions can allow for a richer capacity to experience oneself. Thus, thinking about self in temporal and spatial terms compels rethinking the relationship between body and self. Body-based experiences of sexual desire or rage are not so much primitive pressures located someplace within as they are reactions to various stimuli in relational contexts. And rather than judging some experiential content as more elemental, basic, or primitive, it is more important to see the content in the context of experience. One form of experience is not necessarily more basic or deeper than another, since experience is not layered in space or psychic structure. Experiences shift back and forth over time as forms of self organization. The sense of greater significance of some experiences comes from their spontaneity and freedom from our concern about how they will be received, from their freedom from self consciousness. Body-based experiences of self are simply different ways of organizing experiences; they, like other experiences, shift back and forth as forms of self organization (1993a, pp. 139–140).

In addition to the evocative metaphors of the self as baby and self as beast is the metaphor of the self as damaged, which implies the experience of having been traumatized, crippled, deprived, wounded, or emptied in some fashion by events in one's past. These ways of experiencing oneself reflect a particular kind of relationship between past and present in which one's present self is captive to past events, to resources that have been depleted, and to potentials that have been cut off. Patients experience themselves as deeply damaged and needing care, sympathy, or contempt or in various versions need to see others as damaged so as to care for or feel contempt for them (1988, p. 266).

Mitchell points out that just as other experiential metaphors become established as actualities, so the metaphor of damage can be found in concepts such as developmental arrests, structural deficits, and ego defects. Experiences of defectiveness are assigned literal properties, as if the damage resides in the mind. In actuality, these metaphors need to be recognized as organizational metaphors in an interactional field, serving as paths of connection to others or explaining how ties are maintained once established. For Mitchell, psychopathology probably more accurately means being stuck in a maladaptive relational matrix; patients with repetitive disturbances in interpersonal relations can be drawn to negative kinds of relationships with sadistic, withdrawn, or depriving others (1988, pp. 269, 275).

The relational matrix within each of us can be viewed as a tapestry woven on Penelope's loom, a tapestry rich with interacting figures; that is, representations and various metaphors around which one's self is experienced. Like Penelope, each of us weaves and unravels, constructing and adapting our relational world to maintain the same dramatic tensions, perpetuating the same longings (1988, p. 275). Embeddedness is endemic to human experience. I become the person I am in interaction with specific other people. The way I feel it is necessary to be with them is the person I take myself to be. That self organization becomes my nature, my personality. Those attachments become my sense of the possibilities within the community of others. Those transactional patterns become the basis for my sense of interpersonal security. The additional truth is that all important human relations are necessarily conflictual, since all relationships have complex simultaneous meanings in terms of self-definition and connection to others (1988, p. 276).

Narcissism

Narcissism, another of the central concepts of psychoanalysis, cuts across all schools of analytic theory. In his project of reviewing relational formulations of various psychoanalytic concepts, Mitchell considers narcissism as an arena for comparing and integrating different theoretical perspectives. He also applies his integrated relational approach to clinical situations. The different psychoanalytic traditions all arrive at an essentially similar technical approach to the clinical phenomenon of narcissistic illusions. Narcissistic illusions, usually in the form of grandiose ideas about the self or idealizations of significant others, are a regressive defense against frustration, separation, aggression, dependency, and despair. Illusions arising in the transference (such as idealizations of the therapist or patients' grandiose images about themselves) are to be interpreted, their defensive purpose defined, and their unreality pointed out (1988, p. 187).

Mitchell summarizes alternative views of infantile mental states and narcissistic illusions that are closely connected with the developmental-arrest model. Mitchell specifically highlights the contributions of Winnicott and Kohut about the sense of self. The facilitating environment provided by the Winnicottian mother enables the infant to assume (that is, have the illusion) that his wishes create the objects of his desire. The child's illusion that anything is possible is part of the good-enough mother's facilitating an environment that provides for the child. Winnicott's transitional object, the child's teddy bear or security blanket, exists in the borderline between the child's subjective omnipotence and objective reality. The child's parent allows for ambiguity during the transitional stage. Winnicott (1958) extends this notion so as to see health as capacity for play, as the freedom to move back and forth between harsher objective reality and the soothing ambiguities of self-absorption and subjective omnipotence. This further led Winnicott to see the therapeutic situation in terms of satisfaction of crucial developmental experiences, of missed parental functions. The therapist provides a holding environment that had not been provided in infancy, a kind of revitalization where the frozen aborted self can reawaken and take up development as its crucial ego needs are met (1988, pp. 187–189).

Mitchell also describes Kohut's expansion and development of the technical implications of Winnicott's insights. In two forms of transference (mirroring and idealizing), the therapist and the therapist's responses function in place of psychic structures missing from the patient's own personality. In the mirroring transference, the patient has grandiose feelings that require the therapist's mirroring response to avoid the disintegration of the self. In the idealizing transference, the patient regards the therapist with overvaluing admiration and requires the therapist to allow this idealization to avoid a disintegration of the self (cf. Kohut, 1971). Kohut is pointing out that the patient, by these means, attempts to establish crucial developmental opportunities, a self–object relationship unavailable in childhood. What is happening is the kernel of an aborted developmental process that was stalled because parents failed to allow the child to experience illusions of grandeur and idealization. When the narcissistic illusions occur in therapy, they signal a fragile opportunity for revitalizing the self. As the therapist cultivates the illusions and warmly receives them, the normal developmental process of the patient can be revived and continued (Mitchell, 1988, pp. 189–190).

In his critique of the different technical approaches to narcissistic illusions, Mitchell suggests that the majority of therapists struggle to find a midpoint between different contemporary approaches and the classical approach. Mitchell fleshes out a descriptive framework for locating just such a middle approach conceptually in terms of techniques within his integrated relational perspective. The more traditional approach to narcissism highlights important ways narcissistic illusions are used defensively, but Mitchell feels this approach leaves out the valuable role of illusions in health, creativity, and consolidating crucial relationships with others. That is, the developmental-arrest approach generates a perspective on narcissism that stresses the growth-enhancing function of narcissistic illusions but overlooks the extent to which these illusions can constrict and interfere with real engagements with other people. As an example, Mitchell highlights how Kernberg (1975) proceeds on a different assumption than does Kohut (1971). Kernberg's narcissist lives in an embattled, exploitative world where the only security lies in devaluing and disarming others. Kernberg's therapeutic empathic response is to appreciate this endangered status, point out defenses, and enable some contact. But Kohut's narcissist is a brittle creature living in a bruising world where the only security lies in splitting off aspects of the self in efforts to protect the tender feelings connected to them. The empathic response here is to appreciate the continued threat of self-dissolution. To challenge illusions, in this view, is to perpetuate childhood traumas (Mitchell, 1988, pp. 192–193).

Mitchell seeks an integrated relational approach that draws on the clinical wisdom of both these approaches by viewing the interactive role of narcissistic illusions in prolonging and perpetuating the patient's relational matrix. Thus, narcissism plays an important function throughout the life cycle in perpetuating fixed patterns of interpersonal relationships and phantasied ties to significant objects. All kinds of narcissistic illusions are generated throughout the life cycle from toddlerhood through old age. These narcissistic illusions usually take the form of grand estimations of the individual's own qualities, infatuation with the qualities of others whom the individual loves, and phantasies of perfect merger with a beloved. It is not uncommon for healthy individuals to have experienced feelings and phantasies of considerable grandiosity at times, but in healthy narcissism the individual is able to maintain a balance between illusion and reality (1988, pp. 193–195).

In contrast, pathological narcissism is a character issue where illusions are taken too seriously, where reality is sacrificed to hold on to some idealizing fiction. Mitchell suggests that the pathology of narcissism lies not in the content of narcissistic illusion—what the individual actually thinks—but in the attitude toward those mental contents. Pathological narcissism has an interactional aspect because narcissistic disturbances seem to occur when character is formed in significant relationships where there is a disturbance in the interplay of illusion and reality. In the development of a child with a healthy balance between illusion and reality, the parent can comfortably experience the child and self with both playful illusion and realistic limitations. Illusions concerning self and others are generated, playfully enjoyed, and then relinquished in the face of disappointments. New illusions are continually created and dissolved. But in the generation of pathological narcissism, illusions of overvaluation and boundarilessness are taken too seriously and insisted upon. In some disturbances, illusions are actively and consciously maintained. Reality is sacrificed to perpetuate an addictive devotion to some self-ennobling, idealizing fiction (1988, pp. 194–196).

A healthy parent, engaging with a child, has the capacity to be playful with illusions without losing sight of reality. The parents of some children, however, take these kinds of illusions too seriously, and their own sense of worth and security is contingent upon them. This kind of illusion becomes addictive for this kind of parent and consequently becomes a dominant feature in the kinds of relatedness such a parent offers the child. These conditions for connectedness can exist not just in infancy but throughout childhood and into adulthood. Thus, the children of parents with addictions to such illusions learn modes of contact that can only lead to narcissistic difficulties. These children learn modes of contact that are felt to be the only possible alternative to no contact at all. The myth of Daedalus and Icarus captures nicely the balance required in the delicate relationship between child and parents' illusions, the precarious balance between too high and too low (1988, pp. 197–198).

Applying these interactional ideas to the clinical situation, Mitchell asks how the analyst can help the patient arrive at a balance between illusion and reality and fuse both realms. Mitchell argues that narcissistic illusions are usefully understood neither solely as a defensive solution to an internal psychic hurt nor solely as an efflorescence of infantile mental life but most fundamentally as a form of interaction, of participation with others. From this perspective, grandiosity and idealization sometimes serve defensive functions and sometimes represent unfulfilled developmental needs. But when they reoccur in stereotyped form in therapy, their central function is to serve as a gambit, an invitation to a particular form of interaction. To view narcissistic illusions as invitations means looking at the therapist's response in a different way. The patient needs some participation from the therapist to complete an old object tie. If grandiosity is involved, some expression of admiration or appreciation may be requested. If idealization is involved, some expression of pleasure at being adored may be requested (1988, pp. 203–204). Mitchell offers a therapeutic approach that walks a path between complicity and challenge, a path that reflects a willingness to play. This stance is similar to the kind of ideal parental response to the child's illusions where the parent is receptive to the child's illusions about himself and the parent but the parent maintains a light touch. The therapist's response to the patient's transferential gambits should reflect a similar kind of openness to playful participation (1988, pp. 205–207).

Patients who integrate relationships with others around grandiose fantasies believe these to be the most satisfying sorts of relationships to have. They seek out admirers and discard as uninteresting those who are not admirers. Patients who have secret grandiose claims believe being the object of devoted admiration will be satisfying, but they also fear they will never attain this goal. Patients who integrate their relationships around idealizing others also believe this is the best kind of relationship; in the perils of life, they believe they must link themselves to an idealized someone who seems to offer security and protection. The therapeutic question in all of this is, how did these asymmetrical forms of relatedness become so valued? Therapists often discover that such asymmetric relationships structured around others' admiration or idealization were the means for developing and keeping the closest possible bonds within the family. Thus, "self-organizations centering on narcissistic illusions concerning self or others have crucial functions in maintaining the analysand's relational matrix, by preserving characteristic patterns of interpersonal integrations and fantasied object ties" (Mitchell, 1988, pp. 208, 212).

Therapy

Mitchell believes that the Freudian model of the analytic process no longer works today because of changes in patients, advances in analytic theory, and profound changes in how we think about the objectivity of knowledge. Freud's patients were, generally speaking, individuals adapted to their time and culture except for the intrusion of unwanted symptoms. In contrast, contemporary case studies of analytic patients often depict individuals without bizarre symptoms but whose adaption to their time and culture is problematic. They are missing something fundamental in their experience of living; their subjectivity itself is basically awry. Indeed, the popularity of theories of object relations and self psychology is partly explained by their usefulness in thinking about the kinds of clinical problems that confront today's therapists: feelings of emptiness and inauthenticity, meaninglessness and difficulties in maintaining intimate relationships, the false self and the depleted self (1993a, pp. 22, 64).

Freud and his contemporaries had confidence in psychoanalytic theory as providing a map of the underlying structures of the mind. But what does the analyst or therapist really know? Mitchell feels that advances in theory in the past ten to fifteen years have produced a crisis in confidence about what the therapist can know. This crisis has involved a shift in thinking not only on the level of theory but on the level of metatheory—theory about theory. The crisis concerns what the therapist can know about motives, the structure of the mind, and the development of emotional life. New ideas stress the enormous complexity and fundamental ambiguity of experience, which raises the question of just how little the analyst can really know and how anxiety-provoking that is. This kind of thinking entails a fundamental redefinition of the very nature of psychoanalytic thought and of psychoanalysis as a discipline (1993a, pp. 41–42).

Evolution of theory, especially the theory of how we know, intensifies the contemporary emphasis on the relational aspects of therapy. Indeed, the revolution in theory entails a change in the very way we have come to think about what successful therapy might be. Our contemporary world has declining expectations for rationality and puts greater emphasis on experience. For centuries Western thinkers held that reality was knowable; scientific theories were judged on how closely they corresponded to that reality. Freud and his contemporaries shared these assumptions; they valued scientific rationality and thinking without illusion. But postmodernism marks the radical discontinuity between these earlier views and current thinking, which tends to regard these assumptions as untenable. Knowledge in our day is regarded as pluralistic, not singular and unitary, and contextual, not absolute. Psychoanalysis as a discipline does not escape this paradigm shift in assumptions. This change in analytic thinking manifests itself not only in the fragmentation of psychoanalysis itself into different schools but in how analysis looks at therapy.

Concerning the diversity and heterogeneity of analytic schools, Mitchell is optimistic and positive. He feels that psychoanalysis has not fragmented into conceptual disorder but rather that the different independent analytic traditions, such as the object relations and the self psychology schools, have a great deal to do with each other and can be coherently integrated with each other in a comprehensive framework for clinical practice. This heterogeneity is enriching as well as anxiety-provoking, however, since it becomes evident that there is no longer an exclusive and authoritative method and map for uncovering a singular truth about the human mind. The rich heterogeneity in theory compels us to shift from the view that the therapist knows the truth to the view that the therapist knows one among various possible truths about the experience and inner world of the patient. Accordingly, the essence of good therapy is not the authoritative imposition of one's perspective but an interactive listening process that allows the patient's perspective to develop and emerge (1993a, pp. 45–53).

This revolution in analytic thinking considers therapy an interactive process in which attention is paid to the meaning of events for patients and how patients organize their experience in meaningful ways for themselves. This shift in understanding of what the patient needs, from Freud's day to ours, puts at the center of therapy the reclaiming and revitalizing of the patient's experience of the self, the healing of disordered and deprived subjectivity. What patients need is not a rational reworking of unconscious infantile phantasies, not objective understanding, but a facilitating human environment where they can generate experience that is felt as real and meaningful, where they can develop a more authentic sense of identity and sense of self. Therapists now put less emphasis on rational understanding, insight, and interpretation and more on acceptance, containing, mirroring, and holding the patient's subjective psychic reality (1993a, pp. 24–31, 67).

What does the analyst know? How does therapy generate meaning and foster authentic experience? The revolution in theory and metatheory provides a different vision of the therapeutic process, a shift from objective knowledge to interactions and constructions embedded in the personal experience of the therapist. The therapist is not a mirror or an inert object but a meaning-generating subjectivity; therapy is a highly personal and interpersonal process, an encounter of two perspectives and subjectivities (1993a, p. 78).

In a partial answer to his question of what the analyst knows, Mitchell replies that the therapist "knows a collection of ways of thinking about how the mind works and how experience is structured" (1993a, pp. 64–65). Further, therapy involves a search for a safe therapeutic harbor in which a patient may pursue an authentic personal experience. In contrast to ideas of Freud's that the relationship with the therapist was a recreation of past relationships, contemporary relational views tend to see what is new in the therapeutic relationship. The past is still important as a way for understanding the meaning of the present relationship with the therapist. Healing involves working through the therapeutic relationship. Thus, the therapist uses Freudian tools in exploring personal experiences in ways Freud himself could not have imagined, with the goal of not merely making the unconscious conscious but making personal experiences real and deeply meaningful (1993a, pp. 31–32).

Mitchell points out that in recent decades the therapeutic relationship has been understood more and more as a real relationship, with a shift from therapeutic insight as curative to an emphasis on the relationship as curative. Relational models tend to highlight the therapist as a good object who assists patients giving up ties to bad objects. Further, theorists seem to suggest it is acceptable to give some form of satisfaction to the patient's infantile needs, to provide something that was missing in early development. Soothing and frequent empathic comments, for example, differ from the classical rule of abstinence where the analyst does not gratify infantile wishes (1988, p. 151; 1993a, p. 39).

Freud sought clarity and insight, while contemporary therapists stress enrichment and meaning and allow considerable latitude for ambiguity and confusion. The goal is not clear understanding but the patient's ability to generate experience felt as real, important, and distinctively one's own. Mitchell does not deny the importance of insight and articulating unconscious phantasies; rational thought and clarification of conflicts still play an important part, but they do not occupy the center of contemporary therapeutic work. Control over instincts is no longer the primary goal but rather the establishment of a safe interpersonal arena within which personal experience can be expressed, expanded, and enriched rather than corrected with reference to some rational objective map or standard (1993a, p. 35).

What the analyst knows is not only a repertoire of theoretical concepts but also his or her own experience. From a constructivist perspective, we understand how each person comes to know reality out-side the self only through experience of it. The individual organizes that experience in terms of ideas, wishes, and cultural assumptions. We also appreciate how the therapist's theoretical concepts shape to a con-siderable degree what the therapist sees and hears. Thus, the therapist's understanding of the patient is a construction, and it is not possible to attain a correct and total understanding of any patient's experience. Because the therapist can't grasp the patient's experience directly, but only in terms of the therapist's own experience, attention must also be paid to the therapist's mood, feelings, and phantasies that provide a path into the patient's experience and mode of relating (1993a, pp. 57–61).

If psychopathology often entails an active, willful holding onto maladaptive relational patterns, then it helps to understand therapy as an interactive field in which a patient's new relationship with a therapist as a good object can serve to challenge unhealthy relationships. Un-healthy relationships with their phantasied images and presences often seem to offer safety and connection; the relationship with the therapist offers the possibility of attachment to others along new and more life-giving lines. Patients enter therapy with a narrowed relational matrix. They seek connections with people by projections and by an attempt to recreate familiar, constricted patterns of the past. They tend to experi-ence all significant relationships along the old lines, including the new relationship with the therapist. The central process in therapy, then, is to help the patient break out of the closed system and relinquish ties to these relational patterns and allow an openness to new and richer relationships (1988, pp. 162, 170).

Therapy provides the patient with a richer and more complex adult level of intimacy. According to Mitchell, patients need to become enriched in the present. Mitchell is concerned that some of the developmental-tilt models (especially developmental-tilt models that might reify the metaphor of the baby, where needs and wishes are *felt* as infantile and that neediness is experienced as identical to that of the hungry infant) see the need to correct past omissions and detrimental deficiencies. Mitchell does not want to stress this regressive quality. In other words, issues in the present often seem to be regressive residues of very early disturbance. Mitchell is concerned that relational needs that are aspects of all adult relationships, such as the longing to be held and cherished, should not necessarily be seen only as regressive, sym-biotic yearnings from earliest childhood (1988, p. 156).

Case Study

Sophie was a graduate student in her early 30s, who entered therapy with some depression and a history of failed relationships with men. After a year of therapy with Dr. Mitchell, she had gained understanding of some of her assumptions about relationships with men and her depression lifted. In her third year of therapy, she had concerns about whether she would ever meet a man she could commit to. Mitchell's presentation begins with his return from vacation and resumption of sessions with Sophie. While Dr. Mitchell was away, her relationship with a new man rapidly escalated. Because of the number of failed relationships, she developed a lot of phantasies about marrying this new man but had some distrust of Dr. Mitchell and feared he might try to get her to end this latest romantic interest.

Sophie was the oldest of four. Her parents were of German Lutheran background. Her mother was timid, cautious, and frightened and tended to view Sophie as she viewed herself, as very delicate and different from others. Sophie dreaded her mother and yet relied on her. She absorbed from her mother a vision of the world as dangerous, full of people who were incompetent, base, and inadequate. Pleasure in this stern background was dangerous, and accordingly Sophie entered therapy with social and sexual inhibitions. Therapy helped her realize just how much she worried about petty details, and she began to experience a less solemn and more spontaneous way of living (1993a, pp. 1–4).

Sophie had mixed feelings toward Dr. Mitchell, as she believed that therapy was both similar to the relationship she had with her mother and yet somehow different; she came to think that perhaps therapy represented a way of life more enlightening than that which she had with her mother. Mitchell explored with Sophie these transferential themes, her feelings that he, like her mother, had many ideas about what was best for Sophie. The central relational configuration was powerfully underlined during Mitchell's vacation. In the past, Mitchell had helped her disengage from relationships that were not good for her. Would Mitchell do the same with the relationship she was now engaged in? Mitchell had indeed helped her, did know her family patterns and her history, and he did have ideas about what was real and best for her (1993a, pp. 4, 5).

Mitchell uses Sophie's challenging question about the nature of therapeutic process to consider contemporary ideas about what takes place in therapy. Mitchell does not discount Sophie's real difficulties in living, her anxiety and depression and sexual inhibitions, but he highlights how in a basic way she never viewed her life as her own, how her experience was hostage to her mother's view of the world. He feels that the larger issue in therapy with Sophie was the way she generated her experiences always with a focus on caution rather than expressing and exploring her own experiences. Mitchell explains that Sophie needs to attend to the quality of her passion, to generate a sense of herself and her relationships that feel important, meaningful, and deeply her own (1993a, pp. 23–24, 36–37).

Mitchell is aware that her new relationship was more passionate and rich than any of her previous relationships. He understands that the complex involvement of her mother (the internal presence of her mother) prevented Sophie from feeling excitement about any previous man. Romance, idealization, and excitement were felt as dangerous because they threatened the psychic moorings that the ties to her mother provided. One of Mitchell's themes is that therapy offers Sophie a second chance to find a way of feeling and living spontaneously and deeply, a vitality that was not adequately fostered by her family.

In contrast to a traditional rational exploration and understanding of the unconscious features of her current romance and its oedipal features, Mitchell seeks to find ways to respond with an appreciation of and resonance with her excitement in the new relationship. She had expected a coolly rational response from Dr. Mitchell and had been disinclined to share much with him about her new excitement. Mitchell interprets her feelings not so much as resistance but as a protection of "the delicate and fragile stirrings of authentic excitement and hope to which the analyst poses a genuine threat" (1993a, p. 80). She had previously allowed herself to be shaped by others' ideas of what she should do with her life; now what was therapeutically called for was an alliance with the authentic growth of her personal experience. Mitchell is aware that what he could offer in therapy was a way of looking at things, a perspective different from her usual modes. Mitchell came to appreciate that Sophie had a "much richer and more variegated set of views of herself" than Mitchell ever could have, and she had a "much more complex view of this new man than she had let on" (1993a, pp. 81–82). But Sophie had sacrificed her awareness of what she knew to keep the illusion alive that Mitchell knew better and could authoritatively predict how it would all work out.

Mitchell says that over the course of therapy perspectives on the past change. Views of parents as ideal are replaced by views of parents as destructive, which may in turn be replaced by feelings of love and connection. Mitchell's efforts with Sophie were to help her make use of his interpretations without sacrificing her own perceptions.

Assessment and Critique of Mitchell

The debate over, and assessment of, Mitchell's work proceeds, in part, along "political" lines. That is, traditionalists trained in psychoanalytic institutes that adhere to a conventional reading of Freud tend to be critical of Mitchell's efforts. Bachant and Richards, for example, criticize him for leaving out motivational concepts (Bachant & Richards, 1993). Mitchell's response is that he does indeed take a fresh start at psychoanalytic theorizing. He reminds his readers that concepts are concepts, and if he seems to disregard something it is because he is conceptualizing in different terms; for him, a superordinate motivational principle is object seeking (1993b, pp. 461–462).

The assessment and critique of Mitchell's work hinges on whether his work is judged to be revolutionary or merely evolutionary. Mainstream classical Freudians feel that current developments ought to be extensions of classical tradition. Mitchell acknowledges that he is joining a radical departure from classical tradition. He is taking a revolutionary view and feels that the relational contributions of the past 25 years are revolutionary. Psychoanalysis is different now than it was 90 years ago or even 40 years ago (1993b, p. 466). He feels that "Freud is better served by respectfully discarding some of his concepts and rethinking and reworking others in the light of broad current shifts in theory and sensibility" (1993b, p. 468).

Commentators appreciate the breadth of Mitchell's knowledge and scholarship as well as the enormity of the task he takes on. Mitchell has an extraordinary grasp of classical and contemporary analytic thought. There have been few systematic presentations that compare and contrast the various schools of psychoanalytic theory (cf. Winer, 1985, p. 256), but Greenberg and Mitchell (1983) undertake just such a systematic overview of psychoanalytic traditions with the organizing theme being the idea of object relations. This historical knowledge of theory gives Mitchell an unusual perspective from which to compare, contrast, and integrate analytic ideas. Mitchell and his critics agree that it is not always clear when he is writing about his own particular areas of interest and when he is synthesizing the work of other theoreticians (cf. Hartman, 1990, p. 310). Granting that criticism seems to proceed from where commentators stand on the basic issue of motivation, Mitchell appears to be appreciated for his efforts at integrating the relational branch of psychoanalysis while at the same time appreciating issues of conflict and sexuality in human experience. He appears to be successfully completing the paradigm shift from drive theory to a fully relational model (Hartman, 1990, p. 310). In summary, Mitchell, though scarcely reaching his full peak, is producing work of "major importance in the development of psychoanalytic theory" (Rosenberg, 1990, p. 803).

References

Bachant, J. L., & Richards, A. D. (1993). Review essay. *Psychoanalytic Dialogues, 3*, 431–460.

Freud, S. (1957). Three essays on the theory of sexuality. In J. Strachey (Ed. and Trans.), *The standard edition of the complete psychological works of Sigmund Freud* (Vol. 7, pp. 125–245). London: Hogarth. (Original work published 1905)

Greenberg, J. R., & Mitchell, S. A. (1983). *Object relations in psychoanalytic theory.* Cambridge, MA: Harvard University Press.

Hartman, W. (1990). Book review: *Relational concepts in psychoanalysis: An integration. Clinical Social Work Journal, 18,* 309–310.

Kernberg, O. (1975). *Borderline conditions and pathological narcissism.* New York: Aronson.

Kohut, H. (1971). *The analysis of the self.* New York: International Universities Press.

Mitchell, S. A. (1988). *Relational concepts in psychoanalysis: An integration.* Cambridge, MA: Harvard University Press.

Mitchell, S. A. (1993a). *Hope and dread in psychoanalysis.* New York: Basic Books.

Mitchell, S. A. (1993b). Reply to Bachant and Richards. *Psychoanalytic Dialogues, 3,* 461–480.

Rosenberg, S. E. (1990). Review: *Relational concepts in psychoanalysis: An integration. American Journal of Psychiatry, 147,* 803.

Winer, J. A. (1985). Book review: *Object relations in psychoanalytic theory. American Journal of Psychiatry, 142*(2), 256–257.

Winnicott, D. W. (1958). *Through paediatrics to psycho-analysis.* London: Hogarth.

Chapter Eleven

A Case Study Narrative

Introduction

Different theories affect the clinical approaches of therapists (Fine & Fine, 1990; Morris, 1992). Mitchell (1988, p. 90), for example, points out that therapists listen to patients through the lens of their theoretical presuppositions and that theory helps arrange and organize what is heard. In short, therapists listen more with their minds than with their ears, filtering what they see and hear through the lens of theory and their own experience. The following brief narrative is offered to suggest how to think psychoanalytically or psychodynamically about the data from therapy sessions and how to think about the process of assessment. Ultimately, however, it is the quality of the relationship and the therapist's ability to be tuned to the client's central affective states that leads to successful results (Lindon, 1991).

Brenda

Brenda is 32, a single, attractive but slightly overweight woman. She is an only child, has a teaching job in an all-girls high school, has an active spiritual life, and is currently in the process of preparing for marriage. The prospect of a wedding raised much anxiety for her and brought her back to therapy after an absence of about two years. Specifically, Brenda finds she is worrying a great deal, is distracted in her classes by her preoccupation with her worries, and is getting into arguments with her mother over details of the wedding. The therapist is a male in his mid-50s. He finds Brenda a very appealing person, and he looks forward to their sessions together.

Three and a half years ago, Brenda was referred initially to therapy by her spiritual adviser who has known her since college. The original precipitating incident was criticism from Brenda's female boss, the principal of the school where she teaches. Brenda reported that the incident was objectively trivial but somehow caused intense feelings— a terrible sense of betrayal and hurt that far outstripped the relative mildness of the incident. What made Brenda's response to the incident so intense was that the criticism felt like a very personal attack, and she had a flash of great vulnerability, of not being protected.

Brenda's father died when she was 4, and she has some blissful memory fragments of being held and carried by him. Some of these memories may be based on family photographs that show her father holding the laughing young Brenda. Brenda's mother remarried about four years after, when Brenda was 8. In the course of about 24 months of therapy, Brenda quickly associated the feelings of not being protected with her mother's lack of adequate protection from Brenda's stepfather. Brenda was able to say that the experience felt like a terrible repetition of what had taken place when she was a teenager, a time when she felt her mother did not protect her and left her exposed to abuse from her stepfather, Eddie.

For years Brenda felt or suspected that she had been sexually abused, but fear and some low self-esteem kept her from doing anything about investigating these feelings. With her somewhat chronic sense of not feeling good about herself came the precipitating incident with her principal, and Brenda entered therapy. Brenda did not recall any specific incidents of abuse, but she felt a general sense of being burdened by her stepfather. Her mother had to work nights, and Brenda was often left alone in the apartment with her stepfather. Eddie used to walk around in his underwear, would lay on Brenda's bed, and would say things like he wished she were his wife. Brenda recalls one instance when he fumbled with her bra strap when she was about 13 or 14. When Brenda pulled away from him, he got annoyed and said, "I'm your father; what are you afraid of?"

Brenda's stepfather worked in insurance. He was very meticulous when dressed for work, demanding crisp white shirts. But at home he was sloppy and would often be querulous and unshaven. He tended to get into whining arguments with Brenda's mother and was often critical of and hostile toward Brenda when he was not "mooning around me" or when her mother was home. Her mother was the dominant figure in the family. When her mother was home, the stepfather "behaved and things went relatively smoothly." Brenda's mother may have, in Brenda's words, "struggled with some of her own depression," but in general the impression is that she was solicitous—probably oversolicitous at times—a woman who worked hard for her family and who was devoted to her only child.

Brenda had been an average-to-good student, somewhat reserved, who went to parochial schools, and had friends, but "not many." Although she acknowledges that she was "pretty," Brenda did only occasional dating in high school. Brenda commuted to a local college. She did not reflect on it much at the time, but she was aware that she did not want to leave her mother home alone with Eddie. After her practice teaching and graduation from college, she returned to teach at the high school from which she herself graduated. She continued to live at home and dated only sporadically. She finally moved out about the time she met Eric.

Brenda dropped out of therapy about the same time as she met Eric and was moving out of her mother and stepfather's home. The initial course of therapy enabled Brenda to feel more confident about herself, her dating, and the new relationship with Eric. Brenda dropped out of therapy because things were going well for her, and she was excited by the first "real relationship" she had ever had. She also is now aware that she had some fears of exploring further feelings, especially sexual feelings and fantasies in the transference.

After 18 months, Brenda returned to therapy. What brought Brenda back to therapy was Eric's pressing her to marry him. She has very mixed feelings, and much of therapy now involves exploring the relationship and looking at different courses of action and her feelings about them. Eric and Brenda have had a dating relationship for the past 3 years. Eric is a "very nice man." He is very different from any of the men she has known, and Brenda is aware that she sabotages Eric's efforts to get closer to her because the relationship is "so different from anything" she has known, expected, or is used to. She says she is "not used to being treated so nicely." It makes her feel uncertain, and she tends to be overcritical of Eric. Eric appears to love Brenda and tolerates her nervousness in the relationship. He has asked her several times to marry him. In her fantasies about marriage, Brenda feels both a yearning and fears. She wonders if Eric will actually be powerful enough. In fantasizing about a wedding, Brenda feels she does not want her mother to assist with the planning, and Brenda is determined to pay for the wedding herself.

In exploring Brenda's relationship with Eric, the therapist has found that Brenda has diverse significant relationships. She can point to several key women friends at her high school, early images of her father, and the generally very good relationship with the therapist himself. Brenda is also a religious person and meets occasionally with an older woman for spiritual guidance. Brenda acknowledges the images that she has of God feel similar to the way she felt about her father, images of an enormously loving, powerful, and comforting presence.

All in all, Brenda is a successful teacher, but she worries about her work and the future. She is highly considered by her co-workers. But the adult world does not seem very safe to Brenda, and increasingly the efforts of the therapist are directed in helping her find the path in life that is good for her, feels right for her—especially in making decisions about the relationship with Eric.

As the therapist considers his countertransference feelings, he is aware that he is very fond of Brenda, responds to the little girl quality that she exhibits with him, and is very aware that he feels pulled to be the good father, the guiding father who gives her advice for a successful life. Through regular consultation on his clinical work, he monitors closely how he acts out of these paternal feelings and is trying to enable Brenda to grow up and be an independent adult who is empowered to make her own decisions.

Analysis and Assessment

In brief, Brenda has many strengths and successes in her life. She has the resources of success at work and friends who care for her. There still are key issues she needs to work through in therapy. As she and the therapist explore her inner world, the continued influence of internalized objects becomes clearer, and there are important issues to be faced: her sense of loss of her father, her sense of self that is deficient as the result of the traumatic experiences with Eddie, and her developmental delay in working through her relationship of dependency and disappointment with her mother.

The initial course of therapy dealt with the emergence into consciousness of the abusive elements in her relationship with her stepfather. This relationship, and her sense of not being protected (with feelings of vulnerability and anger), still affect her capacity for close and intimate relationships with members of the opposite sex, in this case, Eric. The issue of Eric's marriage proposal has compelled her to face unresolved intimacy issues and to complete the work of separating from her mother and finding her own path in the world and intimate relationships.

Structural Issues

Structures refer to formerly external functions that have become internalized. Object relations theories refer to self and object representations that shape relationships and patterns of behavior. Psychic structures are metaphorical references to the configurations of self and object representations, internal formations that post-Freudian theory assumes shape patterns of behavior and relationships. Classical Freudian theory implies structures of id, ego, and superego.

Using the resources of object relations theory, some conceptualizing can help to articulate Brenda's personality structures. She has intact but impaired structures, and the therapeutic relationship needs to sort out self representations and object representations that interfere with intimacy. Object relations models tend to view relational issues as structural; hence, the primacy of looking at her key relationships and how these make her the kind of person she is. She does have the positive resource of a richness of relationships with women. Much of her sense of self depends on her powerful mother whom she has internalized with both good and bad aspects. She feels good about her involvement in the world of work, but she is also anxious about moving further into an intimate relationship. Her mother did not enable her to feel sufficiently protected against the inappropriate intrusions of the stepfather.

Therapy provides an opportunity for patients to dialogue with an external object for the purpose of developing increased awareness of their inner world of objects. Brenda clearly internalized her mother as a whole object, but there is the necessity of working through the good and bad aspects of that object relationship as well as confronting the effect of Eddie's threatening abuse. Brenda needs to see how, by her own distance from Eric, she reenacts her mother's distance from her. Good qualities get manifested in Brenda's positive identification with being a woman and a successful teacher. "Bad" aspects are the mother's absence when Brenda needed her to protect against the intrusions of Eddie. As Brenda listens to herself in therapy, she has a growing awareness of her anger at the absent and neglecting "bad" object.

Brenda manifests some evidence of processes of projection and projective identification (Klein, 1946/1975) with her mother in that she feels the *mother* should be protected and made safe. That is, she didn't want the mother to be home alone with Eddie, and it is really Brenda's own continuing inner vulnerability that is in question. Some of her ambivalence toward Eric is her concern that Eric be *powerful* enough to protect her against an unsafe world and other dangerous intrusions. She also likely has unexpressed fears that Eric himself might make intrusions on her. She doesn't know how to respond to his "niceness" toward her since that is not how Eddie behaved toward her.

The loss of her father came at an early age. Such preoedipal losses are sometimes felt by children as punishments or as if they were somehow responsible and should be blamed for them. These preoedipal issues, however, feel less pressing than some of the reality issues of Brenda's current life. The therapist needs to help her see that decisions about marriage need to rest on firm foundations of psychic integration and coming to terms with unresolved developmental issues.

Brenda's essential functioning in the world is good, as manifested in such ego functions (Blanck & Blanck, 1974) as reality-testing, cognitive functioning, and modulating and controlling emotions. She does not fall apart when anxious, nor is there any danger of decompensation or fragmentation. Indeed, Brenda is a "good client," capable of self-reflection and articulating her feelings. She also can draw on other resources, other positive relationships and the positive role of religion in her life, which seems to help make the world appear safer.

Dynamics

The therapist does not conceptualize Brenda's issues as a conflict on a drive level. Rather, her essential dynamics have to do with resolving and completing her relationship with her parents; that is, she needs to resolve her ambivalent feelings toward her mother—both dependency and resentment—deal with the loss of her idealized father and the abuse of Eddie, and develop the capacity for a mutually satisfying relationship with someone at her developmental level.

Developmental Level

Object relations theories are largely theories of how personality structures develop. Perhaps Mahler's (Mahler, Pine, & Bergman, 1975) theories best help focus the issue on the key object relations issues of separating, individuating, and continuing to develop the capacity for intimacy. For a successful emotional investment in a relationship, it is necessary for Brenda to work through the strong feelings about her parents and complete the process of being a self capable of investment in others. Fairbairn (1954) speaks of the mature relational stage in which there is the capacity to give and receive. Most relational issues are from the oedipal and later stages of development. Relational theories point out that a cohesive sense of self is formed through the lifelong process of selfobject experiences; significant interruptions of these relationships affect the sense of self and healthy narcissism or self-esteem.

How can the therapeutic environment foster the continued growth of a positive sense of self? Kohut's (1977) idea of the ongoing need of selfobjects is one way of conceptualizing issues around Brenda's lack of confidence. Perhaps her mother (and clearly her stepfather) were insufficient in supplying appropriate mirroring in certain ways; some of those mirroring needs might be met in the relationship with Eric and appropriately worked through with the therapist. The therapist as self-object can support her exploration, and Brenda can test her perspective and explore feelings and fantasies that were out of her awareness. Mitchell (1993) would probably emphasize that many of her issues of trust in the relationship are appropriate to most adult relationships and that too much attention should not be paid to early and preoedipal issues.

Psychopathology

With Brenda, it is possible to rule out a debilitating impairment from the relationship with Eddie. She does not exhibit the classical symptoms of early abuse and trauma (van der Kolk & Fisler, 1994), such as the inability to regulate intense feelings, self-destructive behavior, erratic attachment patterns, or tendencies toward dissociation and fragmentation. Her trauma, although disturbing and inexcusable, was not overwhelming. She does not seem to have endured such early deficits as to be incapacitated. But there are deficits in her sense of self and an impairment of her confidence in close sexual relationships. The abuse from Eddie took place when she had sufficiently formed structures of self with adequate defenses. Key psychic boundaries between self and others had been well established at the time of the traumatic insults, and good reality-fantasy distinctions were also well established. Nevertheless, the insidious thing about sexual abuse is its eroding effect on a good sense of self. The therapy issues now are to process and metabolize the lingering effects of those disturbing assaults as well as to deal with the limitations of parents. The issues can be conceptualized as relational issues that are structural in the object relations schemas. Kernberg (1976) would probably assess Brenda's structural and character pathology at the higher end of the spectrum of integration; that is, she is essentially well integrated with relatively stable self and object representations. At times, preoedipal conflicts may emerge so her character organization would appear to be at the intermediate level of organization.

Using the categories of the *Diagnostic and Statistical Manual of Mental Disorders* (American Psychiatric Association, 1994), a therapist would want to rule out sexual abuse. Her anxiety and the related relational issues seem to predominate. A differential diagnosis would have to be made between an adjustment disorder with anxiety (309.24) and an anxiety disorder (either generalized, 300.02, or not otherwise specified, 300.00). Her anxiety symptoms are mild to moderate and would be the principal diagnosis. The clinical focus of attention, however, in her return course of therapy would be the partner relational problems (V61.1).

Therapy

The therapist watches for signs of relational patterns that might be expressed in the transference. He and Brenda have a good working relationship, and there are clear signs that she likes and trusts the therapist. This may be evidence of her idealizing and may even draw some psychic energy from the primal images of being held by her natural father. Transference patterns can change, and some of her unconscious anger at her mother could also enter the relationship with the therapist.

The therapist needs to closely watch his wishes for Brenda. He seems to want to keep pulling the patient to a higher level of functioning, which is an understandable tendency for a therapist working out of an ego-functioning model; self psychology allows more time for exploring transference issues that may require temporary regression on the part of the client. For an appropriate exploration of inner self issues and self representations, a certain amount of therapeutic regression may be expected. There may be external time limits, such as deadlines for wedding plans and decisions, but the therapist must stay attuned to Brenda as she both moves forward and has perhaps several sessions in which therapeutic regression is called for. Winnicott's (1963) notion of the holding environment nicely captures the safeness of the therapeutic environment in which the patient can confront scary feelings. As for Brenda's religious imagery, some theorists (Rizzuto, 1979; St. Clair, 1994) point to parallels between representations of God and those from early childhood.

References

American Psychiatric Association. (1994). *Diagnostic and statistical manual of mental disorders.* (4th ed.). Washington, DC: Author.

Blanck, G., & Blanck, R. (1974). *Ego psychology: Theory and practice.* New York: Columbia University Press.

Fairbairn, W. R. D. (1954). Object-relationships and dynamic structure. In *An object-relations theory of the personality* (pp. 137–161). New York: Basic Books. (Original work published 1946)

Fine, S., & Fine, E. (1990). Four psychoanalytic perspectives: A study of differences in interpretive interventions. *Journal of the American Psychoanalytic Association, 38,* 1017–1047.

Kernberg, O. (1976). A psychoanalytic classification of character pathology. In *Object relations theory and clinical psychoanalysis* (pp. 139–160). New York: Aronson.

Kohut, H. (1977). *The restoration of the self.* New York: International Universities Press.

Klein, M. (1975). Notes on some schizoid mechanisms. In *Envy and gratitude & other works 1946–1963.* New York: Delta. (Original work published 1946)

Lindon, J. A. (1991). Does technique require theory? *Bulletin of the Menninger Clinic, 55,* 1–21.

Mahler, M. S., Pine, F., & Bergman, A. (1975). *The psychological birth of the human infant.* New York: Basic Books.

Mitchell, S. A. (1988). *Relational concepts in psychoanalysis: An integration.* Cambridge, MA: Harvard University Press.

Mitchell, S. A. (1993). *Hope and dread in psychoanalysis.* New York: Basic Books.

Morris, J. L. (1992). Psychoanalysis and psychoanalytic psychotherapy—Similarities and differences: Therapeutic technique. *Journal of the American Psychoanalytic Association, 40,* 211–222.

Rizzuto, A. (1979). *The birth of the living god: A psychoanalytic study.* Chicago: University of Chicago Press.

St. Clair, M. (1994). *Human relationships and the experience of god: Object relations and religion.* Mahwah, NJ: Paulist Press.

van der Kolk, B., & Fisler, R. (1994). Childhood abuse and neglect and loss of self-regulation. *Bulletin of the Menninger Clinic, 58,* 145–168.

Winnicott, D. W. (1963). Psychiatric disorders in terms of infantile maturational processes. In *Maturational processes and the facilitating environment* (pp. 230–241). New York: International Universities Press.

Bibliography

Principal Theorists

Fairbairn, W. R. D. (1963). A synopsis of an object-relations theory of the personality. *International Journal of Psycho-Analysis, 44,* 224.

Fairbairn, W. R. D. (1952). Endopsychic structure considered in terms of object-relationships. In *An object-relations theory of the personality* (pp. 82–136). New York: Basic Books. (Original work published 1944)

Fairbairn, W. R. D. (1952). Object-relationships and dynamic structure. In *An object-relations theory of the personality* (pp. 137–151). New York: Basic Books. (Original work published 1946)

Fairbairn, W. R. D. (1952). The repression and the return of bad objects (with special reference to the "war neuroses"). In *An object-relations theory of the personality* (pp. 59–81). New York: Basic Books. (Original work published 1943)

Fairbairn, W. R. D. (1952). A revised psychopathology of the psychoses and psychoneuroses. In *An object-relations theory of the personality* (pp. 28–58). New York: Basic Books. (Original work published 1941)

Fairbairn, W. R. D. (1952). Steps in the development of object-relations theory of the personality. In *An object-relations theory of the personality* (pp. 152–161). New York: Basic Books. (Original work published 1949)

Fairbairn, W. R. D. (1952). A synopsis of the development of the author's views regarding the structure of the personality. In *An object-relations theory of the personality* (pp. 162–179). New York: Basic Books. (Original work published 1951)

Freud, S. (1957). The ego and the id. In J. Strachey (Ed. and Trans.), *The standard edition of the complete psychological works of Sigmund Freud* (Vol. 19, pp. 1–66). London: Hogarth Press. (Original work published 1923)

Freud, S. (1957). Group psychology and the analysis of the ego. In J. Strachey (Ed. and Trans.), *The standard edition of the complete psychological* works of Sigmund Freud (Vol. 18, pp. 65–143). London: Hogarth Press. (Original work published 1921)

Freud, S. (1957). Instincts and their vicissitudes. In J. Strachey (Ed. and Trans.), *The standard edition of the complete psychological works of Sigmund Freud* (Vol. 14, pp. 117–140). London: Hogarth Press. (Original work published 1915)

Freud, S. (1957). Mourning and melancholia. In J. Strachey (Ed. and Trans.), *The standard edition of the complete psychological works of Sigmund Freud* (Vol. 14, pp. 237–258). London: Hogarth Press. (Original work published 1917)

Freud, S. (1957). New introductory lectures on psycho-analysis. In J. Strachey (Ed. and Trans.), *The standard edition of the complete psychological works of Sigmund Freud* (Vol. 22, pp. 1–182). London: Hogarth Press. (Original work published 1933)

Freud, S. (1957). Three essays on the theory of sexuality. In J. Strachey (Ed. and Trans.), *The standard edition of the complete psychological works of Sigmund Freud* (Vol. 7, pp. 125–245). London: Hogarth Press. (Original work published 1905)

Greenberg, J. R., & Mitchell, S. A. (1983). *Object relations in psychoanalytic theory.* Cambridge, MA: Harvard University Press.

Jacobson, E. (1946). The effect of disappointment on ego and superego formation in normal and depressive development. *Psychoanalytic Review, 33,* 129–147.

Jacobson, E. (1954). The self and the object world. *Psychoanalytic Study of the Child, 9,* 75–127.

Jacobson, E. (1964). *The self and the object world.* New York: International Universities Press.

Jacobson, E. (1971). *Depression: Comparative study of normal, neurotic and psychotic conditions.* New York: International Universities Press.

Kernberg, O. (1975). *Borderline conditions and pathological narcissism.* New York: Aronson.

Kernberg, O. (1976). *Object relations theory and clinical psychoanalysis.* New York: Aronson.

Kernberg, O. (1980). Self, ego, affects, and drives. *Journal of the American Psychological Association, 30,* 893–916.

Kernberg, O. (1980). *Internal world and external reality.* New York: Aronson.

Kernberg, O. (1984). *Severe personality disorders: Psychotherapeutic strategies.* New Haven: Yale University Press.

Kernberg, O. (1992). *Aggression in personality disorders and perversions.* New Haven: Yale University Press.

Kernberg, O. (1992). Psychopathic, paranoid and depressive transferences. *International Journal of Psycho-Analysis, 73,* 13–28.

Kernberg, O. (1993). Suicidal behavior in borderline patients: Diagnosis and psychotherapeutic considerations. *American Journal of Psychotherapy, 47,* 245–254.

Kernberg, O. (1994). The erotic in film and in mass psychology. *Bulletin of the Menninger Clinic, 58,* 88–108.

Kernberg, O., Cooper, A., & Person, E. (Eds.). (1989). *Psychoanalysis: Toward the second century*. New Haven: Yale University Press.

Kernberg, O., Selzer, M., Koenigsberg, H. W., Carr, A. C., & Applbaum, A. H. (1989). *Psychodynamic psychotherapy of borderline patients*. New York: Basic Books.

Klein, M. (1975). A contribution to the psychogenesis of manic-depressive states. In *Love, guilt and reparation and other works, 1921-1945* (pp. 262–289). New York: Delta Books. (Original work published 1935)

Klein, M. (1975). Envy and gratitude. In *Envy and gratitude and other works, 1946-1963* (pp. 176–235). New York: Delta Books. (Original work published 1957)

Klein, M. (1975). Mourning and its relation to manic-depressive states. In *Love, guilt and reparation and other works, 1921-1945* (pp. 344–369). New York: Delta Books. (Original work published 1940)

Klein, M. (1975). Notes on some schizoid mechanisms. In *Envy and gratitude and other works, 1946-1963* (pp. 1–24). New York: Delta Books. (Original work published 1946)

Klein, M. (1975). The Oedipus complex in the light of early anxieties. In *Love, guilt and reparation and other works, 1921-1945* (pp. 370–419). New York: Delta Books. (Original work published 1946)

Klein, M. (1975). Some theoretical conclusions regarding the emotional life of the infant. In *Envy and gratitude and other works, 1946-1963* (pp. 61–93). New York: Delta Books. (Original work published 1952)

Kohut, H. (1966). Forms and transformations of narcissism. *Journal of the American Psychological Association, 14*, 243–278.

Kohut, H. (1971). *The analysis of self*. New York: International Universities Press.

Kohut, H. (1977). *The restoration of the self*. New York: International Universities Press.

Kohut, H. (1984). *How does psychoanalysis cure?* Chicago: University of Chicago Press.

Kohut, H. (1987). *The Kohut seminars on self psychology and psychotherapy with adolescents and young adults*. New York: Norton.

Kohut, H., & Wolf, E. S. (1978). The disorders of the self and their treatment: An outline. *International Journal of Psycho-Analysis, 59*, 413–425.

Mahler, M. S., & Gosliner, B. J. (1955). On symbiotic child psychosis. *Psychoanalytic Study of the Child, 10*, 195–212.

Mahler, M. S., Pine, F., & Bergman, A. (1963). Thoughts about development and individuation. *Psychoanalytic Study of the Child, 18*, 307–324.

Mahler, M. S., Pine, F., & Bergman, A. (1968). *On human symbiosis and the vicissitudes of individuation*. New York: International Universities Press.

Mahler, M. S., Pine, F., & Bergman, A. (1971). A study of the separation-individuation process and its possible application to borderline phenomena in the psychoanalytic situation. *Psychoanalytic Study of the Child, 26*, 403–422.

Mahler, M. S., Pine, F., & Bergman, A. (1972). On the first three subphases of the separation-individuation process. *International Journal of Psycho-Analysis, 53*, 333–338.

Mahler, M. S., Pine, F., & Bergman, A. (1972). On the first three subphases of the separation-individuation process. *International Journal of Psycho-Analysis, 53*, 333–338.

Mahler, M. S., Pine, F., & Bergman, A. (1975). *The psychological birth of the human infant*. New York: Basic Books.

Mitchell, S. A. (1988). *Relational concepts in psychoanalysis: An integration*. Cambridge, MA: Harvard University Press.

Mitchell, S. A. (1992). True selves, false selves, and the ambiguity of authenticity. In N. J. Skolnich & S. C. Warshaw (Eds.), *Relational perspectives in psychoanalysis* (pp. 1–20). Hillsdale, NJ: The Analytic Press.

Mitchell, S. A. (1993). Aggression and the endangered self. *Psychoanalytic Quarterly, 62*, 351–382.

Mitchell, S. A. (1993). *Hope and dread in psychoanalysis*. New York: Basic Books.

Mitchell, S. A. (1993). Reply to Bachant and Richards. *Psychoanalytic Dialogues, 3*, 461–480.

Mitchell, S. A. (1994). Something old, something new: Commentary on Steven Stern's "needed relationships." *Psychoanalytic Dialogues, 4*, 363–369.

Ornstein, P. (Ed.). (1978). *The search for the self: Selected writings of Heinz Kohut: 1950–1978* (Vols. 1 & 2). New York: International Universities Press.

Ornstein, P. (Ed.). (1981). *The search for the self: Selected writings of Heinz Kohut: 1978–1981* (Vols. 3 & 4). New York: International Universities Press.

Winnicott, C., Shepherd, R., & Davis, M. (Eds.). (1989). *Psychoanalytic explorations*. Cambridge, MA: Harvard University Press.

Winnicott, D. W. (1958). Aggression in relation to emotional development. In *Collected papers: Through pediatrics to psycho-analysis* (pp. 204–218). London: Tavistock. (Original work published 1950)

Winnicott, D. W. (1958). Primitive emotional development. In *Collected papers: Through pediatrics to psycho-analysis* (pp. 145–156). London: Tavistock. (Original work published 1945)

Winnicott, D. W. (1958). Transitional objects and transitional phenomena. In *Collected papers: Through pediatrics to psycho-analysis* (pp. 229–242). London: Tavistock. (Original work published 1951)

Winnicott, D. W. (1965). The capacity to be alone. In *The maturational processes and the facilitating environment* (pp. 29–36). New York: International Universities Press. (Original work published 1958)

Winnicott, D. W. (1965). Ego distortion in terms of true and false self. In *The maturational processes and the facilitating environment* (pp. 140–152). New York: International Universities Press. (Original work published 1960)

Winnicott, D. W. (1965). Ego integration in child development. In *The maturational processes and the facilitating environment* (pp. 56–63). New York: International Universities Press. (Original work published 1962)

Winnicott, D. W. (1965). From dependence to independence in the development of the individual. In *The maturational processes and the facilitating environment* (pp. 83–99). New York: International Universities Press. (Original work published 1963)

Winnicott, D. W. (1965). A personal view of the Kleinian contribution. In *The maturational processes and the facilitating environment* (pp. 171–178). New York: International Universities Press. (Original work published 1962)

Winnicott, D. W. (1965). Psychiatric disorders in terms of infantile maturational processes. In *The maturational processes and the facilitating environment* (pp. 230–241). New York: International Universities Press. (Original work published 1963)

Winnicott, D. W. (1965). The theory of the parent-infant relationship. In *The maturational processes and the facilitating environment* (pp. 37–55). New York: International Universities Press. (Original work published 1960)

Winnicott, D. W. (1971). *Therapeutic consultations in child psychiatry.* New York: Basic Books.

Secondary Sources and Clinical Applications

Anechiarico, B. (1990). Understanding and treating sex offenders from a self-psychological perspective. *Clinical Social Work Journal, 18,* 281–292.

Appelbaum, A. H. (1994). Psychotherapeutic routes to structural change. *Bulletin of the Menninger Clinic, 58,* 37–54.

Azim, H. F., Piper, W. E., Segal, P. M., Nixon, G. W. H., & Duncan, S. C. (1991). The quality of object relations scale. *Bulletin of the Menninger Clinic, 55,* 323–343.

Baker, H. S., & Baker, M. N. (1987). Heinz Kohut's self psychology: An overview. *American Journal of Psychiatry, 144,* 1–9.

Blanck, G., & Blanck, R. (1987). Developmental object relations theory. *Clinical Social Work Journal, 15,* 318–327.

Borden, W. (1992). Comments on "theories of Kernberg and Kohut: Issues of scientific validation." *Social Sciences Review, 66,* 467–470.

Brems, C. (1991). Self-psychology and feminism: An integration and expansion. *American Journal of Psychoanalysis, 51,* 145–160.

Cashman, P. (1991). Ideology obscured: Political uses of the self in Daniel Stern's infant. *American Psychologist, 46,* 206–219.

Celani, D. P. (1993). *The treatment of the borderline patient: Applying Fairbairn's object relations theory in the clinical setting.* Madison, CT: International Universities Press.

Chernus, L. (1988). Why Kohut endures. *Clinical Social Work Journal, 16,* 336–354.

Dennis, G. S., & Ferguson, G. (1988). An experimental investigation of Kernberg's and Kohut's theories of narcissism. *Journal of Clinical Psychology, 44,* 445–451.

Dublin, P. (1992). Severe borderlines and self psychology. *Clinical Social Work Journal, 20,* 285–294.

Finkelstein, L. (1987). Toward an object-relations approach in psychoanalytic marital therapy. *Journal of Marital and Family Therapy, 13,* 287–298.

Fromm, M. G., & Smith, B. L. (Eds.). (1989). *The facilitating environment: Clinical applications of Winnicott's theory.* Hillsdale, NJ: The Analytic Press.

Goldberg, A. (1988). *A fresh view look at psychoanalysis: The view from self psychology.* Hillsdale, NJ: The Analytic Press.

Goldberg, A. (Ed.). (1988). *Frontiers of Self Psychology.* Hillsdale, NJ: The Analytic Press.

Goldberg, A. (Ed.) (1991). *The evolution of self psychology.* Hillsdale, NJ: The Analytic Press.

Grotstein, J. S., & Rindsley, D. (1981). The significance of Kleinian contributions to psychoanalysis (Parts I & II). *International Journal of Psychoanalytic Psychotherapy, 8,* 375–392, 393–429.

Grotstein, J. S., & Rindsley, D. (1982–1983). The significance of Kleinian contributions (Parts III & IV). *International Journal of Psychoanalytic Psychotherapy, 9,* 487–510, 511–535.

Grotstein, J. S., & Rindsley, D. (1993). A reappraisal of W. R. D. Fairbairn. *Bulletin of the Menninger Clinic, 57,* 421–449.

Grotstein, J. S., & Rindsley, D. (Eds.). (1994). *Fairbairn and the origins of object relations.* New York: Guilford Press.

Hadley, J. A. et al. (1993). Common aspects of object relations and self-representations in offspring from disparate dysfunctional families. *Journal of Counseling Psychology, 40,* 348–356.

Hamilton, G. N. (1989). A critical review of object relations theory. *American Journal of Psychiatry, 146,* 1552–1560.

Hinshelwood, R. D. (1991). *A dictionary of Kleinian thought.* New York: Aronson.

Hughes, J. M. (1989). *Reshaping the psychoanalytic domain: The work of Melanie Klein, W. R. D. Fairbairn, and D. W. Winnicott.* Berkeley: University of California Press.

Jacobs, E. H. (1991). Self psychology and family therapy. *American Journal of Psychotherapy, 45,* 483–498.

Johnson, H. C. (1991). Theories of Kernberg and Kohut: Issues of scientific validation. *Social Service Review, 65,* 403–433.

Kanter, J. (1990). Community-based management of psychotic clients: The contributions of D. W. and Clare Winnicott. *Clinical Social Work Journal, 18,* 23–41.

Kanzer, M. (1979). Object relations theory: An introduction. *Journal of the American Psychoanalytic Association, 27,* 313–324.

Kavaler-Adler, S. (1993). The conflict and process theory of Melanie Klein. *American Journal of Psychoanalysis, 53,* 187–198.

Kavaler-Adler, S. (1993). Object relations issues in the treatment of the pre-oedipal character. *American Journal of Psychoanalysis, 53,* 19–34.

Kramer, S. (Ed.). (1994). *Mahler and Kohut: Perspectives on development, psychopathology, and technique.* New York: Aronson.

Kurzweil, E. (1994). An interview with Otto Kernberg. *Partisan Review, 61,* 204–219.

Lax, R. (1983). Discussion: Critical comments on object relations theory. *Psychoanalytic Review, 70,* 423–433.

Little, T., Watson, P. J., Biderman, M. D., & Ozbek, I. N. (1992). Narcissism and object relations. *Psychological Reports, 71*, 799–808.

London, N. J. (1985). An appraisal of self psychology. *International Journal of Psycho-Analysis, 66*, 95–107.

Nigg, J. T. et al. (1992). Malevolent object representations in borderline personality disorder and major depression. *Journal of Abnormal Psychology, 101*, 61–67.

Paris, J. (1991). Object relations in adolescent girls. *American Journal of Psychiatry, 148*, 1419–1420.

Pessein, D. E., & Young, T. M. (1993). Ego psychology and self psychology in social work practice. *Clinical Social Work Journal, 21*, 57–68.

Petot, J-M. (1991). *Melanie Klein: The ego and the good object, 1932–1960* (Vol. 2) (C. Trollope, Trans.). Madison, CT: International Universities Press.

Petot, J-M. (1990). *Melanie Klein: First discoveries and first system, 1919–1932* (Vol. 1) (C. Trollope, Trans). Madison, CT: International Universities Press.

Rangell, L. (1985). The object in psychoanalytic theory. *Journal of the American Psychoanalytic Association, 33*, 301–334.

Reis, B. E. (1993). Toward a psychoanalytic understanding of multiple personality disorder. *Bulletin of the Menninger Clinic, 57*, 309–318.

Robbins, M. (1992). A Fairbairnian object-relations perspective on self-psychology. *American Journal of Psychoanalysis, 52*, 247–261.

Rosenfeld, H. (1983). Primitive object relations and mechanisms. *International Journal of Psycho-Analysis, 64*, 261–267.

Segal, H. (1981). *Melanie Klein*. New York: Penguin.

Segal, J. (1992). *Melanie Klein*. Newbury Park, CA: Sage.

Seinfeld, J. (1989). Therapy with a severely abused child: An object relations perspective. *Clinical Social Work Journal, 17*, 40–49.

Shulman, D. G., & Ferguson, G. R. (1988). An experimental investigation of Kernberg's and Kohut's theories of narcissism. *Journal of Clinical Psychology, 44*, 445–451.

Spillius, E. B. (1988). *Melanie Klein today: Developments in theory and practice.* New York: Routledge.

Stepansky, P. E., & Goldberg, A. (Eds.). (1984). *Kohut's legacy: Contributions to self psychology.* Hillsdale, NJ: Erlbaum.

Sternbach, S. (1983). Critical comments on object relations theory. *Psychoanalytic Review, 70*, 403–422.

Summers, F. (1994). *Object relations theories and psychopathology: A comprehensive text.* Hillsdale, NJ: The Analytic Press.

Sutherland, J. D. (1989). *Fairbairn's journey into the interior.* London: Free Association Books.

Thomas, K. R. (1992). The wolf-man case: Classical and self-psychological perspectives. *American Journal of Psychoanalysis, 52*, 213–225.

Thomas, K. R., & McGinnis, J. D. (1991). The psychoanalytic theories of D. W. Winnicott as applied to rehabilitation. *Journal of Rehabilitation, 57*, 63–66.

Tuttman, S. (1981). A historical survey of the development of object relations concepts in psychoanalytic theory. In S. Tuttman, C. Kaye, & M. Zimmerman

(Eds.), *Object and self: A developmental approach* (pp. 3–51). New York: International Universities Press.

Weininger, O. (1992). *Melanie Klein: From theory to reality.* London: Karnac Books.

Westen, D. (1989). Are "primitive" object relations really pre-oedipal? *American Journal of Orthopsychiatry, 59,* 331–345.

Westen, D., Ludolph, P., Block, M. J., Wixom, J., & Wiss, C. W. (1990). Developmental history and object relations in psychiatrically disturbed adolescent girls. *American Journal of Psychiatry, 147,* 1061–1068.

White, M. T. (1986). *The theory and practice of self psychology.* New York: Brunner/Mazel.

Glossary

This glossary strives for simplicity, clarity, and freedom from jargon rather than for technical precision. The reader should recall that different authors use the same word with different shades of meaning.

Anxiety. An unpleasant sensation or fearful feeling in response to something in the environment or within oneself.

Autism. Normal autism refers to the first month of life when an infant is psychologically undifferentiated and is turned inward.

Bad object. An object that frustrates and also receives a projection of destructive instincts from the individual in relation to it.

Borderline personality disorder. A disorder, neither neurotic nor psychotic, with a person having problems with object relations, nonspecific ego weaknesses, a tendency toward primary process, and primitive defense mechanisms.

Cathexis. An investment of instinctual or emotional energy.

Cohesive self and fragmented self. The feeling of wholeness versus that of being in parts or the feeling of a loss of continuity.

Death instinct. A drive toward destruction that can be turned inward toward the self or toward the outside world in an aggressive way.

Defense mechanism. A process by which the ego protects itself from threatening thoughts and feelings.

Depersonification. A term used by Jacobson to describe how early relationships with objects give rise to intrapsychic structures.

Depressed position. A Kleinian term for a developmental stage that peaks at about the sixth month during which the infant fears destruction and the loss of the loved object.

Depression. A state of feeling depleted, valueless, and sad.

Development. Growth as a sequence of stages, either from an instinctual perspective or from the perspective of relationships with persons in the environment.

Drives. Instinctual forces (sexual and aggressive) that move a person to action.

Drive vicissitudes. A transformation or distortion of a drive so that the drive takes a new form, such as that which might be manifested in a dream symbol.

Ego. From a conceptual rather than experiential viewpoint, that part of the personality that has consciousness and performs various functions, such as keeping in contact with reality.

Ego boundary. That which gives a sense of (1) the distinction between oneself and external objects, or (2) the distinction between the mind's conscious thoughts and feelings and repressed thoughts and feelings.

Ego dystonic. Feelings, ideas, and actions that are not in harmony with an individual's values and principles and consequently cause anxiety.

Ego functions. Operations assigned to the ego, such as maintaining contact with reality, perception, regulating drives, executing the wishes of the id, defending against impulses, relating to objects, and so forth.

Ego ideal. An aspect of the superego that has an image of perfection that the individual holds up for him or herself.

Ego syntonic. Feelings, ideas, and actions that are compatible and in harmony with one's values and principles.

Energy. The force that motivates or moves a person toward activity.

Externalize. To mentally or imaginatively locate one's wish or feeling as being outside oneself, such as a child being afraid of monsters in the dark.

Facilitating environment. Persons who provide what an infant needs, especially a sense of narcissistic omnipotence necessary for development.

Fixation. A stage of development in which getting gratification or relating to people is highly energized either by excessive satisfaction or excessive frustration; the result is that the individual persists in this pattern of getting gratification or relating to people.

Genital stage. The last phase of instinctual development, with the implication that the chosen love object is another person and that the individual has a biological capacity for intercourse and orgasm.

Good-enough mother. One who sufficiently meets the needs of her child, especially by responding to the spontaneous gesture of the child in a way that fosters healthy narcissism.

Good object. An object that gratifies and also receives the projection of libidinal instinct from the individual in relation to it.

Holding environment. A safe, nurturing environment (or person), with an infant protected from excessive internal and external demands and stimulation.

Hysteric. Suggests, among other qualities, that a person is excitable, emotional, and talkative, but poorly observant of inner feelings.

Id. From a conceptual point of view, a structure of the mind that is associated with instinctual drives and seeks to reduce tension by gratifying those drives.

Identification. A process by which an individual becomes like or gets an identity from another.

Identity. A sense of being the same unique self over time.

Incorporation. A form of introjection suggesting a taking into the mind through the bodily process of swallowing.

Instinct. A drive or biological urge to action.

Internalization. A process by which an individual transforms characteristics of the environment into inner characteristics.

Internal object. A phantasy or image of an object.

Internal saboteur. Fairbairn's term for a split-off part of the ego that punishes in a way similar to the superego.

Introjection. An assimilation of an object or its demands into the ego, or the assimilation of the object representation into the self representation.

Latency. A period in development, extending approximately from 7 years of age to puberty, when psychosexual forces or libidinal interests are inactive.

Libido. A term for sexual drive energy, not sexual desire.

Masochism. Gaining sexual satisfaction by suffering pain.

Model. A set of concepts explaining a complex reality.

Narcissism. An investment or concentration of energy or interest in the self. In traditional psychoanalysis, narcissism refers to a withdrawal of libido from external objects and an investment in the self. Healthy narcissism for self psychology implies the development of self-esteem through a relationship with a selfobject.

Neurosis. A disorder affecting only part of the personality, implying relatively stable and differentiated psychic structures, and with the conflict primarily between the ego and the impulses of the id.

Object. The "other" involved in a relationship or, from an instinctual point of view, that from which the instinct gets gratification.

Object choice. Selection of a person as a loved object.

Object relatedness. Interpersonal relationships as they exist externally.

Object relations. Interpersonal relationships as they are represented intrapsychically.

Object representation. An intrapsychic image of the other in relation to the self.

Obsessive. A way of thinking that is repetitive, insistent, and inhibiting of thought and action.

Oedipus complex. A developmental situation during which the child moves from a dyadic relation with the mother to a triadic relationship with both parents; the child identifies with the parent of the same sex and chooses the parent of the opposite sex as a loved object.

Oral stage. In Freud's model, the first stage of development, which is characterized by libidinal interests centering in the mouth.

Paranoid-schizoid position. A developmental position postulated by Klein that peaks about the third month of life and is characterized by aggression and feelings of persecution.

Part object. When only one aspect of an object is perceived, such as goodness or badness, gratifying or frustrating.

Phallic stage. The third stage of development in Freud's model, approximately from ages 3 to 5, characterized by increasing interest in the genitals.

Phantasy. The mental imagery expressing instinctual drives; different from whimsical fantasies or daydreams.

Phobia. A fear.

Pleasure principle. A regulatory norm for activity that usually involves an uninhibited effort to reduce drive tension and gratify needs; occurs earlier than the reality principle.

Practicing subphase. A period during the separation-individuation phase of development, roughly beginning from 10 to 12 months and lasting through 16 to 18 months, when the child experiences exuberance in being able to distance itself from mother by walking.

Pregenital. The early stages of development when gratification is primarily oriented in the child's own body and to the mother only insofar as she provides gratification.

Preoedipal. The characteristics and interests of the early stages of development before the oedipal complex.

Primary process. A mode of thinking characterized by wishful phantasy and association as found in dreams.

Projection. To imaginatively put onto another what belongs to oneself so that one's subjective reality becomes objectified and externalized.

Projective identification. Imaginatively splitting off part of oneself and attributing it to another for the sake of controlling the other.

Psyche. The mind or mental life.

Psychic mechanism. A process of the mind with a specific function, such as protecting consciousness from inner dangers.

Psychopathology. A psychological disturbance, in contrast to a physical illness.

Psychosis. A serious disturbance characterized by a collapse of psychic structures and a distortion in the perception of reality.

Rapprochement. A subphase of the separation-individuation phase of development; roughly the period from 18 to 24 months of age, during which time the child experiences an increase in helplessness and a resurgence of the need for closeness to the mother.

Reality principle. A regulatory norm that modifies the pleasure principle and aims to keep the activity of the ego in line with the demands of social reality rather than with instinctual demands.

Representation. An affective mental structure made up of a multitude of impressions and feelings; a psychological structure that differs from a merely visual or perceptual mental image.

Repression. The defense by which unwanted thoughts and feelings are kept out of awareness.

Schizoid. Characterized by having intense needs for objects but with fear of closeness with the same objects; the schizoid personality feels isolated, meaningless, and withdrawn.

Secondary process. Mental activity proper to the ego—that is, logical, orderly, and in touch with reality.

Self. A complex term with several frames of reference; can refer to person as subject as distinguished from objects in the environment, the person who I am for myself, or the representation or image of the self contained in the ego.

Selfobject. Kohut's term for the person used in the service of the self or experienced as part of the self, especially with regard to fostering esteem and a sense of well-being.

Separation-individuation. A phase of development and a process in which the child increasingly disengages itself from its psychological fusion with the mother and increasingly gains a sense of being an autonomous person.

Splitting. A developmental and defensive process of keeping incompatible feelings apart and separate.

Structure. Stable, inner psychological patterns.

Superego. Inner controls or ideals that become established at about 6 or 7 years of age.

Symbiotic phase. Margaret Mahler's term for the developmental period from approximately the second to sixth months of life, during which time the infant phantasizes that it and its mother are fused in a dual entity with a common boundary.

Transference. Assigning feelings from a past relationship to a present relationship with a therapist.

Transitional object. Something that a child uses for comfort and security as the child moves from one level of emotional development to another; a teddy bear, for example.

Transmuting internalization. Kohut's term for the process by which functions of persons in the environment are internalized by a child as inner structures and functions.

True self and false self. Winnicott's terms for the feeling of being real, whole, and spontaneous as opposed to the sense of compliancy and covering of one's real needs.

Unconscious. Thoughts and feelings out of awareness of the conscious ego.

Whole object. Perception of an object as a whole person, as a love object, with the implication that the perceiver has the developmental capacity for ambivalence and is thus capable of accepting both good and bad qualities in the object.

Index